Composition Studies in the New Millennium

STUDIES IN THE NEW MILLENNIUM

REREADING THE PAST, REWRITING THE FUTURE

EDITED BY

Lynn Z. Bloom

Donald A. Daiker

Edward M. White

Southern Illinois University Press   Carbondale

Library of Congress Cataloging-in-Publication Data

Composition studies in the new millennium : rereading the past, rewriting the future /
    edited by Lynn Z. Bloom, Donald A. Daiker, Edward M. White.
        p. cm.
    Includes bibliographical references (p.) and index.
    1. English language—Rhetoric—Study and teaching. 2. Report writing—Study and
teaching (Higher). I. Bloom, Lynn Z. 1934– II. Daiker, Donald A., 1938– III. White,
Edward M. (Edward Michael), 1933–
    PE1404 .C626 2003
    808'.042'0711—dc21
    ISBN 0-8093-2521-7 (cloth : alk. paper)
    ISBN 0-8093-2522-5 (pbk. : alk. paper)   2002152306

To honor the living presence of Robert J. Connors,

scholar and friend. His incisive rereading of our past

enables us to rewrite the future of our field.

Contents

Acknowledgments

The national Conference on Composition Studies in the Twenty-First Century: Rereading the Past, Rewriting the Future was held at Miami University in Oxford, Ohio, from October 5 to 7, 2001. For helping to underwrite its costs, we sincerely thank Lynn Z. Bloom, the Aetna Chair of Writing at the University of Connecticut; the Council of Writing Program Administrators; and the Department of English at Miami University and its chair, Dianne Sadoff.

We owe a special debt to Professor Shane Borrowman of Gonzaga University, who served as managing editor for this volume. He took charge of the many details of communication with the contributors, assembled the manuscript and the contributor biographies, prepared the combined bibliography and the index, and generally assisted the other editors in countless small and large ways. We are most grateful for his steady professional, efficient, and cordial work with this book. His quiet and creative efficiency allowed this volume to appear within two years of the conference at which preliminary versions of these papers were delivered.

For help with conference program arrangements, we are grateful to Lori Corsini-Nelson, Aetna Administrative Specialist of the University of Connecticut, and to conference coordinators Kate Francis, Katie Freeman, Brenda Helmbrecht, John Heyda, Connie Kendall, Meredith Love, Moira Miller, Krista Orlando, Tom Pace, Kate Ronald, Jeff Sommers, Paul Teasley, Shevaun Watson, and Morris Young, all of Miami University. For research support, we thank Kathrine Adeylott, Valerie Smith, and Matthew Simpson of the University of Connecticut.

We are indebted to Karl Kageff, senior sponsoring editor of Southern Illinois University Press, for his expertise, patience, generosity, and sheer good will in helping us produce this book. He has our deepest thanks, as do our families, particularly Martin Bloom, Victoria Parker Daiker, Volney White, and Elizabeth Borrowman.

Composition Studies in the New Millennium

Introduction: Challenges and Invitations for Composition Studies in the New Millennium

DONALD A. DAIKER

Perhaps it was because the conference Composition Studies in the Twenty-First Century: Rereading the Past, Rewriting the Future took place less than a month after the series of attacks on September 11 that so many conference speakers invited those in attendance, as they do in their essays here, to consider more thoughtfully where we've been, how we got there, and where we're going. For most speakers, the conference subtitle "Rereading the Past, Rewriting the Future" posed a significant challenge, especially because they acknowledged that the past is not easily read and that the future is even more problematic.

Peter Elbow's keynote address and lead essay, "Three Mysteries at the Heart of Writing," is a rereading of the past that celebrates human intelligence and creativity. Elbow endorses the "principle of mental plenitude," the principle that our minds are always full of things to say, which is one reason that with the help of freewriting, inkshedding, and effort, we enact the first mystery: We move from no words to some words, from nothing to something. The second mystery—making what we've written more clearly reflect what we want to say—can be understood in term of *felt sense,* an inner intention or even bodily sense that enables us almost always to answer the question "Was that what you really meant to say?" If the answer is "no," we can move back and forth between our words and our felt sense in order to express our ideas and insights more accurately. The third mystery—the distinction between words that readily give an experience to the readers and words that make readers work hard to experience them—Elbow explains in terms of *intonation.* Through intonation, which "embodies in language a felt nonverbal experience of meaning," speakers and writers can "pour" their meaning into words. In order to bring intonation into writing, Elbow sometimes asks every student to give a "celebratory reading" of several paragraphs to the entire class. Elbow claims, finally, that students who make progress on these three mysteries are likely to enjoy writing more, to experience themselves

1

as writers, and therefore to keep writing by choice, especially if we writing teachers create "conditions of safety and trust" in our classrooms. Significantly, Elbow celebrates and sings not "composition studies" but "writing" or, more accurately, teachers teaching writing and students (and teachers) writing.

Lynn Z. Bloom and Susan Miller answer the question What Do We Mean by Composition Studies—Past, Present, and Future? in quite different ways. Bloom's discussion of paradigm shifts in composition teaching within the last three decades radiates hope and even joy. Bloom demonstrates that the process model not only continues to influence our composition pedagogy and research but has become "the dominant, default rubric for teaching writing." She recalls the exhilaration that in the 1970s and 1980s greeted the work of Peter Elbow, Donald Murray, Nancie Atwell, and Mike Rose, and she notes that their books "exude the happiness, the euphoria, the sense of discovery and progress that energize teachers and students in the best process classrooms (and indeed the best classrooms of any sort)." Bloom finds "usefulness, elegance, and beauty" in the process paradigm, but it is its "inherently democratic" nature, its emphasis on creation rather than criticism, on active participation rather than passive consumerism, and its recognizing students as writers and even artists that persuade Bloom that writing will be taught as a process rather than a product for a long, long time to come, its principles constituting "a beacon for classroom teachers, glowing through turbulent post-process skies."

In contrast, Miller acknowledges that her view "may seem gloomy in excess." Miller sees the past and present of composition studies meeting in "definitely unsettling ways," in part because she takes issue with both the process and postprocess movements. She finds the post-process paradigm inadequate because it lacks a general theory to explain how composing and texts work, and she dismisses the process movement because, for her, "the friendly pre-writing aura" it introduced is "the only sign *or* substance of changes in most composition teaching." She is especially troubled by what she takes to be the incapacity of the process model to generate new kinds of writing assignments and evaluations. Miller would replace the term *composition studies* with *writing studies,* which she finds less pretentious and less elitist.

Like Elbow, Wendy Bishop unabashedly identifies herself as an "expressivist." Her response to the question What Do/Should We Teach When We Teach Composition? is that we should care about individual writers and about writing with and for them. Like Bloom, Bishop's source—and the focus—of her optimism is "teaching writing. Teachers thinking about teaching writing. Students writing."

Although Bishop finds teaching more than occasionally "unnerving," it is simultaneously "exciting" and "renewing." To Mary Rose O'Reilley's provocative question, "What if we were to take seriously the possibility that our students have a rich and authoritative inner life and tried to nourish it rather than negate it?" Bishop responds with enthusiasm and affirmation, adding several telling questions of her own: "What is the place of emotion in the writing classroom?" and "As a writing teacher, where are my energies best spent?" She challenges us to take "more critical *and* creative approaches to the teaching day," to become as well trained in reflection as we are in criticism. Bishop herself takes student writing as the starting point and central text for the composition courses she teaches. Even with the events of September 11, Bishop believes that the place she matters most is "locally, as a teacher. I should be proud of this." She writes as if, indeed, she is. She invites us, in the words of Jerry Farber, to "view teaching as a career-long process of self-renewal."

No conference speaker issued a more provocative and far-reaching challenge to composition studies in particular and to the humanities in general than Kurt Spellmeyer. From his rereading of the past, he argues that compositionists have made themselves increasingly irrelevant by emulating the model of English literature that privileges graduate over undergraduate study, courses for majors over introductory courses, and theory over practice. For Spellmeyer, who focuses steadily on the impact of education outside the academy,

> The truth is that any literate and moderately thoughtful adult can read, understand, and appreciate a poem, a play, or a novel. While advanced study makes all kinds of sense in fields like microbiology or physics or pediatrics, our society and its literary arts could get along quite healthily without advanced study in the reading of literature, just as it has gotten along without advanced study in the watching of television, the eating of good food, and the enjoyment of sex.

Our challenge, as Spellmeyer understands it, is to extricate ourselves from the legacy of literary studies and cultural studies, marginal fields where scholars write largely for each other in what he calls "autistic gestures" without a genuine constituency outside their discipline.

Spellmeyer believes that society's most pressing issues lie far outside English studies and are far more complex than any one discipline can handle. An adequate response to September 11, for example, would require "a knowledge of the recent history of Saudi Arabia, Egypt, and Afghanistan; some understanding of Islam; and some reading on the culture of the Middle East." Spellmeyer invites us to see composition as the course in which students address complex issues synthetically, as they require. In this way, the composition course becomes the center of undergraduate experience and "the most coherent educational experience" students will ever get. Once we realize that "the glorious empire of the text turns out to be a troubled, stifling little Balkan state," English departments can begin making genuinely useful contributions to our troubled world.

To answer the question Where Will Composition Be Taught and Who Will Teach It? Mark Reynolds believes that we must join Spellmeyer in acknowledging that English departments are in deep trouble, with their very survival at stake. Speaking from the perspective of the two-year college, Reynolds warns that departments of English may follow Classics into oblivion or morph into departments of cultural studies unless they emulate the two-year-college example and make writing the central focus of instruction. Like Brenda Jo Brueggemann, who acknowledges that many compositionists are "significantly out of touch with undergraduate students," Reynolds challenges institutions that permit senior professors to teach only gradu-ate and upper-division literature courses with this penetrating question: "Why should the most experienced and highest-paid faculty members be the most re-moved from the largest number of students to pass through the department and those with the greatest needs?"

Reynolds contrasts the "democratic spirit" of two-year colleges with what he takes to be the antidemocratic elitism of many four-year colleges and research universi-ties. Because two-year colleges are open-admissions institutions, they have become for Reynolds the nation's primary site for educating the academically and economi-cally disadvantaged as well as "the last public vestige of hope for training those with-out adequate language skills." Reynolds concludes by inviting four-year English faculties to join forces with their community-college colleagues for the good of higher education:

> By involving all faculty in the teaching of composition, by acknowledging its service function to the institution, by making its instruction of value to students both in their future course work and in their lives, and by collaborating more often with their two-year-college colleagues,

university English departments will better serve higher education and the public good.

For Art Young, the most important challenge to composition comes not from following literary studies into irrelevance or oblivion but from the business world. Young believes that the corporatization of the academy, "the aggressive importing of staffing and other policies and practices from the business world to what has been popularly perceived as the isolated, protected ivory tower of higher education," means that institutions of higher learning will continue and probably even increase the hir-ing of non–tenure-track faculty to teach writing courses. We cannot passively accept the hiring of more and more adjunct and part-time writing instructors, Young con-tends, because it "devalues composition and mistreats many teachers of composition."

Because the "commitment to teaching as central to our discipline is our strength," Young invites us to accept the reality that composition is primarily a teaching field and then, by working within those limits, to make our faculty and instruction as professional as possible. Young plausibly argues that our best alternative to the corporate model of underpaid, unpromotable, and untenurable writing instructors is a two-track or multi-tier faculty that provides for a parallel—not hierarchical—full-time, teaching-intensive tenure track in composition. It's even imaginable, Young observes, for faculty members to move back and forth between teaching and research tracks depending on their changing personal and professional situation. While Young acknowledges that the two-track faculty may be an unpopular option, he nevertheless sees it as our best hope for professional fairness and equity in a business-dominated academy.

Both Gesa E. Kirsch and Todd Taylor initially respond to the questions What Theories, Philosophies Will Undergird Our Research Paradigms? And What Will Those Paradigms Be? by challenging us to do more in composition research and to do it with greater sensitivity and with higher ethical standards. For Kirsch, the future of composition promises "more interactive, reciprocal, collaborative, qualitative research ... conducted in a range of new settings with increasingly diverse populations" and with increased importance given to the ethical dimensions of our work. Kirsch highlights the award-winning research of Ellen Cushman with inner-city residents, noting especially that Cushman established reciprocal relationships with participants in a project that was mutually beneficial: inner city residents were assisted in negotiating contracts, fighting eviction, and interacting with governmental agencies. With studies like Cushman's that are qualitative, ethnographic, and self-reflexive, the boundaries among theory, methodology, and practice begin to blur, but Kirsch finds no cause for alarm; indeed, she finds such innovative approaches "promising, revitalizing, and exhilarating." In opposition to Steven M. North, she argues that "as scholarship in composition expands and diversifies, it becomes more insightful and valuable."

If Kirsch finds the search for a single research paradigm to be "misguided," Taylor's survey of doctoral dissertations in composition and rhetoric nevertheless locates one: "We are interested primarily in better understanding the way nonfiction language works so that we can teach it more effectively." Taylor goes on to assert that these are good times for compositionists in higher education because most institutions are challenging academic departments to demonstrate (*a*) a commitment to effective teaching; (*b*) the capacity for relating to a more diverse student body; and (*c*) the ability to connect research to undergraduate teaching. Taylor's thesis is that, on the one hand, this paradigm has worked remarkably well to create methodological consensus but that, on the other hand, things are in danger of falling apart quickly. Taylor's essay ends, significantly, with seven pertinent questions, the last being "Will composition studies be left standing?"

The simple answer to the question How Will New Technologies Change Composition Studies? addressed first by Dànielle Nicole DeVoss, Joseph Johansen, Cynthia L. Selfe, and John C. Williams Jr. and then by Lester Faigley seems to be "profoundly"—so long as composition instructors accept, encourage, and even promote the classroom use of those technologies. Both essays demonstrate that more and more students are bringing multiple literacies to our classrooms and that, as a result, texts that include video, sound, images, and animation are emerging with ever-greater frequency and sophistication in and out of the classroom. The problem is that composition teachers by and large are not—or are at least not yet—prepared to work in productive ways either with new technologies or with students who are learning them. Through three compelling case studies of individuals who compose texts in electronic environments, DeVoss, Johansen, Selfe, and Williams show in persuasive detail that composition instructors need, first, to begin with the literacies that their students bring to class but, then, to be prepared to move beyond a narrow focus on language alone or mere alphabetic literacy to embrace new-media texts that transcend time zones, language groups, and national boundaries.

Faigley agrees that student work will be increasingly in multimedia forms while acknowledging that just "a tiny percentage of writing teachers have had any training in graphic design" or related areas. One option for untrained teachers, according to Faigley, is simply to deny students the use of animations, audio, video clips, and images in their compositions. It is an option, however, that Faigley believes our discipline must reject:

> A core assumption of composition studies is that the short-term goals of bringing students up to speed so they can fulfill the writing tasks required in their undergraduate curricula and in the workplace are in the long term aimed at empowering students to become active citizens in a participatory democracy. Herein lies the rub. I can think of no scenario for the revival of public discourse that does not involve digital media.

The challenge to create a technologically informed and competent composition faculty is a formidable one. Not surprisingly, Christine Neuwirth reports that the same conferees who agreed that multimedia literary should be taught posed difficult and perhaps unanswerable questions: Should writing instructors teach it? Can/could they teach it? Where would it fit into an already bulging curriculum?

Whatever the future role of technology in the composition curriculum, both Gary A. Olson and Min-Zhan Lu believe that writing teachers have not sufficiently emphasized issues of power and authority. In the section What Languages Will Our Students Write, and What Will They Write About? Olson observes that our college classrooms are becoming more and more diverse racially, nationally, and ethnically and that both minorities and international students are enrolling in record numbers. Nevertheless, Olson believes that "even a cursory glance at composition scholarship" makes clear that neither writing instructors nor writing program directors are pedagogically or administratively prepared to cope with students of difference. One effective remedy, Olson asserts, is for compositionists to become familiar with critical race theory, an intellectual movement that focuses attention on how power and domination are inherent in race relations. The common project of critical race theorists, according to Olson, is not only to show how and explain why white privilege and minority subordination characterize our society but to change our perceptions and practices. A movement within critical race theory is critical legal studies, whose proponents hold that the law is not and can not be neutral or disinterested. Rejecting the notion of "color blindness," they believe that the way to eradicate racism is through a heightened race consciousness that leads to understanding how often race is a submerged issue in law and academic subjects. Another emerging movement is critical whiteness studies, whose aim is to understand how whiteness is constructed and represented. For writing instructors, Olson believes that "race consciousness is an important analytical tool that allows us to examine our own pedagogies, writing programs, and institutions and, perhaps, to alter them for the better." Critical race theory prepares us to be more sensitive and responsive to an increasingly diverse student body.

Lu joins Olson in challenging us to highlight the connection between language and power. To do so, we must treat "language as a dynamic process involving competing ways of seeing, thinking, and talking." In particular, we need to emphasize the rights of students "to deliberate over how they do language." What we've done instead, Lu claims, is to relegate students to the role of passive learner, while we follow the traditional top-down approach to student writing, marking as errors any deviation from the rules established by the powerful few. To oppose what Lu calls "the tyranny of linguistic imperialism," she urges composition teachers to foster the deliberative rather than the functional use of standardized rules. In her first-year writing classes, for example, Lu invites students to interpret the logic of "errors" in student papers, in one case the construction *can able to* with its implications of individual capacity and will power. Lu's goal is what she terms "a more sustainable world for all," a world less structured along the axes of domination like class, race, gender, and education.

In confronting the question What Political and Social Issues Have Shaped Composition Studies in the Past and Will Shape This Field in the Future? Keith Gilyard joins Young in protesting the "creeping corporate tendencies" in higher education and joins both Lu and Olson in challenging composition instructors to embrace a broader mission than the teaching of writing and reading. As critical pedagogues, Gilyard asks that we first grasp for ourselves and then help our students attain "a thorough understanding of the political economy and its attendant discourses in order to achieve an informed evaluation of the social order." Gilyard accepts Ira Shor's characterization of critical literacy as

> an effort to discover alternative paths for social and self-development. This kind of literacy—words rethinking worlds, self dissenting in society—connects the political and the personal, the public and the private, the global and the local, the economic and the pedagogical, for reinventing our lives and for promoting justice in place of inequity.

For Gilyard what binds together critical pedagogues like Shor, Henry A. Giroux, Lu, and Robert P. Yagelski is what he terms "a shared commitment . . . to undermining oppression, alienation, and subordination." However, because the aim of critical pedagogy is not merely the understanding but rectification of social inequity, compositions must go beyond asking questions, offering critiques, and mediating discussion in their classrooms. They must take the next step by "model[ing] a process of full participation in civic affairs."

If Olson, Lu, and Gilyard seem to be demanding much of writing teachers, challenging us to understand economics, political science, critical race theory, and globalization, as well as current events, Harriet Malinowitz wants perhaps even more—especially in light of September 11 and its aftermath. Her starting point is that critical literacy is central to the teaching of the English language arts:

> Liberatory pedagogy, cultural studies, multiculturalism, and other socially based teaching practices took root in composition in the last decades of the twentieth century because reading, writing, rhetoric, language, and discourse came to be seen as constitutive, rather than merely descriptive, of events in the world.

Malinowitz asserts that corporate culture and its domination of American media make critical literacy difficult to achieve, particularly, she passionately argues, "in a climate in which asking questions, reading skeptically, and analyzing closely—three essential components of intellectual work—can lead to charges of anti-Americanism or 'justifying terrorism.'" But because politics is shaped by language and rhetoric, it is the responsibility of composition teachers to do our homework, to use independent media in our teaching and research, and to encourage our students to "read" the world so as intelligently to approach key events like globalization and the suicide attacks on the World Trade Center. Politics, Malinowitz concludes, cannot remain solely the concern of the social sciences because politics is dependent upon the formation of mass opinion, which is shaped by rhetoric and language and which is best studied through these lenses. For Malinowitz, there is no goal for writing teachers more important than helping our students in the complex task of reading their world, especially because "critical literacy is on the critical list."

Richard E. Miller agrees that we must teach our students to propose viable solutions to the intractable problems of the new millennium; to do otherwise, he cautions—to write only for each other and to analyze the past without attention to future action—is to make ourselves increasingly irrelevant.

Perhaps the central question that the conference Composition in the Twenty-First Century and this volume frame for writing instructors at the start of the new millennium is, how do we balance our obligations to teach writing with our obligations to teach the world? In her conference journal, Miami University graduate student Rebecca Fleming describes that dilemma in concrete and powerful terms:

Dr. Gilyard was the first at this conference, of the speakers I listened to, to link the September 11 tragedy to composition, to a responsibility of composition teachers to connect composition to larger social issues. He mentioned that composition has to be larger than economic interests. I guess he wants the composition class to be a realm of subversion, instead of a market primping good little capitalists. I struggle with how far to go with this idea—there are so many good ideas for the composition class; I don't know which is more important or essential. And I think about the options. I hear a Peter Elbow voice emphasizing writing in and of itself, and I don't know who to listen to. There just isn't enough time. I don't know what to critique, what to gently prod towards, and what to preach. I don't know when to encourage and when to challenge. I don't know how to balance race, gender, social class with politics, economics, history, literature, and popular culture—there are so many choices.

Like Fleming, most of us struggle with our many choices. But what the challenges and invitations issuing from this volume make clear is that our choices carry serious consequences for our students, our discipline, our institutions, and our world.

1 Three Mysteries at the Heart of Writing

PETER ELBOW

In this essay, I explore three murky processes that writers must deal with if they are to find lots of good words and thoughts and get readers to hear them. In a sense, I'm exploring a key doorway into the so-called process movement: a new insistence on exploring a realm of rhetoric that had been largely ignored for a long time, namely *invention*.

But doesn't an essay about invention and the writing process belong in a book about the *twentieth* century, not the twenty-first? Maybe I've been a bad student and run away from the writing assignment set by the editors of this book to "look forward to the rest of the century." I'd insist I'm looking forward to important issues that people will need to struggle with if they want to get things written. Whether I'm looking forward to where *scholarship* and *research* will go is anybody's guess. I think the present collection of essays shows (among other things) that both concepts—"the process movement" and "the process of writing"—have become bones that scholars need to chew on. The question is whether they will swallow and digest them—or spit them out.

First Mystery: From No Words to Words

An old friend and excellent teacher, Bob Whitney writes of a student who kept stopping during a freewriting session. "So what's on your mind?" he asked. "Nothing," she said. "*Nothing* begins with N," Bob replied. A pretty ordinary exchange— at least the first part of it: "What's on your mind?" "Nothing." But let's pause over it. Possibly, she did have words in mind that she couldn't or wouldn't put on paper, even in private freewriting. Yet if we're willing to take her word for what was going on, we have a story about the first mystery: she started out with no words, but then in response to a question, she transformed her nothingness into a word: *nothing.*

How do we get from no words to words? What is the doorway or hinge between the experience of nothing and the experience of having words? A certain number of students experience full emptiness: "I have *nothing* to write about." "I have *nothing* to say about that topic." Far too many teachers believe such students and thus make a terrible compact with them. "These kids are too young. They have too little experience. They have nothing on their minds." When teacher and student agree that the student's mind is empty, we have a killing stalemate.

Both parties are simply wrong. Words and thoughts are always available even when they seem unavailable—however strong the experience of emptiness. The mind is always full of things to say. Even *nothingness* is an experience for which there is at least one word. Even when the topic is boring or alien, there are lots of oblique words and thoughts about why we don't like it or why it feels stupid or what it reminds us of. If you don't believe this principle of mental plenitude, I would ask you to *try* believing it—or at least to try adopting it as a hypothesis to test. See whether it *might* be true. In a moment I'll suggest two ways to test it.

First let me explore a mental emptiness that's less total and more common. Most people sometimes have the experience of starting out working on a topic for which they *have* thoughts—but not enough. And yet sometimes, for some reason (we've cleaned our plate or done the right rain dance?), we end up with lots to say. When that happens, *how* does it happen? I'm not talking about getting words and ideas from books or from someone else. We didn't have much to say at first; we get no "input"; yet we end with lots to say. How?

I call this a mystery and won't try to explain it, but I think I can throw light on it by suggesting two activities that are fairly reliable for making it happen.

1. Talk to someone. Not to get input from them but to get interaction with them, and above all, good listening. With the right kind of person, we love to talk and we come up with lots to say. It's usually someone who listens well, who respects us and probably even values us—who thinks we are smart or interesting. (Occasionally it's someone who disagrees and fights us about our views—but a person who is nevertheless rewarding to argue with.) This is my first hypothesis for evoking the first mystery: Set up these dialogic conditions and see whether it helps you or your students to get from no words or few words to lots of words.

But it's not always easy to find this kind of person. Even if we know just the right person, he or she may not be available right now when we need more words and thoughts; or this person may be so uninterested in the topic that it's not feasible to have this kind of generative conversation. It's fortunate to have another reliable activity to call on.

2. Freewriting. (My wife says that for me, whatever the question is, freewriting is the answer. Can I help it if freewriting helps everything?) The essence of free-

writing is to push ourselves to write or keep on writing even when we don't have words in mind and we don't know what will come. Most people can't do this well without conditions of safety. That's why the default form of freewriting is *private*—so we can push away worry about mistakes or poor quality.

I won't try to explain the mystery of why freewriting leads from no words to words. Only to assert that it does. But if you want to test it, you need to make the test fair before concluding it doesn't work: (*a*) People need to give freewriting quite a few tries and with some regularity, instead of just a couple of random attempts; (*b*) People need to have the experience of continuing to write when they have run out of what's "in mind." That's why it's helpful for teachers gradually to increase freewriting times: five minutes, ten—but then sometimes fifteen, twenty minutes, and even longer. A new freewriter needs the experience of "running out" in order to get that experience of a door opening up to unplanned or unrehearsed or unexpected words and thoughts; (*c*) Finally, people need to exert a certain kind of *care* or attention to the process of freewriting. I realize now that in the past, I've tried too hard to make freewriting sound easy and foolproof: "You can't go wrong. Just keep writing for ten minutes and you've done it perfectly." I've too often neglected to say, "But you still have to *try* a bit. You don't have to try for quality, but you have to exert some focus of attention. Don't struggle or clench, but exert some energy and care."

Inkshedding. Many writing teachers in Canada (through the writings and leadership of James Reither and Russ Hunt) have developed a particular use or application of *focused,* and *public* freewriting for academic purposes that they call *inkshedding:*

> Briefly, it entails informal or impromptu writing that is immediately read and used and responded to by others, and then discarded. A typical inkshedding situation might occur as a response to a conference paper—the audience might immediately write for a few minutes, then read a half-dozen other participants' writing, and then move to oral discussion based on the reading. The writing might then be thrown away. (Hunt, "Speech Genres" 249)

Before the advent of networked computers, Reither and Hunt wanted to heighten the social, dialogic dimension of writing by finding the most efficient technology for getting everyone's thinking into everyone else's head in a classroom or academic gathering. (Since 1984, the annual working conferences of the Canadian Association for Study of Language and Learning have been called *inksheds.* I attended Inkshed 18 in the spring of 2001 and saw inksheds from individual sessions typed up and made available the next day to people who had been at a different session. For an extended definition and history of inkshedding, see <http://www.stthomasu.ca/hunt/dialogic/inkshed.htm>.)

Inkshedding, as a way of getting from few words to many words, addresses two difficulties that some people experience with freewriting. That is, some people feel freewriting is a waste of time. Because they can't see any reason to give care and attention to such a useless activity—no doors open. For them, the stakes are too low. Inkshedding raises the stakes a bit because the writing is always doing academic work, and it always goes to at least a few readers. Here's a passage from an inkshed in response to my conference presentation about the relationship between freewriting and inkshedding: "I stayed away from Inkshed conferences for years because I was intimidated by inkshedding. Now I am (almost) totally unselfconscious about it." A few people, interestingly enough, find that it's freewriting that raises the stakes too high. It's themselves whom they experience as the most critical audience of all. They would rather share their writing with a reader, even a critical reader, than be left alone with their words.[1]

Freewriting and timed exams: the dialectic between soft and hard. Freewriting often sounds hopelessly "soft" to teachers who feel a strong pressure for hard results, quality, and excellence: "Freewriting might be nice if there were world enough and time—but there just isn't." Many students and parents want all writing to be graded; there's been an explosion of externally mandated standards and testing. Yet consider this simple practical question: When do students most strikingly need to move quickly from no words (or few words) to lots of words? On timed essay exams. More and more students have to write an essay in twenty or sixty or ninety minutes under exam conditions—very often on a question they've never seen. Frequent focused freewriting or inkshedding is ideal practice for timed exams: again and again students have to answer a question about a new topic or a topic they've studied and to come up with as many thoughts as possible as fast as possible in readable prose. When students get to try this over and over in conditions of safety, they get good at it. Focused freewriting lowers the stakes in order to zero in on what's hardest about high-stakes exam writing: not being able to stop and having to come up with as much as possible.

Second Mystery: Figuring Out What We Really Mean

The second mystery is simple and obvious—yet also subtle. One day in seminar, a graduate student explained his point about something, but then he emailed me that evening to say that his earlier words didn't really capture his thought—and now here is what he really meant to say. An unremarkable event, but let's pause over it. Here's an important question we mostly forget to ask: *How* did that speaker know that his words weren't what he really meant to say? What did he measure his spoken words against? He didn't say that his words were wrong or incorrect about the topic—nor awkward or unclear for listeners. He said they weren't what he was trying to say. On what basis did he decide? He must have compared his spoken words to something else—to some internally experienced intention.

Felt sense is the word that Eugene T. Gendlin coined for this inner intention, and Sondra Perl brought the concept of felt sense to the world of composition many years ago ("Understanding Composing"). Gendlin insists that this inner intention is a *nonverbal* and indeed bodily sense. For even in the unlikely event that the student compared his spoken words to some unspoken words in his mind, the same question would remain: How would he decide whether *those* words were what he really meant? Ultimately, Gendlin argues—and I think I see it frequently borne out—there is always a felt or even bodily sense that is possible to be found behind most of our utterances.

Thus it is not only interesting but remarkably important that we can almost always answer that simple question, "Was that what you really meant to say?" (Steven Pinker makes the same point in his *Language Instinct* 47.) Occasionally, we can't answer it: "Gee, I'm just not sure *what* I was trying to say." But almost always we have an answer: sometimes "Yes," more often something like this: "Well, that was sort of it. The first part was pretty close, but something was off in the last part. In that part, I was really trying to get at . . . "—and then usually some more words come out of our mouths. After we speak these new words, we may say, "Yes, that's it"—but often we feel, "That's still not *quite* it, but it's closer."

So far, I've tried to emphasize how natural it is to consult felt sense—how we do it all the time. Indeed, in my story about the graduate student, he didn't need to consult felt sense; felt sense jumped out and bit him on the nose. But it's important to notice the opposite state of affairs and reflect on why people often *don't* consult felt sense when they speak or write.

On the one hand, sometimes we don't *feel* or notice that quiet feeling that our words don't match our inner felt intention, because we are paying so much attention to *outer standards* for words: whether our words are any *good*—right, valid, interesting, well said, or correct. On the other hand, I think I see some people who notice felt sense too strongly. Actually, it's not that they notice it too much but that they get too discouraged from noticing it.[2] When we attend to felt sense, what we usually notice is that our words fail the test and don't really say what we were trying to say. If the smoke detector goes off too often, it's tempting just to remove the battery. I see two sorts of people who take this route and learn to ignore felt sense: (*a*) People whose words have been criticized a great deal. They lose all trust in their power with words and finally decide that it's not worth paying attention to felt sense because what they really meant to say is probably wrong anyway. (*b*) People who must constantly speak their thoughts clearly and coherently and off the cuff to a demanding audience. In those conditions, it's hard to pay much attention to felt sense and make delicate adjustments of meaning because doing so tends to disrupt clarity and coherence of utterance: One must constantly interrupt one's speech to restate differently what one has already just said.

What about felt sense and writing? Writing makes us more likely to ignore felt sense. Our goal for speaking—at least for informal speech—is usually just to say what we mean. Notice the contrast with writing. In writing, our goal is more often to say what's right or good: not so much to *match* what we mean but to *adjust* or *change* what we mean till our words are true or well argued or valid or interesting—and clear and well organized. "Yes, what I just spoke may be wrong and awkward, but damn it, that's what I want to say right now." We're much less likely to say this kind of thing about what we've written. (The exception is illuminating: we might say it about a personal letter we've just written.) When we write, we usually feel the weight of that nagging question: "Why write something that's wrong or poorly expressed?" So it's not surprising that felt sense is more likely to be drowned out during writing.[3]

But even though it may be frustrating to notice felt sense ("No. You've failed again to say what you really mean")—or tempting to ignore it when writing something for tough, external standards—the "No" of felt sense needs to be seen as a *positive* or even happy event. It's our best leverage for getting things clearer. Socrates said in the *Apology* that he had a voice that often spoke to him, but it had only one word, "No." Gendlin used the term *focusing* for the process of using felt sense in order to get closer to what we really mean—a process that tends to follow steps like these:

- We find ourselves uttering words for some idea or insight or feeling on our mind.
- Then we pause to attend inward to felt sense—and often we notice that our words don't quite say what we were trying to say. (Or sometimes we start with that wordless feeling of something we would like to say.)
- But we welcome that felt sense of mismatch and put attention on it charitably as a nonverbal experience—turning away from words for a few moments.
- From that nonverbal and bodily experience, we invite new words—and they usually get us closer to our meaning-intention.

With any topic that feels important, we often have to go through this process repeatedly, but the process can lead us to that remarkably rewarding experience of having actually said *just* what we mean.

Note that this whole train of thought assumes the reality of *nonverbal knowledge* and invites us not to be so skeptical when someone says, "I know what I want to say, but I just can't find the words." This statement annoys some theorists who deny the possibility of nonverbal knowledge. "There is nothing outside the text," says the Derridean, deconstructive slogan. And impatient teachers sometimes declare, "If you can't say it, you don't know it." But artists, musicians, and dancers laugh at the claim that all knowledge is linguistic—as does a Chomskyan linguist like Pinker. In a long chapter on "mentalese," he undermines "the idea that thought is the same thing as language" (47) and "languages dramatically shape their speakers' ways of thinking" (48).[4]

One of the principal strengths of most good writers and talkers, it seems to me, is the ability recurringly to pause, even if only briefly, to consult and stay in touch with their felt sense. Yes, they try to think about whether their words are any *good;* but they don't let that external standard of goodness overwhelm their monitoring of their internal standard of how well their words reflect their felt insight.

When I think back over my own history of writing, I see two general turning points. The first corresponds to the first mystery: getting out of a writing block by learning that if I just keep putting down whatever words that come to mind (no matter how bad), more will come; there are always more. The second corresponds to this second mystery: learning that when this stream of words leads me to inadequate, messy, inchoate words, I can trust that I *do* know something and that I will learn to say it if I keep going back and forth charitably between words and felt sense. We can teach our students to be better at expressing their insights more accurately by means of noticing and using the leverage of felt sense.

Third Mystery: Words That Give

How is it that some writing seems to do more of the work of *giving* us its meaning, while other writing seems to make *us* do more of the work? In truth, of course, readers must always do the entire job of constructing meaning. Strictly speaking, there are no meanings *in* words; meanings are only in people. The only meanings that readers find *in* words are ones they themselves had to project there. Otherwise, *chat* would contain the same meaning for French and English readers. The rules of communication are perversely double-barreled: writers have the whole job of choosing words with the right meanings—thus, in effect putting the meanings "in there;" yet readers have to do the work all over again of putting meanings into the words they find on the page—hoping that these projected meanings match what the writer had in mind. Still, some writers do better work than others, so some writing seems to make less work for readers.

Of the many ways in which writing can be easier for readers, I will explore one particular virtue. That is, some writing makes less work for us by somehow making us seem to *hear* the meaning coming to us from the silent words on the page. I'll try to illustrate my point with two passages from an academic book by Stephen Booth:

Any reader committed to reading and paying attention to the book that follows can profitably skip this introduction. Everything I want the introduction to do is done in the essays it introduces. I am writing an introduction only because experience has taught me that people who read academic criticism—usually authors of academic criticism—do not so much read critical studies as "check them out." (1)

The difficulty in dealing with the relation of *shall not perish from the earth* and the Bible is that the specificity of the evidence can overwhelm its presenter and lead him to posit an audience as finely tuned to biblical echoes as his research has recently and temporarily made him. (32)

I suspect that most readers found less work in the first passage and had to expend more effort and attention to experience the meaning of the second passage than the first. Admittedly, the second passage suffers because we're not caught up in the context, but even so, imagine how much more clearly we would *hear* the meaning in that complex syntactical construction if Booth or some good reader *spoke aloud* that second passage—skillfully and strongly out of a rich and full understanding of its meaning. Listening to a good reader, we would experience the meaning with little or no effort.

I'm pointing to a simple but powerful fact: A speaker can, as it were, "pour the meaning into words" for us so that we *hear* that meaning almost without effort. The key here is *intonation* or prosody. Intonation *embodies* in language a rhythm and melody of meaning—a nonverbal experience of meaning. (Note that my second mystery centered on the *speaker's* or *writer's* experience of meaning; this third mystery centers on the *listener's* or *reader's* experience of meaning.) It's not just syntax that intonation makes us hear; it also makes us hear semantic meaning:

- *I* didn't say he stole the money.
- I *didn't* say he stole the money.
- I didn't *say* he stole the money.
- I didn't say *he* stole the money.
- I didn't say he *stole* the money.
- I didn't say he stole *the* money.
- I didn't say he stole the *money.*

(American Accent Training)

As these sentences show, we tend to pour meaning into our words even more clearly and naturally when we speak in normal conversation than when we read text outloud. In normal speech, it's almost impossible to say words without giving them a felt meaning that listeners *hear* without the effort of extracting it.

It's worth quoting Mikhail Bakhtin on the central force of intonation:

> Articulated words are impregnated with assumed and unarticulated qualities. . . . Intonation lies on the border between life and the verbal aspect of the utterance; . . . [intonation] pumps energy from a life situation into the verbal discourse, . . . [intonation] endows everything linguistically stable with living historical momentum and uniqueness. ("Discourse in Life" 106)

My focus for now is only on how intonation carries simple literal meaning. Bakhtin is casting a wider net.[5]

I've argued so far that words give their meaning most readily when someone *speaks* them easily and clearly out of felt meaning. Audible intonation somehow carries meaning to us. How can we apply this phenomenon to writing? Can we get intonation down onto a silent page along with this gift of heard meaning?

Yes. It simply happens that *some* written words give us their sound more than others do—we hear them in our mind's ear with seemingly little or no effort. Robert Frost made the point a kind of manifesto: "All that can save [sentences] is the speaking tone of voice somehow entangled in the words and fastened to the page for the ear of the imagination" (13–14). This kind of hearing is one of the things people mean when they speak of writing with a strong voice. (Not the only thing. See my "Introduction. About Voice.")

But since intonation isn't *in* written words as it is in spoken words, the intonation that readers find there must have been supplied by themselves. (Punctuation and italics are exceptions; they do put *some* intonation down on the page.) How is it, then, that certain words on the page lead us to hear their intonation more than others? After all, we *can* sound any written word or phrase in our ears—no matter how ungainly or obscure; but only some writing somehow sounds itself in our ears. We hear intonation most obviously when written words awaken actual oral memories. "Get your paper! Read all about it." The distinctive intonation is already in our ear—ready to be triggered because we've heard the words so many times. "Forgive us our trespasses as we forgive those who trespass against us." What an awkward, uninviting sequence of sounds, but people who have said it and heard it over and over again are likely to hear it even when it's silent on the page.

But of course, we hear intonation in lots of written passages that are *not* familiar to us. Why? Musicians speak of certain passages of notes being easier to play because the notes "lie under the fingers." Even when sight-reading these passages, the fingers fall easily and naturally into the patterns or sequences that the notes

call for. Words can be like this. Even new words in new patterns of syntax can probably invite us to hear them (invite us to project the intonation), if they are easy
and pleasingly speakable or inviting to hear. Of course, different people or groups
will sometimes find different passages inviting. Grace Paley's New York Yiddish
cadences will not ring in the ears of readers who have heard only Southern speech.
This third mystery of words that give their meaning through intonation will not
operate exactly the same for all readers, but there will be large overlap.

Look again at the two passages from Booth, and notice how the first one is built
mostly out of syntactical patterns that are fairly familiar or inviting to the ear and
even to the tongue. I've italicized the parts that seem most notable in this regard:

> Any reader committed to *reading and paying attention* to *the book that follows*
> can profitably *skip this introduction.* Everything *I want the introduction to do*
> is done in the essays it introduces. *I am writing an introduction* only because
> *experience has taught me* that people who read academic criticism—usually
> authors of academic criticism—do not so much *read critical studies* as *"check
> them out."*

He's put words in combinations that invite poured in or intonational meaning.

The second passage doesn't bring as much intonation and felt meaning to our
ears as the first one—even though it does have some chunks of audible or familiar phrases that invite the ear (I've italicized them). It's a long and difficult piece
of syntax that is less inviting to say or hear:

> The difficulty in *dealing with* the relation of *shall not perish from the earth* and
> the Bible is that the specificity of the evidence can *overwhelm its presenter* and
> *lead him to posit* an audience as *finely tuned to biblical echoes* as his research
> has recently and temporarily made him.

Perhaps a reader will say, "Why make such a complicated fuss when it's all just a
difference in register between a more informal introduction and a more scholarly chapter?" Of course, that's true, but what matters here is the *effect* of changing the register on the syntax and vocabulary—and the corresponding effect on
how much we hear intonations from the page. (Note that the linguistic term *register* is borrowed from its application to the different *voices* of an organ [OED]. I
can't help wondering *why* scholars should invite each other to sound more informal in their introductions—when the subject matter is just as academic.)

Intonation is a complex topic in linguistics, but I'm content to put my case here
in the simple terms I use with first-year students: We hear more intonation and

thus hear more meaning in writing when the words, phrases, and clauses "lie beneath the fingers" of our mouth and ear—that is, when the words are inviting and comfortable to speak aloud.

If this is true, the pedagogical consequence is equally simple. When students have the repeated experience of reading their writing aloud, they are more likely to write sentences that are inviting and comfortable *to recite*—and thus to hear on the page. Putting the pedagogical principle a different way: The sound of written words when recited has an important effect on silent readers—yet far too few people *hear* the words they write. When students frequently read their words aloud and thus hear them, I see them more often writing words that *give* their meaning—words in which readers hear meaning.

Therefore, as often as I can, I try to get students to read aloud what they have written. When I ask my class to do public freewriting or inkshedding (as opposed to private writing), I almost always have us all read our words aloud in pairs or small groups. When students are working on essays, I have them read very early drafts to each other in pairs and small groups—just for discussion of the ideas, not for feedback on the writing. I have them read their middle drafts in pairs or groups for feedback. Even when I ask students to give paper copies of their drafts to each other for responders to take home in order to write more-considered feedback, I always ask them to start the process by reading their draft aloud to their responders in class. When we get to final drafts, I sometimes ask everyone to give a celebratory reading of a couple of paragraphs to the whole class. Furthermore, it's become a staple in my teaching of first-year writing to have frequent, fifteen-minute conferences with students during which they read aloud whatever version of the current essay they have in hand, and I give my feedback on the spot.[6]

So am I just asking for more speech in writing? Yes and no. I can clarify a crucial point if I articulate a common criticism: *Speech may carry meaning well because of its intonation, but speech is a terrible standard for writing. If we put speech on the page, we get a fragmented, incoherent mess.* True enough. But it is not *speech* that I am calling for in writing, it's *intonation.* I'm not asking students to reproduce speech on paper, I'm asking them to write sentences that are inviting and pleasing to read aloud—that feel good in the mouth and sound good in the ear. This is a standard that much speech fails to meet.

Nevertheless, speech is the natural home of intonation, so I don't want students to fear speech or run away from it as they write. In fact, when I ask students to freewrite or do exploratory draft writing, I frankly invite them to "talk onto the page," if that helps them write more copiously. I think teachers do harm if they try to build a fire wall between the mentalities of speech and writing and warn students to keep all speech elements out of writing (see my "Shifting Relations

Between Speech and Writing"). Casual speech may be loose and fragmentary, but if people call on their easy, intimate skill with spoken language, they can find one of the most powerful engines to make written words give their meaning to readers. The test is always reading aloud. Messy, fragmented, elliptical speech is not inviting for reader or listener.

Let me briefly address another objection: *Reading aloud will serve as a harmful crutch. It will lead students to write sentences that work when given a good performance but that don't work on the page for silent readers.* This *can* happen. Here's an example: "Divine predetermination of what shall be imposed constraints on both thought and behavior." (This problem sentence is perfectly clear if spoken because of a natural pause after "what shall be.") Nevertheless, I see students' prose helped more often than harmed when the students frequently read their writing aloud and thereby heighten their awareness of the intonation of words in the mouth and the ear. Of course, the mouth and ear can also invite some violations of written grammar, but here, too, the benefits outweigh the harms. (Cases of wrong grammar that sound fine are useful for illustrating the difference between what linguists and teachers mean by grammar. Concerning speech and grammar, see appendix A about using intonation for teaching the basics of punctuation.)

Applying Intonation to the Reading Process

I've focused on writing and the process of giving readers a stronger experience of meaning. What about reading? Can we help students as readers to *extract* a stronger experience of meaning from written texts—especially when the texts are difficult? For this goal, too, intonation is powerful.

Suppose we ask students to read a hard text, for example, a Shakespeare sonnet. Many cannot get a clear meaning without a hard struggle. Students do much better when I set them the following concrete exercise: "Work out a *speaking* or *recitation* of these lines. Your only goal is to make listeners *hear the meaning without effort.*" After students work out their readings in class or for homework (either way, I ask them to work in pairs), we hear three or four performances and then have a fairly simple but interesting discussion: "How well did each reading work? What made the good ones work?" That simple discussion leads right to the heart of the syntax and meaning—and very quickly to complex nuances of the poem.

All my work on intonation has convinced me that the cause of many students' poor reading is their lack of skill at *hearing* words on the page. They've mostly been encouraged to think of reading as a silent process of extracting purely cognitive or mental meanings from the page. Even when they're not under a stopwatch in a testing situation, they are usually in a hurry. I think I see students reading more skillfully and with more pleasure when I give them constant practice in learning to hear words on the page.

The principle at work here is the same one I've been drawing on throughout my treatment of this third mystery: *Intonation embodies meaning* (syntactic meaning especially, but also some semantic meaning). Words won't sound okay unless the meaning has been embodied into sound.

The principle applies not just to literal meaning but also to *interpretation*. It turns out that we also can't make a text sound okay unless we embody (pour in) an *interpretation*. This was Bakhtin's larger point: intonation always embodies a wide set of attitudes and implications. In our classrooms, we ask questions like these: What is Woolf's attitude toward a certain character or event? Is the Faulkner scene tragic, ironic, or slapstick funny? What kind of a person is Othello? Most class discussions of questions like these involve students trying *silently and mentally,* to infer interpretations of words *they have never heard.* But if we hear four or five readings of the same passage—where the only assignment was to "make it sound the way it's supposed to sound"—we get an interpretation already *embodied* in each reading. Instead of students scrambling to "invent" interpretations that don't yet exist, they can spell out and contrast and evaluate the multiple interpretations that are already live and physically present in the classroom air. Furthermore, students are often far more sophisticated in their interpretational skills when they try to make a text sound right than when they try to figure out an interpretation—and this skill increases the sophistication of the discussion. This process makes it quite natural to say things like, "*His* reading made the scene tragic, but *her* reading made it both tragic and slapstick all rolled into one." (For more about the performative dimension in teaching literature, see my "Breathing Life into the Text.")

Mark Levensky, my friend and colleague at Evergreen State College, liked to say, "Peter, you spend all your effort just trying to get to zero." Mark would point how *little* of the teaching of writing is covered by my three mysteries. What about the rigors of logic, good thinking, correct language, copy editing? What about the mysteries of revising and organizing? I'll conclude by arguing that the scope of these mysteries is not so limited as it might seem.

1. If we can get students to make good progress on these three mysteries, they are far more likely to *enjoy* writing and to experience themselves as writers. Discovering more words and thoughts in your head than you thought were there—the sense of a door opening and the ability to open it when you need it—what a pleasure. The experience of working your way through to words that say just what you meant to say—what a pleasure. And finally there's the pleasure of finding

words that feel good in the mouth and ear. These are experiences that keep people writing by choice and make them experience themselves as writers.

2. Work on these mysteries is not *work*. It's neither difficult nor drudgery. I'm not saying that students never resist. A few students feel that freewriting is a waste of time (though inkshedding helps here, with its social and academic payoffs). Some students roll their eyes when I try to explain felt sense to them (though they all know the feeling of not managing to say what they really mean). And many students *hate* to read their writing out loud and can sabotage the process with mumbling nonintonation and inaudibility. (They don't really hate it, but they are embarrassed. I stage most of the outloud reading in pairs and small groups—and in my office where I can encourage and cajole them not to sabotage their own words.) Still, none of these activities requires work, and I can restrict them all to five-, ten-, and fifteen-minute bits of time—dropping seeds and not being in a hurry about results.

3. Even though work on these mysteries *seems* to ignore the whole dimensions of quality (or perhaps *because* we are ignoring quality), the activities bring some surprising progress towards excellence in writing:

- Regular freewriting leads not just to writing that is alive and flexible but to a number of explicit prose excellences (see appendix B).

- When students learn to listen to felt sense and use it to work their way closer to what they really mean, they get better at thinking. The focusing process gets them to make repeated subtle differentiations or distinctions between similar meanings.

- When students write prose that feels good in the mouth and sounds good in the ear, they seldom need much feedback on clarity or even style. Yes, reading aloud can lead to prose that is too colloquial for the most academic genres, but even good academic prose should appeal to the mouth and ear while it goes about meeting other standards.

- Consulting felt sense and getting closer to our exact intention *are* revising—and teach substantive rather than merely cosmetic revising.

- Trying out one's prose by speaking it aloud is also one of the central activities in good revising and heightens one's awareness of felt sense.

4. Work on these mysteries is not work for *us* either, as teachers. It doesn't even involve responding to what students write—though it does imply reading some of what they write.

In short, if we help students work on these three mysteries, they will be much readier to engage in the inevitable work, struggle, and even drudgery of writing—and we will find it more rewarding to respond to their writing.

But I don't want to fall again into that mistake that somehow always tempts me—the mistake I made about freewriting: "Piece of cake!" I mustn't pretend there is nothing difficult here. If students are to freewrite, to consult felt sense, or to read their words aloud to a listener with full intonation, they need to do what in some ways is the hardest thing of all: to invest or even *give of themselves* with a kind of caring attention. It is hard for them to do that unless *we, too,* do something that is difficult, namely, to set up conditions of safety and trust. We see this principle strikingly illustrated in the first method for getting from no words to words: What makes good listeners so powerful is that *they* provide invested caring, safety, and trust.

Appendix A: Intonation and Punctuation

The third mystery involves an important distinction that is too little noted: the difference between the syntax of live speech in conversation and the syntax of sentences that speakers find most inviting to say and listen to. This distinction permits me to do something that many teachers view with suspicion, namely, to use intonation and performance to teach punctuation—or at least the basics of punctuation.

In my first-year writing classes, I do periodic mini-workshops on commas and periods. Using samples like this—"First it was rain then it was snow"—I do voice training and ear training. For voice training, I ask students to come up with as many different performances of these words as possible that sound right. The question is always, "Does that sound okay? Acceptable to the mouth and ear?"— so this rules out nervous monotone mumblings. I always push a little harder for odd or extreme versions so we can debate the limits of acceptability. How about no pause whatsoever between clauses? or a full stop after *then*? A student might have once heard or imagined the sentences so, but do speakers judge these as right or acceptable?

For the ear training, I have to help many of them notice the subtle differences among the ways they themselves pause in different readings—in effect, the difference between the sound of a comma and that of a period. Many of them start off assuming that a short pause stands for a comma and that a long pause stands for a period. When I get them to listen more carefully, they can hear the difference between the not-quite-letting-go sound of a comma and the letting-go sound of a period—*even when* the comma pause is very long and the period pause is very short. This is not new knowledge. Their voices have been making these oral distinctions since childhood and their ears registering distinctions of meaning on the basis of them. The knowledge tends to be tacit and nonverbal—a bodily knowledge that the students have been *using* but not consciously attending to and certainly not applying consciously to punctuation in a writing classroom.

Indeed, many students have been warned *against* using their ears for punctuation, for there is understandable resistance to this approach. Consider the title of one notable research report: "How 'Normal' Speaking Leads to 'Erroneous' Punctuating" (Danielewicz and Chafe). But this study, like others (see Chafe) focuses on normal speech and on the empirics of what students or adults do naturally without any training in the use of intonation for punctuation. The training is crucial—and even with it, the process only leads to what I'd estimate to be 80 percent conformity to the conventions of written punctuation. However, this is enough to keep untrained students from being hammered as stupid or illiterate because of end-stop mistakes. We badly need research about which intonational or prosodic shapings feel right or okay to what groups and proportions of students? How about ESL students?

This is obviously a tricky and debatable topic that I can't treat fully here. I have an essay in progress. But I can give a quick illustration of the power of harnessing intonation for help with difficult punctuation. Consider these two sentences that illustrate the pesky problem of *that* versus *which*:

The concert that is taking place on Saturday is sold out.

The concert, which is taking place on Saturday, is sold out.

Both sentences are correct; they contain no clue at all for choosing one over the other. Yet in most contexts, one will be right and the other one wrong. Not many students have the explicit knowledge needed to avoid a mistake: first they must understand the grammatical rule for *that* and *which;* but then in order to apply the rule, they must understand the difference between restrictive and nonrestrictive phrases—and be able to analyze the surrounding context well enough to know whether the phrase about the time of the concert *is* restrictive or nonrestrictive. Daunting.

The performance of intonation comes to the rescue here with a very simple and reliable rule: If you pause, use *which* and commas—if not, use *that* and no commas. I offer this example not because I think that mistakes about *that-which* are life-threatening—far from it. I want to illustrate a profound theoretical point: Many or even most punctuation rules in grammar books are built on rough *approximations* of the author's felt intention. That is, the rules try to guide us when we don't really know the writer's intention. For example, the grammar-book distinction between restrictive and nonrestrictive clauses ultimately depends on the speaker's or writer's intention—on how the speaker-writer *felt* the role of *Saturday night* in his sentence about the concert. The best window into a speaker's intention is through intonation. In short, the grammatical rule for *that-which* is tricky and not very helpful to many people; the performance rule is simple and helpful. (My explorations here were spurred by the germinal essay by John Dawkins, "Teaching Punctuation as a Rhetorical Tool.")

Appendix B. Specific Excellences Promoted by Freewriting

- Variety in syntax or sentence shapes—the opposite of stiffness and repetitive rhythms and patterns.

- Variety in vocabulary when students are writing about academic or non-personal topics. Freewriting helps students use homely and felt and often metaphorical language for these topics. (When students freewrite about informal or personal topics, the vocabulary is likely to be limited to what they use in speech.)

- A strong and lively voice in writing. *Voice* is a loose term, and so it's useful to distinguish some related but different virtues: (*a*) audible voice: writing that makes readers hear the intonation or that sounds lively and energetic, (*b*) dramatic voice: writing that gives readers a sense of a *person*, (*c*) distinctive or recognizable voice, and (*d*) voice with authority or courage to speak out. (See my "Introduction: About Voice.")

- Active thinking. There are two related virtues here: (*a*) writing that shows a spirit of inquiry or questioning or perplexity and (*b*) writing that shows movement of thinking and reflects a mind actively in the process of thinking.

Notes

I'm grateful for feedback on drafts of this essay from many participants at the Miami conference, Abigail Elbow, Helen Fox, Eugene T. Gendlin, Paul Matsuda, and Edward M. White.

1. Most young children are pleased with the words and thoughts that come out of their heads and are proud to share them, but some students have heard so many critical responses to their words that they gradually internalize that response and can't hear anything but criticism from their own inner voices. Yet charitable and nonjudgmental readers can help these students use the same process of gradually internalizing what was external in order to *learn* to read their own words in a charitable or nonjudgmental way when they want to use low-stakes writing for exploratory invention. James Britton et al. talk about the important role of "trusted adult" in the teaching of most anything.

2. The way this sentence corrects the previous one is just the kind of adjustment that comes from noticing felt sense—a process of getting closer to the insight you were feeling.

3. I'm describing the assumptions about speaking and writing that we find in our culture. As I understand it, other cultures—Native American? Asian? early Anglo-Saxon?—have less tolerance for light or unconsidered speech. By the way, this distinction between attending to internal felt sense versus external standards of excellence corresponds to what Sondra Perl spoke of as "retrospective structuring" and "projective structuring."

4. Caryl Emerson, writing about Mikhail Bakhtin and Lev S. Vygotsky, declares, "Individual consciousness is a socio-ideological fact. If you cannot talk about an experience, at least to yourself, you did not have it" (26). She quotes a remarkably doctrinaire statement from Bakhtin: "Experience exists even for the person undergoing it only in the material of signs. Outside that material there is no experience as such. . . . Thus there is no leap involved between inner experience and its expression, no crossing over from one qualitative realm of reality to another" (Bakhtin, *Marxism* 28). When I or Gendlin stick up for the possibility of knowledge or experience that is nonverbal, we are not making a naive claim that experience is entirely *unaffected* by language or culture—just that there is a crucial space or leverage to work with.

5. In the same essay, Mikhail Bakhtin stresses something else important about vocal intonation: the need for what he calls "choral support." That is, the intonational wind usually goes out of our voice if we feel that others are likely to criticize us or feel unsafe in some other way. That's why people often speak in gravelly monotone voices when they are in high-stakes academic or business situations—and why students often mumble their speech in class. However, Bakhtin fails to note an important exception: Strong feelings or passion will often preserve vivid intonation in our speech, even in the absence of choral support.

6. I *think* I see this process helping ESL students, too, but most of those that I teach already have a fair command of English. Do ESL students benefit as much from an emphasis on the ear? I don't know if there's research on this. We certainly need research about this matter with native speakers. By the way, my individual conferences are not so much of a time burden as you might think. I have conferences with half the class each week. Because I don't have to take these papers home for written response, the process doesn't actually cost me extra time: fifteen minutes of conference time is less than it takes me to write a response at home.

Part 1 What Do We Mean by Composition Studies—Past, Present, and Future?

2 The Great Paradigm Shift and Its Legacy for the Twenty-First Century

LYNN Z. BLOOM

> Most post-process theorists hold three assumptions about the act of writing: (1) writing is public; (2) writing is interpretive; and (3) writing is situated . . . and therefore cannot be reduced to a generalizable process.
> —Thomas Kent, Introduction to *Post-Process Theory: Beyond the Writing-Process Paradigm* (1999)

> My lessons cover ways to compose with computers . . . to manage the time that completing a beautiful text requires, to collaborate practically with others, and to revise and evaluate one's own writing. Without these lessons in composition, typically called a 'process' but lately identified by 'post-process' theorists as an activity comprising too many distinct tasks and minute-by-minute choices to be a teachable algorithm, my students retain their awe of . . . printed texts and their writers. But demystifying lessons in the acts and habits of confident writers . . . focuses students' learning.
> —Susan Miller, "How I Teach Writing," *Pedagogy* (2001)

The Great Paradigm Shift, from the "traditional prescriptive and product-centered paradigm" (Hairston 80) to "teaching writing as process, not product" (Murray, "Teach Writing"), remains a significant influence in composition studies because process philosophy and research-based pedagogy continue to retain their power in textbooks and in the classroom. With modifications and contemporary upgrades, they will do so as long as one of the major aims—and responsibilities—of the profession is to continually improve our teaching of writing. Meanwhile, theory and research in the current post-process era and in the as-yet-to-be-labeled future enable the profession to move beyond the limitations of process theory and models to address a host of other issues from diverse social, multicultural, ethical and other perspectives. Because process remains the default mode in much of our thinking about writing, I will divide this chapter into three parts: Where

We've Been—The Process Paradigm; Paradigm Drift—Post-Process Definitions, which includes a rereading of *Lives on the Boundary* (1989); and a look at composition studies of the future in Process, Post-Process, and Beyond.

Where We've Been—The Process Paradigm

Let's begin with a brief, nostalgic look at the good old days of the process era—when process theory, process research, and process teaching were in harmony. What we think we know, we forget, as familiarity neutralizes and blurs distinctive features of even the most vital entity. In another decade or two, the term *process,* once as cataclysmic as the explosion of the atom bomb, may become as bland and unremarkable as *current-traditional rhetoric* is to the entire profession at present. And though still viable, just as vague.[1] In "Stepping Yet Again into the Same Current," George Pullman offers an insightful, relativistic contemporary definition of current-traditional rhetoric, which differs significantly from the implied definition of fifty years earlier:

> The expression refers to how traditional rhetoric influences our current understanding of composition, which means that current traditional rhetoric is today concerned with understanding how the tradition is written, with the work of people such as Richard Enos, and Jarratt and Schiappa, while the current traditional rhetoric [fifty years ago] was concerned with how to apply Aristotle's insights to Freshman Composition. (22–23)

So first, a definition.

Process Definition. "What's the magic word?" asked my interviewer in 1977, looking for a codirector of a National Writing Project affiliate. "Process," I shot back, in the spirit of "plastics" as the mantra of the future in *The Graduate.* We grinned conspiratorially, for we had the keys to the kingdom undiscovered by our indifferent literary counterparts. "You're hired," he said.

Here's what turned us on. In "Toward a Post-Process Composition: Abandoning the Rhetoric of Assertion," Gary A. Olson provides a contemporary interpretation of ten essential characteristics of the thirty-year-old process paradigm that remain significant in the new millennium:

1. Writing is an activity, an act composed of a variety of activities.

2. The activities in writing are typically recursive rather than linear.

3. Writing is, first and foremost, a social activity.

4. The act of writing can be a means of learning and discovery.

5. Experienced writers are often aware of audience, purpose, and context.

6. Experienced writers spend considerable time on invention and revision.

7. Effective writing instruction allows students to practice these activities.

8. Such instruction includes ample opportunities for peer review.

9. Effective instructors grade student work not only on the finished product but on the efforts involved in the writing process.

10. Successful composition instruction entails finding appropriate occasions to intervene in each student's writing process (7).

Although these writing-process principles have been interrogated, expanded, adapted, and modified from the time Hairston articulated them in the classic "Winds of Change,"[2] they remain today a beacon for classroom teachers, glowing through turbulent post-process skies.

The Joys of Process

There are many reasons why the process paradigm won the hearts and minds of English teachers and researchers. In contrast to the current-traditional paradigm, which it either replaced (Murray, "Teach Writing as Process, Not Product") or supplemented (Crowley, "Around 1971"), the process paradigm was dynamic, not static. Coming of age in a revolutionary era that gave power to the people, especially to women and minorities, this paradigm was empowering to teachers and students alike. It was reality based, focusing on actual writers—from the most sophisticated to the most naive—in the act(s) of writing. It was obvious—to the converted, anyway, and accessible in principle and in practice. As John Clifford explains, "Like New Criticism a generation earlier, process gave writing professional credibility. It could generate theory" and, I would add, research—"while allowing for an accessible pedagogy" (Clifford and Ervin 180). Arriving at the same time as deconstruction and other critical theories that were armored in thick abstractions and expressed in darksome jargon, process was a welcome alternative that—in research and in practice—could be discussed in plain, understandable concepts and everyday language.[3]

Because process seemed so clear and straightforward, teachers could quickly understand its concepts and put them into effect without much (if any) training, though the National Writing Project and its affiliates were created to help translate theory and research into classroom application.[4] Particularly if teachers were writers themselves, they could recognize how the general process framework—prewrite, write, rewrite, and variations—could accommodate their own practices and those of their students. This is true despite the fact that some teachers and whole school systems voided both theory and practice by reducing the writing process itself to a formula: "Prewrite on Mondays, Write on Wednesdays, Revise on Fridays" (Couture 30). Nevertheless, when employed as intended, the process paradigm allowed for considerable individuality, particularly when readers were regarded as part of the transaction (as in the revival of Louise M. Rosenblatt's *Literature as Exploration* 1938, 1983). Process research of scholars as diverse as Janet Emig, Donald Graves, Sharon Pianko, Nancy Sommers, Sondra Perl, and Mike Rose focused on a variety of students in school settings. The elasticity of the process paradigm was demonstrated in research by Carol Berkenkotter, Lee Odell and Dixie Goswami ("Writing in a Non-Academic Setting"), and Linda Flower and John R. Hayes ("Images, Plans, and Prose"), among others,[5] whose studies expanded to include people of differing ages, abilities, jobs, and status performing varying tasks in diverse settings. It is axiomatic that process research was cutting edge in the 1970s and 1980s and established the reputation of these scholars.

In its days of youthful exuberance—the 1970s and early 1980s—the process paradigm was exhilarating. Inherently democratic, it was calculated—through accommodating a wide variety of writers and writing processes—to produce a nation of good writers committed to their own process and invested in their own writing. Its promulgators, such as Murray (*A Writer Teaches Writing* and *Write to Learn*), Peter Elbow (*Writing Without Teachers*), and Mike Rose (*Lives on the Boundary*), themselves epitomized the four Cs—compositionists of competence, confidence, and collegiality—and thus became instant gurus with large followings of teachers who to this day remain loyal to the pedagogical philosophy embodied in their works.[6] Examining "the process of writing as followed by most professionals" (xi), in *A Writer Teaches Writing*, Murray showed teachers how to help their students discover a subject, sense an audience, search for specifics, that is, "to show instead of tell," create a design, write, rethink, and rewrite (2–13). By decentering the classroom and encouraging teachers, as Nancie Atwell put it (4), to come "out from behind [the] big desk," the process paradigm was compatible with Paolo Freire's liberatory pedagogy, and a fitting response to the turbulent 1960s, "the years of Kennedy, King, Vietnam, urban riots, student protests, and Watergate" (Harris, *Teaching Subject* 26).

Paradigm Drift: Post-Process Definitions

American academics are a dissatisfied lot; the academy seems to function most happily in an adversarial mode. Popular paradigms can't be all good, popular research can't be always right.

The critical tradition of literary scholarship, whose antagonistic character Olivia Frey labels "literary Darwinism," has obliged composition students to "invent the university" by adopting its argumentative stance (Bartholomae, "Inventing"). Thus it is inevitable that even the most widely adopted paradigm and the most respected process research have drawn fire. Time and knowledge move on.

Process research and its resultant pedagogy were initially centered on the individual writer and the writer's private views of the world. Teachers worked with individual students to enable them to discover an effective process to liberate these nascent ideas struggling to breathe free. Critics equated such process orientation with expressivism—self-indulgent writing in contrast to real-world demands for meaningful, goal-directed communication; their hostility to personal-sounding writing persists to this day. Yet the process paradigm—and virtually all of the process-oriented textbooks after the 1970s—allowed for many different kinds of writing, especially narratives, expositions, and arguments. Scholars in the early 1980s sought to open up these conceptions. In well-received articles, Lester Faigley ("Competing Theories of Process") and Patricia Bizzell ("Composing Processes") "identified three main strains of process thinking (expressive, cognitive, and social)." James A. Berlin ("Contemporary Composition") labeled the "major pedagogical theories" as "classicist, positivist, expressionist, and new rhetorical" (Harris, *Teaching Subject* 54–55). The seeds of post-process were planted in these critiques, particularly the social-constructionist view that understands writing to be "culturally and socially mediated behavior" (Petraglia 54).

While the process paradigm today remains paramount in teaching writing (to which I shall return later), its survival as a subject for research has been superseded by a host of other issues and methodologies, many addressed by other contributors to this volume. Although some label the times we live in *post-process*, *post-process* is a term that, like its counterpart, *postmodern*, seems vague in comparison with its referent. A poll of teachers-on-the-street might elicit a post-process acknowledgment that writing is a social action in a variety of social contexts. Even among those who use the term with confidence, there is no readily identifiable configuration of commonly agreed-on assumptions, concepts, values, and practices that would comprise a paradigm. In a forthcoming book, Lisa Ede examines "The Writing Process Movement and the Professionalization of Composition," concluding—among other things—that process never really disappeared, because

> arguments for writing as a social process rely upon the same strategies used to establish the writing process. Just as scholars arguing for writing as a process reified and essentialized a diverse group of scholarly and pedagogical projects into current-traditional rhetoric, so, too, did scholars arguing for writing as a social process reify and essentialize a diverse group of process-based products.

(outline, chapter 2)

In its minimalist sense, post-process may simply be a chronological marker to indicate the passage of time, with various topics of current concern grafted onto an essentially process-oriented view of composition studies. This seems to be the perspective of Libby Allison, Lizbeth Bryant, and Maureen Hourigan's *Grading in the Post-Process Classroom: From Theory to Practice,* one of the few books with *post-process* in the title, whose editors claim that "lettered grades demanded at semester's end are at odds with post-process composition theory" (back cover). Yet the contributors concentrate on the phenomenon of grading—in student-centered classrooms, the heart of the writing process.[7] Victor Villanueva Jr.'s afterword reiterates the pervasive theme: "Writing is a process. Ultimately, first-year composition emphasizes awareness of writing as a process—from a process of jotting meaningful marks on a page . . . to a process of discovery, to a potential process of change (of the self and others)" (178).

Nevertheless, post-process scholars themselves do agree on the following. Process theory is too big, too encompassing, say the post-process critics, who begin where the 1980s critiques leave off. Process theory proposes a common writing process, about which generalizations can be made. In contrast, post-process theorists accept as a fundamental truth, proclaims Thomas Kent in his industrial-strength definition that introduces *Post-Process Theory: Beyond the Writing-Process Paradigm,* that "no codifiable or generalizable writing process exists or could exist," and thus there is no Big Theory that can capture what writers do (1). Kent explains why in three major assumptions about the act of writing:

1. Writing is a public act—a public interchange between the writer and "other language users" to whom the writing must be accessible. We "could not write at all if it were not for other language users and the world we share with others." Thus there can be no possibility for "private" writing. Because any given act of writing is specific to individuals at specific moments in time and because these individuals and relations are always changing, no single process or account of a process can capture what writers actually do (1–2).

2. Writing is "a thoroughly interpretive act"—making sense of what is going on in both the "reception and the production of discourse." Writing means more than translation, paraphrase, or moving from one code to another, which process pedagogy encourages. Writing is always context-specific: too much of the 1970s and 1980s process research decontextualized writers, or created arbitrary, unreal laboratory settings. Post-process theory, says Kent, is sensitive to the circumstance that

> When we read, we interpret specific texts or utterances; when we write, we interpret our readers, our situations, our and other people's motivations, the ap-

propriate genres to employ in specific circumstances . . . Writing requires interpretation, and interpretation cannot be reduced to a process. (2–3)

3. Writing is situated. That "writers always write from some position or some place; writers are never nowhere" is a tenet both process and post-process theorists share. The latter suggest that to communicate we need "a cohesive set of beliefs about what other language users know" and about how they will "understand, accept, integrate, and react" to our communication. This constitutes a "prior theory." Indeed, the advice given in process textbooks (meaning all textbooks today) rests on this assumption. According to post-process theorists, however, "no two people ever hold precisely the same prior theories"; we actually use a "passing theory" to communicate, and this shifts depending on the context. What matters is how we employ our "beliefs, desires, hopes, and fears about the world" to formulate passing theories "in our attempts to interpret one another's utterances and to make sense of the world." Because passing theory never "stops" to let us "capture some sort of unitary, complete, or determinate meaning," it "passes" away. It "never endures, never works twice in quite the same way." Thus our acts of writing, always dependent on a situated, improvisatory "hermeneutic dance," can "never be reduced to a predictable or generalizable process" (4–5).

Kent's definition of post-process theory is to composition studies what deconstruction is to literary criticism. Its extreme situational specificity precludes the "model-making," derived from a coalescence of "law, theory, application, and instrumentation," that Thomas S. Kuhn defines as a paradigm (*Structure* 222). Post-process theory, strictly applied, would make a composition class an oxymoron—as well as an unteachable algorithm, to paraphrase Susan Miller's definition in this chapter's epigraph from "How I Teach." Only individual tutoring adapted to the specific paper of the individual student (or collaborative writing group) at a particular time in a particular context would be possible.

Joseph Petraglia is not as arbitrarily dismissive of the process paradigm as is Kent. In "Is There Life after Process?" Petraglia analyzes the influence of "social scientism" to explicate the connections between process and post-process. His explanation of their relations is analogous to the phenomenon of *pentimento* in painting, where an underlying image in an older painting shows through in the newer paint that has been applied on top of it. For Petraglia says that "the fundamental observation that an individual produces text by means of a writing process has not been discarded. Instead, it has dissolved and shifted from figure to ground." The process paradigm "infuses our awareness of writing, it tinctures our thoughts about writing instruction, and trace elements of it can be found in practically every professional conversation" (53).

While to some this would indicate that the composition culture is steeped in the process paradigm, to Petraglia this signals that we are *past* process, for we "now have the theoretical and empirical sophistication to consider the mantra 'writing is a process' as the right answer to a really boring question. We have better questions now." In the late 1980s and throughout the 1990s, the conception of how writing works had been animated by three complementary sets of questions and observations, he says: (1) "Writing genres, audiences, and writers themselves are socially and culturally constructed"; (2) "The ways in which writing gets produced are characterized by an almost impenetrable web of cultural practices, social interactions, power differentials, and discursive conventions governing the production of a text, making writing more of a phenomenon than a behavior"; and (3) The notion that the writing process is a predictable and regular system has been critiqued from "political, social, philosophical, linguistic, and socio-cognitive perspectives." As with many other movements and theoretical schemes, the label is applied ex post facto to the phenomena it encompasses. As the new millennium approached, *post-process* could be attached to what Petraglia calls "not a paradigm at all, but a shorthand for an eclectic assortment of frameworks devised for the study of human activity" (53–55).

Rose's *Lives:* Process and Post-Process Fused

Lives on the Boundary may be read as a work embodying the fusion[8] of process and post-process theory and practice. That this is not a contradiction may be one major reason for the book's enduring popularity and iconic status.

Mike Rose didn't start out that way, but then, nobody did in the 1980s. His early work, epitomized in *Writer's Block: The Cognitive Dimension* (1984), is traditional though ingenious process research, derived from his doctoral dissertation. He interprets laboratory case studies of students with writer's block, "a composing process dysfunction" (3) manifested, for instance, in an absence of "planning strategies," premature editing, or rigidly misapplied rules: "Writing has to be logical. . . . Writing is not good if it's not clear, vibrant prose" (49). *Writer's Block* epitomizes in theory and method what Petraglia calls the "old social scientism" that sees "writing as a compendium of discrete general skills used by individuals." Rose's research seeks to discover "the processes by which effective writing can be produced [and] taught"; he offers "heuristics to assist teachers and students of composition"; the book is "practice and pedagogy centered" (Petraglia 55).

By 1989, Rose had rediscovered his roots, literally and figuratively, in the brilliantly innovative *Lives on the Boundary,* the blockbuster book that had more influence on composition studies in the first half of the 1990s than any other work.

At first glance it looks like a process book, a literacy autobiography embedded in a characteristic American bootstraps narrative. In Rose's version, a poor but bright youth awakens to the possibilities and the promise of higher learning and "enter[s] the conversation" as a Loyola undergraduate (69). John Trimbur summarizes the plot:

> We follow Rose on a kind of pilgrim's progress, from his struggles as a high-school student who arises, miraculously, from the slough of Voc-Ed despond, through college and the temptations of literary studies in graduate school to his redemptive work as a teacher of the neglected and underprepared. ("Articulation Theory" 238)

This progress is full of vignettes that serve as case studies and group ethnographies of the students' "struggles and achievements" in the arduous path toward literacy and the engagement with ideas that is "the essence of humane liberal education" (Rose, *Lives* 48).

Rose's scenarios are scenes from the theater of guerrilla teaching rather than a scripted series of stages through which all writers must pass to arrive at the promised land. Rose does not have to spell out step by step the process approach that he uses to writing—as a way to learn, as a means of self-expression and self-fulfillment, as the antithesis to a rulebound orientation. His readers already understand the process that emerges in fragments throughout Rose's discussions of classroom practice. Thus he considers his returning Vietnam veterans at UCLA "strangers in a strange land" who want to "change their lives" through education. Rose's "careful sequencing" of reading and writing assignments, moving "slowly" from summarizing "through classifying and comparing to analyzing" assumes that the veterans will "pick up the details of grammar and usage" as they go along, without formal instruction (*Lives* 137–43).

Although process underlies Rose's pedagogical method, post-process dominates his philosophy. For Rose, as for Kent, learning—as manifested in thinking, reading, and writing—is public act, situated, and "thoroughly interpretive" (Kent 1–3). As a post-process work, *Lives on the Boundary* incorporates—in humanistic terms, without later post-process jargon—the principles that Petraglia attributes to the "new social scientism" that undergirds post-process views of writing. From this perspective "writing is a socio-cognitive phenomenon dependent upon historical and cultural context" (Petraglia 55). Rose is acutely aware of issues of "background and social circumstance . . . intersections of class, race, and gender" (*Lives* 177). Thus he presents every group of students he teaches—as a member of the Teacher Corps in El Monte, as a tutor for Veterans and other underprepared (often minority) students at UCLA—in multiple contexts, reinforced by his own comparable experiences. As students ten years younger, the veterans, for instance, might have been "a high school teacher's bad dream: detached or lippy or assaultive," Rose's Voc Ed "comrades reincarnated" and out of reach because of "the poverty and violence of the neighborhoods," family dynamics, peer culture. But "different life experiences" bring "different perspectives on learning"; the "sullen high schoolers" metamorphose into mature believers in the American dream, "bringing with them an almost magical vision of what learning could do for them"—"'I'm givin' it a hundred percent this time'" (*Lives* 137). Through such "'thick' description" of "writing [and learning] behavior and patterns of writing behavior," Rose seeks to provide a "deeper and more complex understanding" of the contexts of learning and of writing (Petraglia 55). However, although post-process is in general theory-centered, *Lives on the Boundary* is all about teaching and learning and how to do both better. Theory can be extrapolated from this compendium of best practices.[9]

Process, Post-Process, and Beyond

It is hazardous to predict the future of theories and the evolution of paradigms, even though the reckoning lies on the indefinite horizon. Along with a number of speculations, I will offer here one true thing about teaching writing in the foreseeable future.

The one true thing. The process paradigm—once radical—is now the dominant, default rubric for teaching writing. It will continue to prevail in textbooks and presumably in the classrooms in which these books are used.[10] Teachers entering the profession since the late 1980s take process for granted, as Nancy DeJoy confesses in "I Was a Process-Model Baby."[11] The textbooks following Elbow's liberating, liberatory *Writing Without Teachers* (1973), including Elbow's own *Writing with Power* (1981), have been process oriented. Yet as Sharon Crowley ("Around 1971," 1996), Faigley (*Fragments*, 1992), Robert J. Connors (*Composition-Rhetoric*, 1997), and others have observed, most if not all of the most widely adopted books have grafted process terminology onto the preexisting current-traditional paradigm. Among these are such staples as James McCrimmon's *Writing with a Purpose* and Connors and Andrea Lunsford's own *St. Martin's Handbook*. In creating an amalgam of the two paradigms, these researchers say, the textbook authors made no significant changes; it was current-traditional business as usual—a critique that Joseph Harris levels against the textbook that Flower derived from her process-protocol research, *Problem-Solving Strategies for Writing*. This paradigmatic blend continues to dominate rhetorics and many readers

(David Bartholomae and Anthony Petrosky's *Ways of Reading* is the exception rather than the rule).

Yet, even Harris's perceptive analysis does not raise the most potentially damning question of all, which is dauntingly difficult to investigate: Do students actually write better—however one defines this—in a process curriculum than under other competing models?[12] Success stories from master teachers notwithstanding, I can find no compelling research on the subject—large-scale, long-term, or otherwise—to demonstrate the clear-cut efficacy of process teaching.[13] Because this subject does not appear to be a compelling issue in contemporary research, as long as process continues to feel good, teachers will continue to use it.

Now for some speculations.

1. The current split between theoretically sophisticated research and process-model composition classrooms will continue and will probably widen. Petraglia's hypothetical worst-case scenario, that "the writing field hunkers down into the general writing-skills trenches and reverts to the purely service status it has struggled to overcome" is unlikely. The large numbers of composition-studies specialists trained in the past twenty years can be counted on for a militant defense of their hard-won turf. Nevertheless, the current orientation of postprocess theory, which sees writing "as another site of cultural studies lending itself to theorizations of power, ideology, and the construction of identity" will continue, at least for awhile, unconcerned with "validation from empirical research" (Petraglia 60–61).

2. Radical changes are occurring in the ways we think about genre. Barbara Couture explains that "textual theory has deconstructed the foundational belief that truthful writing corresponds to a single concrete reality and that facts are disassociated from beliefs." Cultural studies, for instance, has "led us to rethink assumptions about the neutrality of certain discourse forms favored in the academy or in the business world." Discourse modes and styles—such as the model of the scientific method—"establish power relationships, exclude some groups, and mask underlying ideologies and assumptions." Moreover, some researchers (Berkenkotter and Huckin, *Genre Knowledge in Disciplinary Communication;* John Swales, *Genre Analysis*) now see genre not as the static designation of a rhetorical mode but as the entire, dynamic "context of textual production and reception" (Couture 41–42).

3. We will continue to rethink and revise what it means to write and to teach writing in and beyond the composition classroom. The following list illustrates some of those areas currently under (re)consideration.

- *New conceptions of what it means to write.* These include developing "rhetorical sensitivity" in students—awareness of the rhetorical possibilities in particular social situations, considering "verbal alternatives," attempting to "process and to choose among all possible verbal strategies *before* giving utterance to an idea" (Hart and Burks qtd. in Petraglia 62). This can be translated into "knowledge design," in which students, through analyzing others' "situated rhetorical performances" can apply the same "reflective sensitivities" to their own texts (Kaufer and Dunmire 230). In *Reflection in the Writing Classroom*, Kathleen Blake Yancey expands on the analogous concepts of *reflection in action, constructive reflection,* and *reflection in presentation* (13–14). And there is the by-now familiar concept of *Writing as Social Action* articulated by Marilyn M. Cooper and Michael Holzman.

- *New types of students.* As culture becomes truly global, its concerns are reflected in the changing campus that models the world. The now-familiar perspectives of race, class, and gender are now being supplemented by concerns with sexual preference, disability, and age (Malinowitz, *Textual Orientations;* Brueggemann, *Lend Me Your Ear;* Rinaldi, "Journeys Through Illness"; and Ray, *Beyond Nostalgia).*

- *New areas of the curriculum.* The well-established conceptual underpinning of writing in the disciplines, in law and business schools, in and with ever-higher technology, grows increasingly sophisticated (Russell, "Activity Theory").

- *New places in the extracurriculum.* Reading and writing are now taught in community settings—youth centers, inner-city communities, book clubs, sites of service learning, hospitals, nursing homes, homeless shelters, prisons, governmental offices, and granting agencies (Flower, Construction of Negotiated Meaning; Cushman, The Struggle and the Tools; Gere, Intimate Practices; Herzberg, "Community Service and Critical Teaching"; Ray, Beyond Nostalgia; Winslow, "Poetry, Community, and the Vision of Hospitality").

- *New emphasis on qualitative issues.* This focus includes lore, values, ethics, emotions, intuition, inspiration, power and powerlessness, therapy and healing, spirituality (Bishop, *Teaching Lives;* Mortensen and Kirsch, *Ethics and Representation;* Fontaine and Hunter, *Foregrounding Ethical Awareness;* Brand and Graves, *Presence of Mind;* Foehr and Schiller, *Spiritual Side of Writing).*

- New conception of relations between the academy and the world beyond. David Russell observes:

  Although there has been important research in the writing processes (genre systems) of nonacademic settings, there has been comparatively little research into the relation between writing processes in activity systems of academic disciplines, professions, families, neighborhoods, and activity systems of formal schooling. (89)

In "Activity Theory and Process Approaches," he shows how this can change.

4. Most dramatically, the nature of the entire relationship of humanities teacher to student to subject has the possibility of being completely transformed. As Kurt Spellmeyer asserts in *The Arts of Living: Reinventing the Humanities for the Twenty-First Century,* ever since Matthew Arnold, we have given higher priority to criticism—"a reactive, consumerist mentality"—rather than to creation. This needs to change, for learning should once again become an active *process* with creation rather than criticism as its aim. "Our task is to democratize the arts, not simply by making more accessible the work of 'great artists' . . . but by creating a world in which everyone participates in art and feels entitled to be an artist" (483, 500).

A paradigm, whether the process paradigm or any other, may be seen as a model that enables those who adopt it to tell a story, or a nest of stories, about what it means and how those meanings may be used. Newcomers become initiated into the community of paradigm-users through the stories they hear. They become members of the same community through the stories they tell—of new applications of the paradigm, variations on it, extensions of it, always pushing the boundaries, as is true of post-process developments and projections. You are reading in this book the stories, familiar and comforting, new and exciting that our colleagues past and present are telling and will embellish in the future. As long as the fundamental narrative retains its usefulness, elegance, and beauty—and the process paradigm does so to this day—it will not perish from the composition studies universe.

Notes

1. Try this quiz. Q: Name at least ten features of the current-traditional paradigm, some aspects of which (especially concerns with form and style) still remain current. A: We'd all get this one: "An emphasis on the composed product rather than the composing process" (Richard Young qtd. in Hairston 78). A corollary is the resultant emphasis on prose models, epitomized in the four modes of discourse—description, narration, exposition, and argument. However, would we still remember that the emphasis is on "expository writing to the virtual exclusion of all other forms," that this paradigm "neglects invention almost entirely" (Berlin and Inkster qtd. in Hairston 78), concentrates on style and usage (Richard Young in Hairston 78), and "posits an unchanging reality which is independent of the writer and which all writers are expected to describe in the same way regardless of the rhetorical situation" (Berlin and Inkster qtd. in Hairston 78). Hairston supplies three additional features: "Its adherents believe that competent writers know what they are going to say before they begin to write"; thus their most important task at the outset is to find the appropriate form that will orga-

nize this content. The adherents also believe in a linear composing process, and that "teaching editing is teaching writing." Unlike the process paradigm, which is derived from the "composing processes of actual writers," research, and experimentation, the current traditional paradigm "derives partly from the classical rhetorical model that organizes the production of discourse into invention, arrangement, and style"; and is a "prescriptive and orderly view of the creative act" (Hairston 78).

2. Hairston's account shares with Olson's the holistic view that regards writing as a "recursive rather than linear process" and a "way of learning." However, whereas Olson treats this paradigm "first and foremost [as] a social activity," Hairston focuses on "the writing process," teaching "strategies for instruction and discovery," considering "audience, purpose, and occasion." She explains that its recursive nature involves a combination of overlapping, intertwining "pre-writing, writing, and revision" activities accomplished through rational, "intuitive and non-rational" means. Writing is a "disciplined creative activity that can be analyzed and described" by linguists and process researchers, anatomized in textbooks, and taught—preferably by teachers who themselves write. The underpinning of cognitive psychology and linguistics, and the "variety of writing modes," from expository to expressive (Hairston 86), have faded from Olson's rendering of this paradigm.

3. Because it can be discussed in accessible language does not mean that the process paradigm is devoid of theory nor that theory can only be expressed in abstract, difficult concepts and language—"the smart for the smart," as Susan Miller characterizes it ("Writing Theory" 62). That this accessibility has meant that some literary critics consider composition studies as "theory lite" (in contrast to the more dense, abstruse language of critical theory) in no way diminishes the value of either the theory or the process.

4. While English and language arts teachers have a disciplinary advantage in understanding and applying writing process principles, teachers in other disciplines have more problems. Their impulse is to use the model they remember from their own high school or undergraduate schooling rather than the process(es) they engage in as publishing professionals. Typically, they assign specific topics, providing few if any directions on how to write the paper. They read and comment only on the final draft, using intermediate drafts (if any) to ensure against Internet plagiarism. Revision opportunities are few. Instructors in Writing Across the Curriculum faculty development programs often have to spend considerable time convincing participants of the inadequate pedagogy of this approach; even when teachers are unhappy with the papers written in this traditional manner, they are often reluctant to change—usually on the grounds that responding to drafts is too time consuming.

5. It would not be too great a stretch, in my view, to include among highly influential works embodying process concepts James Moffett's *Teaching the Universe of Discourse* (1968) and his *Student-Centered Language Arts Curriculum K–13* (1992); James Britton, Tony Burgess, Nancy Martin, Alex McLeod, and Harold Rosen's *The Development of Writing Abilities* (1975); Mina P. Shaughnessy's *Er-*

rors and Expectations: A Guide for the Teacher of Basic Writing (1977); and much of the 1960s and 1970s sentence-combining research and pedagogy (O'Hare; Morenberg, Daiker, and Kerek) and pre-writing (Odell; Kytle).

6. The common sense, friendly tone, and accessible language of these authors not only ensured their popularity but seem to have protected them from destructive, negative criticism until after their work and reputations were well established. Murray and Rose, I believe, have no significant detractors except for the generic argument espoused by J. Elspeth Stuckey in *The Violence of Literacy* that school-sanctioned literacy practices deracinate the culture of those who must conform to middle-class language and embedded values. Trimbur, however, defends Rose against this charge by showing that

> what allows Rose to evade the class-bound limits of the self-made coming of age narrative ... is his refusal to separate himself from the lives on the boundary and to take on the kind of distanced lucidity that Sartre finds characteristic of the genre. . . . Rose never quite leaves his neighborhood or his youth behind. ("Articulation" 248)

Those who tar Elbow with the expressivist brush and dismiss all expressivism include Elbow's primary antagonist, David Bartholomae, in "Writing With Teachers: A Conversation With Peter Elbow," which dented neither Elbow's following nor his reputation.

7. For example, in the book's lead chapter, David Bleich concludes:

> It is about time that we stop wringing our hands about grading and, instead, commit ourselves—teachers and students—to the principles of teaching without competitiveness, hierarchy, and authoritarian value, to teaching through cooperation, interaction, mutual respect, and communication. (33)

These are Freire's liberatory principles articulated in the works of teachers most closely associated with process—Murray, Elbow, Rose, and Atwell.

8. I use the term as physicists would, to denote "a nuclear reaction in which nuclei combine to form more massive nuclei with the simultaneous release of energy" (*American Heritage Dictionary* 714).

9. Rose, who often interprets student writings as records of struggle, "testament[s] to the power of desire" (*Lives* 147) has been criticized for providing ways to help students accomplish what they themselves want to do—to learn the lingua franca, a "discourse of possibility" (*Lives* 79) and to learn the values of the upper-middle-class mainstream rather than encouraging them to resist these (see Stuckey, *Violence of Literacy*). This narrow, elitist argument is not particularly post-process, and it ignores the pervasive message of *Lives on the Boundary:* "Philoso-

phy, said Aristotle, begins in wonder. So does education"—and that sense of wonderment and delight is within the reach of everyone on earth (223).

10. Lisa Ede discusses the implications of this in chapter 4, "Thinking Through Practice: On the Resistance to Theory," of her forthcoming book *Situating Composition: Composition Studies and the Politics of Location.* She examines how "scholarly practices of writing may (unintentionally and ironically) contribute" to the resistance of students and teachers to theory in composition, with a particular focus on her own changes over the years in directions to students on the processes of how to write papers and other contextual considerations. (The quotation is from Ede's annotated book outline, thoughtfully supplied to the author.)

11. Newer teachers cannot experience the "heady sense of breakthrough" of 1970s teachers who encountered Elbow's *Writing Without Teachers,* the quintessential anti-textbook of its time. Smitten with "desire to operate outside oppressive institutions and avoid the errors of the past," recalls Trimbur, newly liberated teachers embraced "freewriting," "growing," "cooking," the "teacherless writing class," and other manifestations of process pedagogy that remain serviceable today ("Taking the Social Turn" 110).

12. Elbow's *Writing Without Teachers,* Murray's *Write to Learn,* Rose's *Lives on the Boundary,* and Atwell's *In the Middle: Writing, Reading, and Learning* exude the happiness, the euphoria, the sense of discovery, and the progress that energize teachers and students in the best process classrooms (and, indeed, the best classrooms of any sort, as exhibited in the works of Wendy Bishop *(Teaching Lives: Essays and Stories),* Pat Hoy *(Instinct for Survival),* Susan H. McLeod *(Notes on the Heart: Affective Issues in the Writing Classroom),* Richard J. Murphy Jr. *(Calculus of Intimacy: A Teaching Life),* Joseph Trimmer *(Narration as Knowledge: Tales of the Teaching Life),* Victor Villanueva Jr. *(Bootstraps: From an American Academic of Color),* and Kathleen Blake Yancey *(Reflection in the Writing Classroom),* among others). These books are full of individual examples and anecdotal evidence that process works, but because their authors are such gifted teachers, anything they do might work equally well.

13. There are many reasons why such research doesn't exist. Even if distinctively positive results could be demonstrated—for a class of process writers or a process-oriented curriculum or a group of teachers, it is almost impossible to conduct the research in a way that could replicate the results. Various sites of the National Writing Project have at times been under pressure to demonstrate the efficacy of process teaching in the schools of funded teachers. Why spend taxpayers' money on a major pedagogical change that has little or no measurable impact? The attitudes and knowledge of National Writing Project teachers can be measured pre- and post-participation. That is often done, supplemented with information about curricular changes, in-service workshops, and other in-school evidence of the exposure of teachers and students to the National Writing Project's philosophy and practice. For instance, the National Writing Project evaluation, as reported in 2001 by the Academy for Educational Development, focuses on the amount of time NWP teachers spend per week in teaching writing, "an analysis of teacher assignments and corresponding student work, written surveys, and

telephone interviews with NWP teachers," focusing on "'authentic intellectual work'—the original application of knowledge and skills rather than the routine use of facts and procedures . . . and the emphasis NWP teachers place on such work in their assignments" (Bradshaw 1).

None of these phenomena, however, address the quality of student writing or how well teachers and students retain and apply process principles over time. The same sorts of illustrative examples that buttress the professional literature can shore up the general impression of success (no one wants to demonstrate failure) in a given year of a particular program—just as they can in college writing programs—but definitive, replicable data is hard to come by (see, for instance, Witte and Faigley, *Evaluating College Writing Programs*). Large-scale, longitudinal studies are plagued by high attrition rates of student participants, even from one course in a composition sequence to the next. Writing project teachers do not necessarily have the same students before and after their project participation. Student writing is subject to a myriad of influences, for better and worse, in addition to those they encounter in composition class. Over time, writing ability deteriorates unless it is used and reinforced continually—but according to what criteria? And more problems too numerous to identify here.

3 Why Composition Studies Disappeared and What Happened Then

SUSAN MILLER

On the morning after Pearl Harbor in 1941, my stepfather went to the Japanese embassy in Washington, D.C., my hometown. He took everyone there to Union Station and a train that went somewhere else. That day the embassy closed, a suddenly silent witness to the worst possible failures of relationship. I was a child accustomed to the quiet around staccato raps of guns and swords and salutes, so I understood exactly what my father meant when he much later told what that morning was like. I could see each person, ambassador to cook, filing out, carrying only a few permitted possessions, boarding a bus, equal in this one day of delayed recognition. It was very scary, he said. No one said a word.

My responses to sudden and enforced change are also wary. I would like, especially so soon after we begin to learn from terrorists, to avoid certainty about meanings and definitions. Instead, this is what George Pullman calls a rhetorical narrative, a case that performs experience (21–22). This Tarot-deck sort of proof depends on uncovering figures of thought that may help us discern human edges and new emotional declivities in the planes and patterns that until recently have made the term *composition studies* legible. My argument, however, is that the overlayered past and present of composition studies meet in definitively unsettling ways. Thus, in a specifically disheveled, postcomposition moment, I take comfort from my father's memory of another time when the world seemed suddenly disintegrated. Everything had already changed that next day. No one said a word. Yet, a future in which we ask new questions and expect new stories to answer them was already in progress.

Any analysis of this memory of course most emphatically points toward changed relationships that are suddenly uncovered as fully disrupted identities in moments that mutually collapse theories and practices. Such moments are complicated. They create a simultaneously active resilience and a passive inertia—

a gaggle of emotions experienced as observations. Here, composition studies continues to enact results similar to those of public-educational agendas that were first articulated in America in the late-nineteenth-century and to reproduce many of this project's teaching methods, established soon after. Yet, both that public project and its methods themselves meshed past and present to enact existing, constitutive cultural ambivalence toward postsecondary mass education. We know too well that in the context of that mixture, later heroic attempts at a class-blind professionalism by composition studies are after all realized in hierarchical patterns that produce academic celebrities but mostly unrealized improvement in the status of composition teachers and estimates of their students.

This is not to set aside our appropriate celebrations of the achievements that make any of us object to calling this time a postcomposition era of disintegrated identity. However, those attainments may now also be late-age memorials, remnants of a more generally lost confidence in identity politics and its creation of both academic celebrity and the positions of students who have been its fans. Composition studies became a solid field, that is, just when a client-based, product-oriented, community-embedded New University foretells an unfamiliar, fragmented, and to us a newly trivializing view of its traditional work.

The volume of collected essays that represent the earlier version of this forward-looking conference implies that I have a very small burden of proof in making this point.[1] First, it certainly identifies composition studies as an overlayered novel-traditional circle. Most directly, the Robert J. Connors–Sharon Crowley exchange about abolishing the first-year course requirement tells of continued energetic wishes to erase freshman composition as against the energies, and the inertia, devoted to maintaining it.[2] That discussion shows that little novelty results from the process movement that is everywhere a fulcrum in our modern histories. That is, apart from the friendly prewriting aura that movement has successfully installed, the assignments and evaluations of the early century continue in a field that deploys that happy inventive moment as the only sign *or* substance of changes in most composition teaching. Stephen M. North adds in the wake of Connors and Crowley that our research has as well not been a sterling "code of conduct and a set of promises to be lived up to" ("Death" 200) but "directed at perfecting a set of institutional practices that . . . are objectionable" (201), and, he implies, holdovers from the past.

Respondent C. Jan Swearingen lists other difficulties with the identity of composition studies ("Prim Irony"). For instance, insiders critique pseudo reformism and the Marxist devotion to a social justice that frets all the way to publishers' parties. Many condemn histories that deny what they take to be the obvious individual agency of teachers and students. However, many equally berate individualistic teaching and learning, admit everyone's complicity in using wretched textbooks, and note the pressures imposed on teachers who haven't resources to write their own. Many bemoan too much introspective writing; some claim that the results of introspection will be calls to and acts of revolution (76).

A few in this earlier collection also support my second claim that unfamiliar demands on a New University will trivialize circular dissatisfactions like these and the traditional *ethos* that is at stake in their persuasion on any side. Certainly, neither my view of composition studies nor theirs portends revolution, not as an internal *coup* nor as a benign fulfillment of a discipline-in-progress. We instead look to a shift we will not control, one that brings up the relevance of our practices in administration, curricula, and research. The formerly inconceivable landmark projects of this shifted formation are already underway, as witnessed by Sarah Freedman, Linda Flower, and Shirley Brice Heath. They describe responses to demands that the New University incorporate its dependency on its immediate surroundings, not merely tolerate it. They especially point to a new instructional model that acknowledges the diversely situated language practices of its valued clients. Freedman and Heath separately argue that this reenvisioned ad hoc writing takes place in what Heath calls "a field of communicative and visual arts" (240). There, Flower argues in her similar "Literate Action," writers are not meant to read and interpret texts but to produce writing that is "not autonomous but . . . parts of social actions and events" ("Literate Action" 252). They engage activist composition with people who already move in and out of college to supplement individual and group self-teaching, and they foretell the community learning-health centers that John Trimbur also describes ("Writing Instruction").

Having remembered the range of these thoughtful critiques and prescient visions, I might now say no more, but in addition to my noticing inattention to technology and Lynn Z. Bloom's reference to a very telling indifference to creative writing ("Conclusion" 276), I want to interrupt this earlier conversation, at least momentarily. My claims, that is, are contextualized elsewhere, in what I understand as a crucial failure of ethical persuasion, a change that has disrupted our profession's constitutive relationships. This failure, I think, makes novel-traditional dissatisfactions, the assumptions that Heath, Freedman, Flower, and Trimbur tacitly undo, pale against new premises about writing and the academy. Authority as prestigious influence is now detached from composition, even in its self-parodic "nonauthoritarian" classrooms. Our unstated root metaphor—promised growth in people, not in the sophistication of their skills—no longer advances interest in the limited range of approaches we take to the teaching of writing. In sum, composition in its current incarnation as a profession devoted to students about whom the institution remains tolerant but ambivalent still honors the ancient Platonism that imposes the goal of improvement on us all. We lead students to a transcendent status, or more accurately, to desire for that status: to a wish to be better, not specifically practiced and informed. In so doing, we have inadvertently assured that composition studies has disappeared.

In *Post-Process Theory,* George Pullman explains this primary idea that well-formed language and supposed universal desire for it equal an improved being. This belief is, he says, a humanistic prejudice that "writing is a way of life." That prejudice, until recently a premise of authorship, also normalizes slogans like "'writing is rewriting' and 'vision is revision,' and the frequently enacted belief that (essay) writers are somehow better than non(essay) writers because they have keener insight and more polished self-reflecting mirrors." Evidence of this privilege for the writing life abounds. We regularly project the power of properly internalized writing instruction to fix a self that is, he says, "a text to be constantly revised, amplified, polished, and presented for critique and praise" (25).

That daunting goal warrants generalized attention in composition studies to self-revelatory writing assignments that often expose student values and ways of realizing them that we pretend we never share, yet hope, precisely, to improve. This ambivalent belief system similarly transposes liberatory pedagogies onto those students who are already deeply committed to shoring up traditions that oppose their leftist foundations and who are certainly not the peasants on whose cultures that pedagogy may work wonders. Following Plato in the *Republic,* not Aristotle's *On the Soul,* many think writing instruction has power to overturn family wisdom and to untie students from community, religious, occupational, economic, and regional heritages whose positive impact on academic history we largely deny. No early English journal or professional debate denies this divisive social-cultural mission. All assume that writing teachers mediate relations to higher culture and to a higher status, that the interior lives of students can be enhanced by composition's more and better ways of moving them toward Idealist realities.

My point is that its persistent worries about novel-traditional self-definition divert composition studies from its unbroken cooperation with one ethical persuasion, the privileging of the always emerging, never realized ethos, with results apparent in its administrative practices, curricula, and research. Nonetheless, a culturally norming ethos is increasingly experienced as trivial by students, colleagues, changed institutions, and a larger profession, whether it is sought straightforwardly as aestheticized sensibility or displaced onto flat vocationalism, the universal practicality of composition. Colleagues and students would admire composition studies if it asserted its expertise in the conventions of any sort of text but expertise is not the point of ethical proof nor the primary result of the field's judgmental evaluative practices. Instead, we embody and privilege a better, writing life, an ineffable quality of experience. We hereby slight specific knowledge in ways that undercut our hotly voiced demands that teachers be compensated equitably in institutions that do reward demonstrations of expertise but do not usually prize the unrealized value of personalities. Composition studies thus enforces evaluative judgments while rejecting as common opinion, as mere *doxa,* the respect already accorded them as knowledge of the increasingly secret secrets of producing traditional texts. It focuses on selected readings, not on rhetorical actions that warrant wars, laws, and consent to them. It equally admires but names as aesthetic, and thus mystified, the control of language production that enriches imagination, for whatever purposes.

Unfortunately, the field's commitments to enhancing the identities of its students and its own members often also result in substituting unexplained evaluations of its students' good guesses about their teacher's preferences for measurements of well-explained techniques in their texts. Unlike the elite students drilled in rhetorical methods to communicate an already realized ethos, contemporary recipients of the lessons of composition are thus left with longing for power, not access to its symbolic habits. Whether topics of essays are derived from literature, personal experience, or from quick-cut sound-bite versions of culture, and whether they are prescribed or in Janet Emig's term are "self-sponsored," their execution and its possible results are not so vivid as their place in our trademarked growth toward an elevated ontology.

This focus on the ethos of teachers normally results in its evaluative disposition and emphasis on prestige as both a manner and a content for a discipline. Prestige and the rewards that go with it in the academy follow those whose work and expectations imitate the celebrity of insightful interpretative readers, not those who work on behalf of teaching and learning to write. Time for research and writing especially comes from and goes to faculty members who do not teach writing, or appear not to, and who measure those judgments, paradoxically, against others who do admire anyone with knowledge about writing both well and poorly. Celebrity thus becomes an inadvertently firm obstacle to bringing to teachers theorized information about syntax, stylistics, pedagogy, classical rhetoric, literacy studies, history of usage, public-language policy, or relatively successful, situated writing processes.

In support of these claims, David Bartholomae also noted in the previous collection on composition studies that "composition has produced and justified a career that has everything to do with status and identity in English." He says it is "increasingly common to find a specialist [kept] from the scene of instruction that defines his or her specialty" ("What Is Composition" 23). He verifies the paradox I describe, that the reward for going into composition to purvey the writing life is to evade all but its ethical images by avoiding teaching and responding to writing. That diverted career and training for the field lead away from the margins many complain of, but they do move toward full interpretative collegiality in a composition studies whose study is hermeneutic. This path around what is known across disciplines about how to write starts at the deeply held belief that a proper relationship to writing is personal, already realized, never learned, never the result of practice. It circumvents canons of arrangement and style, prescriptive text linguistics, and a better pedagogy of process, or appears to, because those bodies of information are now firmly associated with the unfortunate need for mass education in vernacular language, not with pure research or with texts that are interesting enough to interpret precisely because they realize that knowledge.

I'm well aware that these claims seem willfully peripheral to those too busy with administrative persuasion and teacher training to overthrow outworn values just now. I also know composition studies, just *as it is,* has made enormous theoretical contributions to the humanities by taking up the writing subject as an object of study. It hereby has encouraged critiques of authorship and has enabled analyses of political and other culturally effective prose as products of situated composing, not of reading. The field also hugely supports the fresh materialist textual histories that many in literary studies now undertake because they see all textual forms and their sites of production as routine objects of study. However, composition studies itself most often avoids this recent textual scholarship. It is irrelevant to students' ethical shortcomings, which as Heath has demonstrated are actually imposed stereotypes of gender, race, and class deficiencies. That is, composition studies prefers a safe identity politics, one that can focus where Jean Baudrillard, in "Plastic Surgery for the Other," says it must to assimilate its Other as a nonwriter, the unschooled and unaestheticized who are voiceless and incapacitated outside the writing life.

Many local variations on research, curricula, and effective public projects like those of Heath and Flower would seem to refute these points with a different proof from projects based on the motives and purposes of audiences for composition studies, not on its self-definitions. However, such evidence is also to my point, that a certain persuasion based on the ethos of a writing life has gone missing. Its alternative is visible in the ways these different, nonevaluative projects appreciate very well-developed and smartly managed, indigenous writing practices, even those in academic discourses that vehemently ignore insight and consciousness. Yet, we retain even in these interests a notable unwillingness to explore new projects that value situated literacies apart from their spiritual access to elevated consciousness.

This recalcitrance may result from fear of losing hard-won, still-uneven support from colleagues who depend on composition studies to attract graduate students who share their own interpretative writing life. However, for whatever causes, only a small number of professionals in composition studies appear to feel the pull of EFL, of critical discourse theory and genre studies, or even of the emotion studies exploding throughout the humanities and scientific psychology. Many hire computer and composition specialists, not to reeducate colleagues about the details of electronic curricula but to relieve them of its mechanical implications. All know that expertise about how to find, use, and evaluate research sources, now databases, has long been a sign of a writing life, not of a library's information technology. As a graduate student in composition in my program recently put it, relegating research methods to libraries, applications of computerized composing to technology-assisted instruction centers, and concern about graduate students' professionalism to centers for teaching excellence all suggest an abdication in English departments of their only remaining applied, systematic interests in the production of texts.

Such a view may seem gloomy in excess, certainly irrelevant to the pleasures of teaching and its evident results. Yet, insofar as students and institutions themselves now set aside the four-year-hiatus model of attendance and the shape of curricula based on this outdated norm, it is reasonable to explore alternatives. What happens after the failure to elevate permanently the quest for a superior, self-monitoring introspection and its attendant protocols for projecting human universals onto texts? We may not be convinced with Crowley's *Methodical Memory* that difference and diversity are discouraged by the methods of novel-traditional composition. We may not have cross-cultural experience of how stereotypes of student Others are retrogressive nor infer this point from recent, forced recognition of stereotypes imposed on the American ethos internationally. Most of us do now accept the limits on insisting that Shakespeare and Hugh Blair knew a universal human nature and do acknowledge the element of voyeurism in studies of cultures that never reference the indigenous literature of the cultures under investigation. In sum, the teeth in equating clear, correct English with a personae—in deference to the recent novel by Zadie Smith, the *White Teeth,* in this equation—have less bite. The foundational ethos that centers traditional, current, and postmodern composition studies slips into history as a construction whose purchase on conventional teaching is past.

Now, I imagine a different writing studies forming around writing processes that are investigated beyond cognition and abstract thought and consciousness. Writing studies would still contain required and elective writing instruction so long as graduate programs need support and a larger community thinks that the content of this instruction is expertise about how to write. However, insofar as it directs attention to practices rather than an interiorized writing life, it will also respond to an otherwise obvious, happily fragmented, social emphasis on production. We have many examples of that emphasis, even if we rarely generalize from them to reinform our own practices. Instances include the eager, widespread composition of Web pages and restriction of that form of writing in prisons; the music tapes, home videos, and CDs that students regularly turn out for each other and their own sense of craft; the emerging young artists who focus on novel ways of making images and texts at least as energetically as they attend to the representations these experiments create; and the myriad public writing groups across the country turning out fiction, autobiography, memoirs, family history, and children's stories.

These and many other elected alternatives to sanctified composition multiply across both publicized and self-contained sites of production. They suggest that in a client-based New University, we have increasing difficulty in maintaining the ethos that knows better than students the appropriate uses of writing and that defines them as ancillary to personal, not social, development. That University, finally noticing the community—often the slums—around it, places cooperation at stake as much as it does canons. The liberal arts certainly thrive but now as "the liberal arts," in quotation marks, a reference to but one cultural heritage among others that it is increasingly crucial to study. Teachers turning to writing studies mediate among such mixtures of academic, professional, and institutional desires. They and their students emphasize craft, not personal relationships. They devise family literacy centers and open community writing centers—not for remediation but to offer sites that acknowledge the mutual enrichment that results from ordinary literate habits: storytelling, senior reading groups, and Cicero for executives. Writing studies, that is, praises a satisfying completion of texts and sharing them, not just vision as revision.

I'm sure it is finally obvious that emerging writing studies does not celebrate the post-process movement now said to theorize composition anew. That theory claims, in Gary A. Olson's words, that "any attempt to construct a generalizable explanation of how something works is misguided in that such narratives inevitably deprivilege the local" ("Toward a Post-Process" 9). Certainly, many generalized explanations may be misguided, as I think this one is. That is, without a stake in a general theory of how composing and texts work, there is no justification—as some already suspect—for hiring composition specialists who claim more interest in generalized explanations of reading than in general theories of writing. There will certainly be no reason to support graduate degrees in composition studies whose recipients do not acknowledge that writing is both process and product. Writing studies, that is, may occasion vital new attention to writing practices from activist teachers. Should the claims of post-process theory become a model for the field, its administration will be in the diffident hands of those with no general ideas about writing and no disciplinary mandate to develop them.

Eight years ago, Kurt Spellmeyer said at this conference that "the freedom that people are pursuing in their private lives they increasingly expect" (but do not find) "in the public sphere," especially not in classrooms ("Inventing" 38). He noted that many social achievements for which the academy wants credit have begun outside it. In my parallel view, new, decentered ethical ideals that emphasize making also begin in practices outside the academy, much like those glimpsed in interviews with those stunned by the attacks on Washington, D.C., and New York City. These diverse yet almost uniformly articulate adults and children composed their responses to horrific events with grace, citations, and marvelously artful narratives. Few contemporary, media-inundated Americans, that is, are without the rhetorical skill or discursive energy whose ownership composition studies and the writing life want to retain. If we do not engage this local knowledge and venture to make informed generalizations about it, we will not only look in vain for the missing audacity about the best minds that has made composition studies cohere in all its versions. We will also be without all power but that to read, not write, our own, now ended, history.

Notes

1. See Pullman 21–22.
2. See Connors, "Abolition Debate," and Crowley, "Around 1971."

4 No Discipline? Composition's Professional Identity Crisis

RESPONSE BY CHRISTINE FARRIS

> The major argument used against lifting the requirement is ideological, and it invokes composition's traditional service ethic. It goes like this: "Our students need what we teach."
> —Sharon Crowley, *Composition in the University*

Not long ago, while serving as acting chair of my department, I was summoned to the dean's office because the history department had decided it wanted to offer freshman composition. Ever more shrewd interdisciplinarians occupy department foxholes these days, especially if their institutions have adopted responsibility-centered management (RCM) or some similarly titled plan whereby deans' and departments' budgets are tied to course enrollments. As both a writing program administrator and a writing-across-the-curriculum veteran, I felt I should go armed with more than just a "Composition R Us" turf-war speech. With little time to mount a defense, I took along our materials for preparing new composition instructors—a ten-pound, three-ring binder known as the Black Notebook, complete with color-tabbed sections devoted to our course aims, variations on the main syllabus, the six-assignment writing sequence, prewriting and peer review exercises, how to teach analysis, converse with sources, and respond to drafts.

The administrator from the history department brought a slim volume on writing for history and the social sciences. Pointing to a page listing sample writing assignments, he said, "We thought we'd do a few of these in a history lecture–discussion section format. After all, you write about literature and culture in those composition courses. Literature, culture, history, what's the difference?" "It's the difference," I said, "between an intensive-writing course and a composition course. It's the difference between that little book about writing-to-learn and the contents of the Black Notebook, which includes the collective knowledge of composition experts as well as the faculty and instructors in our program, who teach together and regularly revise these materials, and who will continue to teach writing for the rest of their professional lives."

This was an ironic if not heretical moment, as I had spent a good part of my professional life collaborating with faculty from departments like history to complicate the very expertise I was now defending. We spent the rest of the meeting sorting out matters having to do with composition's disciplinary authority (what it is that we know better about how students produce written texts), what might be termed composition's use value (*why* students need to learn to write), and its exchange value (seat time, credit hours, teaching-assistant stipends). Clear distinctions among these interdependent categories, are, of course, impossible.[1] For instance, if no one in the university believes that students need to learn to write (use value), composition will cease to have exchange value, despite the empire-building desires of English or any other department. To suggest the inseparability of these matters, however, is not to endorse a hermeneutic that grants composition exclusive claim on students' literacy instruction. Just as we would now question any one theoretical model for organizing our knowledge of writing, so should it be difficult to comfort ourselves with any seamless narrative of theoretical coming-of-age, disciplinary success, or inalienable rights. As John Trimbur suggests in *Composition in the Twenty-First Century,* composition, like any discipline, is a social, not merely an intellectual formation ("Writing Instruction" 136). Consequently, "we ought to consider how the politics of professionalization affects writing teachers, writing programs, and writing scholarship in unequal and contradictory ways" ("Writing Instruction" 134). Nevertheless, does our inability to agree on a unified theory mean that composition ought to give up its disciplinary authority? Or, despite the intellectual contradictions caused by the politics of the institution, can composition find a way to ground itself in disciplinary expertise? Our conference session, "What Do We Mean by Composition Studies— Past, Present and Future?" with Lynn Z. Bloom and Susan Miller, addressed these and other questions by considering the extent to which composition can serve its disciplinary ends while still tied to the agendas of the institutions that discipline it. Continuing a conversation begun at the first conference, Bloom and Miller explored the field's trajectory by distinguishing between process and post-process theories and their implications for research and practice. While Bloom sees little threat to composition's disciplinary authority, Miller feels that a combination of outmoded institutional assumptions about students and increasingly disparate research agendas call that authority into question.

Attention to process in the last thirty years has made it possible to view writing not merely as a product but as a social activity amenable to teacher intervention, a view that Bloom and Miller agree still shapes instruction. However, there is widespread post-process acknowledgment that because writing is situated and interpretive, no generalizable theory of the writing process exists for the field to work from. Consequently, Bloom and Miller wonder whether the research made possible by wider disciplinary boundaries provides evidence that students write better as a result of composition instruction, and they suggest that in the absence of this proof, the split between theory and practice(s) in the field will widen.

Bloom downplays the split, however, normalizing the process–post-process difference with an examination of the changing praxis of Mike Rose. In the self-reflexive but instructive *Lives on the Boundary,* Rose exemplifies for Bloom the ways in which an earlier focus on growth can remain at the center of an invigorated composition studies committed to a more situated view of writing processes mindful of students' multiple subject positions.

Miller, on the other hand, sees post-process scholarship threatening to undermine the basis of composition's authority at the same time that writing instruction masks these threats in holdover practices from the past. More important to Miller than epistemological hand-wringing, however, is what she views as composition's failure to defend its use value. Although composition has grown as a respectable discipline with scholarship focusing increasingly on "indigenous writing practices," its original mandate to improve student writing and the working conditions for writing teachers has not changed. Although we may have given up what Stephen M. North terms "paradigm hope" ("Death of Paradigm Hope" 194) (that research will provide us with the best way to improve writing), we have not, Miller says, relinquished the power supported by the composition imperative. The unexamined assumption that all students *need* to acquire a feel for the writing life still forms the basis for composition's holdover requirement, its gatekeeping function, and its complicity with English and university hierarchies.

Speakers at the 1993 twenty-first-century conference (North, Anne Ruggles Gere, Linda Flower, and Shirley Brice Heath) predicted the expansion of research beyond the traditional classroom to literacy sites promising change in both curriculum and community. In the absence of a paradigmatic top-down model for composition research that determines practice, new sites for investigation, including new configurations of writing instruction like WAC and service-learning, invite new questions, methodologies, and responsibilities (North, "Death of Paradigm Hope" 203). However, this absence of "validation from empirical research," Bloom believes, will not result in a return to a belief in general writing skills. Rather, she is confident that, influenced by extracurricular and cultural studies as well as diversity, ethical, and spiritual issues, we will reconceive "what it means to write and to teach writing."

Miller acknowledges these new directions for literacy inquiry but is leery of compliance with the production agendas of noncomposition English studies and the "client-based New University." Post-process reluctance to make any generalizations about writing from the investigation of situated literacy practices risks reinscribing the untroubled "improvement of writing" while threatening unified authority for composition. Miller envisions these disparate projects loosely organized under the umbrella of a less institutionally powerful interdisciplinary writing studies. The extent to which such a program could house composition courses that reflect the variety of new knowledge produced in its various research settings (and do so without overcodifying that knowledge) remains to be seen.

Bloom's prediction that compositionists will defend their hard-won turf was realized immediately in the response to our panel from audience members, who tended toward a post-process reluctance to accept even this much generalizing about the field. Despite composition's institutional position, discussion reflected the ways in which teachers and WPAs will struggle, as Bruce Horner claims ("Traditions" 371), to make their work and the discipline meaningful in practice. Consequently, discussants were more comfortable with Bloom's vision of an expanded usable notion of the writing process than with Miller's more deterministic and cautionary one. Some participants indicated that they did not recognize themselves in Bloom's and Miller's presentations, given, as Trimbur points out, the differences in the material conditions of their work, that is, types of schools, students, writing programs, and opportunities for research ("Writing Instruction" 139). Several took issue with the research-teaching split, claiming that either their own or someone else's scholarship had indeed contributed to a reshaping of their pedagogy in ways that challenge the current-traditional status quo. Others, either directly or indirectly, revealed they had no problem with composition's or the university's endorsement of the desirability of "the writing life." One respondent, citing Miller's reference to September 11 discourse produced outside the university, said that now more than ever such events justified, rather than rendered superfluous, the composition classroom as a space for dialogue and reflection. I read the audience response not as a resistance to post-process theory, however, but rather as an enactment. As Gary A. Olson remarked later the same day, post-process theory is not a replacement top-down paradigm but what permits us to better understand the practices we have.

After the conference, in light of our session, I thought some more about the history department's incursion into English territory. I agree that we would strengthen our stake in student writing and make our public arguments more persuasive if we were drawing evidence from relevant disciplinary scholarship. We should strive to bring into a better (and less hierarchical) alignment theoretical claims, research agendas, course content, and conditions of work. Certainly, the expansion of disciplinary boundaries and scholarly venues with little to no change in the status of most writing instructors makes visible contradictions that now leave English departments open to future turf battles, if not ideological embarrassment. However, finally, I believe composition will be forced into realignment, not so much through an ethical or theoretical argument but a material one. Along with new general-education initiatives aimed at recruitment and retention, it is no wonder that departments looking to amass revenue and territory in an ever more corporate university will want, despite our expanded disciplinary redeployment efforts, to trade on the extent to which composition is as much about inclusion and exclusion as it is about writing (Miller, *Textual Carnivals* 55; Crowley, *Composition* 253). In the end, exchange value presupposes all other categories. If we produce good, if not better, products—courses, notebooks of smart materials, well-prepared instructors, and students whose writing is "parts of social actions and events" (Flowers, "Literate Action" 252), we have no apologies to make. This is the work we do. To quote Hyman Roth's reminder to Michael Corleone in *Godfather Part II,* "This is the business we've chosen." Composition will only maintain control of the exchange value, however, as long as we continue to redefine its use value. The cross-curricular and extracurricular sites for the production of discourse, including community literacy work, virtual-community Web sites, service-learning venues, that are changing our assumptions about what it is that students need in order to analyze and produce discourse, are also changing our expertise. Furthermore, there is more than one kind of writing expert whose local practices—teaching, research, and consultation—can produce local change. As Trimbur suggested at the 1993 twenty-first-century conference, WAC, for instance, can work "within the contradictions of professional life by producing new producers of knowledge outside existing monopolies of expertise" ("Writing Instruction" 145).

The meeting with the dean ended with a suggestion that interested and experienced history TAs collaborate with us in the composition proseminar and the teaching of first-year writing. As a result, they might return to the history department to design and teach intensive-writing courses. In the proseminar, they will enhance our English-centered understanding of interpretation and production and, ultimately, the use value of all our writing courses. I am confident that we can make more of the institutional structures in which we work and draw from an ever-changing disciplinary expertise to convince the university and the public that there is value in more than one kind of writing life.

Note

1. As Bruce Horner points out, in Marxian terms, all scholarly labor, including publications, grants, and courses, is a commodity, and both use value and exchange value reside within a commodity (*Terms of Work* 5, 211).

Part 2 What Do/Should We Teach When We
Teach Composition?

5 Because Teaching Composition Is (Still) Mostly about Teaching Composition

WENDY BISHOP

> If we approach teaching as a career-long process of constant renewal, we're going to have to work much harder at it, but, as students may learn when they take a fascinating and very demanding course, some things can be more work and yet less like work.
> —Jerry Farber "Learning How to Teach: A Progress Report"

Imagine three composition teachers—one from 1980, 1990, and 2000—visiting each other's classrooms. The 1980 teacher would certainly be impressed with 1990's students' small-group draft-sharing and the quality of the writers' discussions, and both might be impressed by 2000's on-line conferencing capabilities, but none would be particularly uncomfortable entering the other's physical and intellectual workplace. Because United States universities continue to pair one writing teacher and twenty to thirty writing students and set them on a term-long path of creating and responding to texts, the majority of our first-year writing courses still take place in the general classroom, amidst clumsy patterns of desks, chairs, and book bags; with hard copy, pen, imagination, story, persuasion, time limits, and talk; in the form of drafts, drafts, drafts.

Despite the intense attention of compositionists over the last forty years to disciplinary history and the creation and evaluation of a great amount of field scholarship, the majority of writing classrooms remain much as they were when our field's senior scholars entered them as teaching assistants or first-time writing instructors, probably because most of these courses continue to be taught by similarly credentialed faculty. And it is within these writing classrooms that we most often address the problems and pleasures of teaching and learning writing. It seems important, then, to return those sites, to reconsider pedagogical roots, to discuss anew both acts and actions, and to focus on teaching. Teaching writing.

Teachers thinking about teaching writing. Students' writing. Students thinking about and learning to write. Students' identities as writers. Students' written texts.

As I drafted this chapter during the dramatic and disturbing events of September 2001 following the destruction of the New York World Trade Center and the attack on the Pentagon, I was reminded that whatever my allegiance, my region of preference, my theory pod's place on the map, I'm part of the whole, acting, reacting, contributing, and constructed. Immediately, it felt like a joke or a bad dream that those in composition who cared about individual writers, who allowed themselves to be labeled expressivists, who wrote with and for their students through the tumultuous 1960s and 1970s, should have been marked down as having embraced a pedagogy that reflected little-to-no-social awareness.

Who doesn't walk from the house to the car to the parking lot to the classroom? Who doesn't stop at the store, pass the newsstand, share the world's words, talk to family, support charity, attend local events, and observe larger ones? Perhaps a change in our national consciousness—as we come to a renewed understanding that we all do these things—can mark a change in our intellectual consciousness also. We need to be collegial and generous—within and without our profession— and to do so on our own best terms, because enforced generosity or legislated belief matter not a whit. In fact, they are destructive oxymorons. The place I matter most, I believe, is locally, as a teacher. I should be proud of this, engaged by this, articulate about this: I should study my writing classrooms, I should report back.

In a recent term, I began teaching an undergraduate course about theories of composing with a very mixed enrollment of students due to the coveted Tuesday-Thursday early-afternoon time slot. Although not officially a writing-workshop course, the plan, as in all my classes, was to use writing to learn and to study ourselves as writers. Due to a misguided presemester cut-and-paste syllabus-making moment, I arrived in class with course-information sheets where the page with the journal-assignment component read:

> For all assigned chapters, please do the following: [Here my students found a great big BLANK—no directions at all]. Although you're welcome and encouraged to make additional entries, please be aware that these are public journals. That is, at times, peers will be reading them. *Please bring your journal to each class.*

In class, looking at this page and seeing what I had done—or rather what I had not done—I gulped and thought, "Ah, a teaching moment." Two students sitting to my left had enrolled in a previous term's workshop and I already knew they didn't like journal requirements. Looking to where they sat, I saw their resistance hardening. I also thought, "Well, do something quick, begin by asking students what they find valuable or problematic about keeping course learning journals. Keep today's class moving. *Try not to look too stupid.*" Three minutes into our discussion, it became increasingly clear that the entire class was significantly antijournal. Another teaching moment. "Give them their resistance," I thought as I decided on the spot that we'd create our own journal assignment.

The next class period, I asked each group to look at a handout, from Toby Fulwiler's edited collection *The Journal Book,* listing attributes of good journals. I mentioned the basic role journals would play in the course, that the goal of keeping one was to help class members think informally about composing, and that the journal would provide one-fifth of the course credit (along with three short, multidrafted papers and class participation). Then I asked each group to create the language that should have been included in the syllabus: that is, to design their own preferred yet meaningful course-long assignment. I would post those group options on our course discussion list and ask class members to commit to the version that seemed most valuable to them.

A cautionary lesson in student empowerment ensued. Three of the four groups agreed quickly on their requirements. One group could not agree, and I asked the members to send individually designed options to me via a follow-up email. Each set of class-group–generated options turned out to be very much the same and to be surprisingly like what I might have asked for except for the infinitesimal paring away of length; clearly, the class remained unconvinced, and no one much wanted to write no matter how eager I was to read. Members of the group that couldn't agree on their own criteria during class discussion also failed to send me individual versions. Then, Corey's solitary, days-late message skidded onto my email screen:

> I apologize for the tardiness of my reply. After some thought, I have decided that a Journal for this class should be structured as an intense personal examination. Each journal entry should reflect a wide range of expressions on a specific personal focus which begins, ideally, with strictly the empirical form (e.g., face, hands, navel, etc.) employing wide ranges of media if necessary to convey an image either visual (pictures, words, random colors, hell even video), auditory (short recordings of sleep, songs of original composition which could be written or recorded), olfactory (the verbal expression of the skin exposed to metal, collected scents, b/o), or digital (glued in textures that resemble/elucidate on what it feels like to be one's self). These entries will hopefully grow from there into complex and intimate verbal representations of the personal emotions one feels with the various parts of one's self (e.g., frustration with my stationary mouth). Rather free-form granted, but a process that will hope-

fully allow its proponents to move from extrospective examination to introspective bonding with self. By shifting the writer's scrutiny from that which is
other than self to that which is purely self, may or may not be an effective way
of touching the parts that examine the writer's relation to his/her approach
to craft. These should be epic free writes that have been reexamined, possibly
using areas of the text that apply, and reworked to present an adequate representation of one's vision of and feelings toward the various facets of self.

Mulling over what to make of this comment, because I was only then getting
acquainted with that class and that student, I found myself asking whether the
writer was feeling facetious, playful, stoned, exploratory, sloppy, or serious (his
email handle was *kidprodigy*, after all). Whatever the answer, I was interested in
the way this email made me consider my own course position: Was this response
bullshit and should I address it as such? Was this response a confirmation that
students do see themselves as writers, contrary to the cyclical and predictable bad
press about any current generation? My response to this student would draw on
my entire teaching history, my constructed-self-in-culture, as I reached out to
understand Corey and his constructed-self-in-culture.

Lynn Z. Bloom reminds me that I'm a middle-class white woman teaching
generally middle-class students:

> When we teach composition (and anything else to undergraduates), we teach
> a complex of the teacher-class values (read *virtues*) embedded in every main-
> stream institution of higher education in the country. Even at the risk of sound-
> ing politically incorrect, the message is plain: we want our students to share
> our class values. ("Teaching" 28)

And I wonder what it would mean for a change not to respond with guilt to this
fact, to move from useless apology into exploration as I consider the benefits and
strengths of caring about teaching writing. That is, I don't find it productive to
spend a teaching life assuming that I'm teaching for suspect, seldom-interrogated,
and impoverished reasons. If I do, what becomes of me as a classroom teacher?
Do I become burned-out or endlessly apologetic? Do I turn defensive, snobbish,
or jaded? If I'm not careful, I could find Corey crude, immature, or boring. I could
continue the tradition of professorial snobbery that reaches back to the beginnings of the last century:

> 1911: Professor Thomas Lounsbury in *Harper's* "ridicules the very possibility
> that most college students could learn to write well or that students might
> actually have something interesting or important to say. At various points in

his essay, he describes students as 'crude,' 'thoughtless and indifferent,' and 'immature.' [Robert J.] Connors refers to Lounsbury's 'thinly concealed opinion that undergraduate students were ignorant barbarians' (7). (Roemer, Schultz, and Durst 379)

The almost embarrassing fact is that I found the entire "design your own journal assignment" teaching moment very interesting. I found it exciting—in the "Duh . . . of course" sort of way that is the hallmark of most day-to-day teaching moments. Why, when transferring computer files, did I cut and yet *not* paste in this assignment text block? In a remarkably Freudian manner, I *lost* something that my students for several semesters had been telling me wasn't productive, due to journal saturation via successful campuswide writing-intensive initiatives. I needed to respond to the obvious but important implications of the students' message: journals assigned routinely evolve from useful technique to useless task. I needed to take the time to keep the baby and throw out the bathwater, to reinvent and reinvigorate a writing-to-learn practice that I still very much believe in. If writers' attitudes toward journal keeping have changed, I need to change. This is the kind of teaching problem I mull over when grocery shopping, waiting for a haircut, clipping the hedges, watching a movie that fails to engage. Sometimes I feel like mine is an egghead response, but more often lately I decide that it's not, for I find teaching exciting, unnerving, and renewing, even as I become more expert at it, and expertise, oddly, can lead to self-consciousness and discouragement. In this chapter's opening quote, Jerry Farber suggests that when I view teaching as a career-long process of self-renewal, I need to understand it will appear to be harder rather than easier work, with the confusing benefits of hard work: weariness *and* satisfaction. This is why I continue to study writers, my own teaching, and the scholarship of teaching.

Because it is the twenty-first century and not 1911, I would substitute for Professor Lounsbury's "thinly concealed opinion that undergraduate students were ignorant barbarians" Mary Rose O'Reilley's question: "What if we were to take seriously the possibility that our students have a rich and authoritative inner life and tried to nourish it rather than negate it?" (102). I would add my own: What if we teach as if everything matters?

It seems crucially important to rediscover what is fundamentally sound about what we do when we support our writing students: make meaning, engage minds, improve practices, tap deep and meaningful rituals, inculcate life-changing habits of thinking and persuading, reflect, and revise. It is crucial to explore the dividends of time-on-task for writers and teachers. To praise what *is*—no matter how undersupported. Why does college composition as a field often fail to claim what

its members really do so well and to publicize what our students have been doing so well and for so long with our support?

For me, learning begins with questioning. I find it useful to list the particular
and local questions I have as a teacher because I have been thinking globally until my head hurts and my teaching suffers. Every writing teacher knows how
quickly the questions arrive. For me, teaching questions are generative, each a
meditative koan. For none of them do I have final answers, measurable outcomes.
At this point in my teaching life, I'm curious about—which means crucially interested in—the following:

1. How can each one of us personally change the climate of our writing
   classrooms for the better?

2. What have we done for our writing classes today? For our teaching
   minds?

3. Why don't I have a good sense of how my colleagues in the profession
   teach? I have biases, impressions instead. How can I correct this?

4. Why are my first days in the writing classroom so different from last days
   of each term? What transpires and needs to transpire? How can and do I
   better understand the journey we take together for a term?

5. Does it matter that we ask students to write three or ten pages, on a set or
   self-selected topic, to use portfolios, to respond to cases, to study in
   nonschool settings? How do we know? How do we explain what we know?

6. Why don't we say "practice into theory" on a regular and productive basis?

Most writing teachers I know could double and treble this list with one typing
hand tied behind their back.

I am teaching a graduate-level course on theories of composing, and we are taking a fast march through the writings of the last forty years. As we do, I'm pleased
to find these readings hold up: Janet Emig on thinking, Nancy Sommers on revision, Linda Flower and John R. Hayes on cognition, P. J. Corbett on rhetoric, Lisa
Ede and Andrea Lunsford on audience, and onward. In fact, it takes only time to
find new applications for each of these works. Flower and Hayes, for instance,
remind me that expert writers are able to utilize and shuttle between both short-
and long-term goals, so these authors' explorations of goals makes me reexamine my teacher's goals in a parallel key, asking how, across a term, I shuttle between short- and long-term goals, goals for individual students and goals for the
class ("A Cognitive"). And while I know time is so scarce as to seem laughable for
writing teachers, it is, too, for all workers in the world, for all who live full lives.

Beginning as a field in which writing teachers joined to share concerns, our constituency has increased and diversified over the last forty years, making it harder, perhaps, to continue to amass a canon of resonant, key research texts like these. So I want key, shared texts but I want more. I want to recruit an entire class-room-based research community; I want help answering the questions that matter to me and to the teachers I know. My questions include the silly and the sublime and the complicated. They propagate; they multiply: What is the place of emotion in the writing classroom? How can we better understand creativity? Where did teacher research get to, and where can it still go? How can we cultivate and disseminate our expertise? As a writing teacher, where are my energies best spent?

As I ask these questions, I find I want to throw off the yokes of category. I don't feel just liberal nor do I feel overly conservative. I don't like labels so I appreciate a student who doesn't either. That's why I could (but won't) spend a whole chapter meditating on this email:

From: KCM1978@

I want to thank you for your advice and instructive criticism regarding my draft. I also thank you for setting aside your political and ideological views when reading this paper. As I mentioned in the paper, I wasn't trying to force my beliefs or opinions on anyone, but it is something that I have wanted to write for quite a while. In fact, the only reason I hadn't written before was because every chance I got, I had teachers who were clearly Democrats and this essay would not be welcome. I got the feeling you were a Democrat as well, but based on the impression I got of you, I realized that you would evaluate this writing based on its substance and quality, not your ability to agree or disagree with it. I appreciate that, and I appreciate the opportunity to write it. Once again, thank you for your help and I'll see you on Monday.

I know that many writing teachers vote liberal to socialist and that Myers-Briggs tests suggest that we are introverted and more bookish than our students, so I wanted to move carefully with this student who wrote a passionate yet (at that point in his drafting) poorly argued and exceedingly conservative paper. Because I didn't want to fail in addressing the complexity of this teaching moment, much discussion and revision of KMC's paper followed. We conferenced in person and by email, and I moderated a full-class workshop where peers' responses to the form and substance of his argument became heated and then more productive.

Like any number of my students, I feel buffeted by the agendas of politicized pedagogies (or politicized colleagues):

> As Henry Giroux points out, conservatives and radicals have taken different positions about schooling as a reproductive public sphere: conservatives wanting more attention to what would suit corporate needs, radicals wishing not to be complicit with legitimation of the established order and its concomitant tracking and differentiation along class, gender, and racial lines. . . . But Giroux claims that both conservatives and radicals have concurred in failing to see the complexity of the teaching transaction, and of cultural transmission in general. (Roemer, Schultz, and Durst 383)

According to certain compositionist trends, I'm damned if I pay attention to the individuals gathered together in our classroom space, yet I'm drained if I try to teach civics to writing students, for that is not my expertise or interest. When I look at a group of writing students, their desks circled, discussing each writer's paper, I don't think about reproductive public spheres or corporate needs or cultural transmission. I think, "Why doesn't Summer have a draft again?" and "Can I usefully keep Justin from overdominating the discussion?" and "Great, Colleen has taken a wonderful chance with her draft that will probably demonstrate a lot to her peers about the possibilities for this assignment." I can be there, or I can be somewhere else, second-guessing my pedagogical position and letting my students' needs get lost amid uncertain professional battles. Marjorie Roemer, Lucille M. Schultz, and Russell K. Durst's observation above suggests to me that I owe as much or more to the actual as to the possible. Like all writing teachers, I need more time and space and support for tending to daily teaching transactions.

I feel I have a great deal at stake in this discussion as a writing teacher, as a citizen of my city *and* university. In his introduction to *Composition in the Twenty-First Century: Crisis and Change,* Donald A. Daiker claims, "Perhaps the central fact of the new geography of composition is that the most exciting things are happening outside and away from the college classroom. Or to put it another way, the college classroom is in the process of expanding to include segments of the larger community, both on and off campus" (2). While I can agree with the second statement, I don't agree with Daiker's initial premise. A writing teacher's life is often so hard and engrossing, the work begins to seem less like work. The students I teach rise each day and try to shine. They arrive in the classroom, and as Bloom suggests, we are them; they are us.

Beth Daniell enlarges on Bloom's assertion that we are inculcating our own, generally middle-class values:

> It would take either an incredible optimist or a complete ignoramus to deny the inequities in American society and in American education. But by the

world's standards, most of the students who enroll in the classes we teach—especially in private colleges and large state universities—are not oppressed. They are not Freire's Third World adult illiterates, and our job is not now, if it ever was, to recruit for the leftist revolution. Rather, our task is to help students learn to read and write critically so that they can carry out the tasks of their lives with some control in an increasingly complex culture in which levels of literacy 'accumulate' quickly (Brandt, "Accumulating"); this includes giving them the machinery by which to critique the world around them. (401)

As usual, I both agree and disagree. I agree that our students are living in a complex culture, but I believe *all* cultures are complex and that they have been equally so throughout human history to those who experienced them. I don't agree that my primary teacherly purpose is to shore up just the critical side of the equation. I want to explore all dimensions of my own and my students' humanity. And I want to because they are us. Our university system is one that students enter with many hopes, but they have not arrived here as aliens nor are they all alienated.

I also agree and disagree with David Bartholomae. I agree with his 1993 goal of trying

to imagine a way for composition to name a critical project, one that is local, one whose effects will be necessarily limited, but one, still, of significance and consequence. . . . I think of the question this way—what does it mean to accept student writing as a starting point, as the primary text for a course of instruction, and to work with it carefully, aware of its and the course's role in a larger cultural project? ("What Is Composition" 24)

However, I want to use a language in and around the classroom, in and around my professional life, that is richer, more evocative, and I think ultimately more precise. Bartholomae's critical project or Daniell's machinery by which to critique or no doubt a good deal of my own scholarly writings run the danger of distancing us from our work even as it allows us to reflect on that work. This language does not greatly help the classroom writers I know, nor does the flabby and dubious student-writer language of flow suffice either. Projects are not simply critical, writing does not simply flow. What we say and how we say it make a difference in our classrooms. Think of the initial aftermath of the terrorism of fall 2001, of the degree to which so many turned to words, to writing, consulting the spiritual and creative sides of our natures for sustenance (and how often in the recent decade we've been suspicious of the same in our classrooms). Vigils, prayers, litanies of names, each syllable reminding us of an entire complex life lost. We heard

Walt Whitman quoted and stories told, large, small, terrifying, transformative. Immediately, the nation was awash in socially constructed memorial, celebration, rhetoric, communication.

I believe we can be taking more critical *and* creative approaches to the teaching day. Some of us contribute through analysis and critique; an equal number of us can contribute deeply to the profession through action or reflection. Through course assignments and through teaching journals. Through teaching poems, like William Snyder Jr.'s that provide important and uncapturable-in-any-other-way analysis, argument, and evocation:

Preciousness of Imperfection

I'm getting so frustrated, *she says,* this is so
confusing. *Angela sits in the student chair*
in button-down blue shirt, white sweater-shirt
beneath, jeans—front of one cuff flipped up
exposing oval of sock. Could she
not have noticed? The computer hums.
Students chatter down the hall. We consider topics
for the argument essay, small topics
from the heart, from experience. What about
bilingual education? *She asks.* That will need
research, *I say.* I'm so frustrated, *she says,* and I hate
to choose a simple topic, you know, like abortion
or euthanasia, ones everybody does. Maybe like,
I'm just saying, I like the little topics, you know,
like that one in class: you shouldn't tell white lies.
Yes, *I say,* I like that one too.
I'm the kind of person, *she says,* who likes to be
challenged. I know, *I say.* What about
stay-at-home-dads? *she says.* I'm skeptical, *I say.*
Like, that they shouldn't be ostracized.
That there is nothing really truly womanish about
working in the house, nothing that says just women
can do those things. I think you have something, *I say.*
Brown shoes, knobby soles. Eyes that see you
when she speaks. This young woman, Angela,
sits by my desk, and as we talk, figure, plan—
that cuff. Curled in the dryer perhaps, creased
in the folding, or at some small moment

of thinking or dream she scratched her shin, forgot
to flip it back. I fall in love with this odd cuff,
the white-ribbed sock, with Angela too—her trial
of choosing. And with those kids in the hall.
And with me even. With all of us, gone as we are
To confusion and flaw.

(46)

This poem is one of the best writing-conference transcripts I've ever read, in that it captures, analyzes, and conveys the detailed wealth of a particular yet shareable moment. It offers a wise report of writing instruction: computers hum, and students chatter down the hall, the persuasion topic, the difficulty of choosing a subject. It is an assertion of individuality: "I like the little topics," and an assertion of community: "I like that one too" and "I think you have something, I say." It is an illustrated enactment of teaching, the engrossment with and difficulty of the task, the diversions that appear, like that student's tender and distracting cuff, curled in the dryer at some small and distant-from-the-classroom yet important and unobserved moment. It is intellectual—"I'm the kind of person who likes to be challenged" and emotional "I fall in love," and it points to commonality: "With all of us, gone as we are to confusion and flaw." The poem succeeds due to its attention to language, due to this teacher-author's attempt to capture what was, is, and might be. This is one important way that we make meaning, as writers, readers, speakers, and audiences.

I wish that we had as large a bank of teaching poems and shared and analyzed teaching narratives as we have of historical, experimental, and naturalistic research. I would have us stockpile it all and also spend it freely. I would prefer not only to be searching my current classroom for quotes, mining old essays for nuggets but also to be turning to anthologies of landmark essays, stories, *and* poems, as well as to a Bartlett's of teaching quotes.

I do not believe I can have a smorgasbord pedagogy, but I do feel entitled to range widely, as a teaching generalist, as a writing specialist. Then I'm obliged to think systematically about my practice, even if I do so in snippets of time—at the market, on the commute, between classes, and during the department meeting. I am obliged to define, refine, name, and explain my practice and to build new knowledge from which to set out again. It is the building and the appreciating and the setting out strongly that matter to me. Writing teachers who get up each day and do their work are doing their work; they do not have to apologize for having values and beliefs, for coming from one section of a field and for moving—perhaps—to another section—from one understanding of instruction to another understanding of it—as long as they are willing to talk, to share, to travel on in company.

Of course, I want and choose to affiliate. I believe I do have a core identity. I came to composition and will be carried out again as a writing teacher. I study disciplinary writing, and I study creativity and critical thought: that is, I study the thoughts of individuals engaged in literate behaviors. I need my students as much as they need me: we are mutually engaged in learning together:

> What does become of 'teacher' if there are no 'students'—or if, to put it another way, we are all students, some of whom have made a career out of helping others learn? Well, as a relatively straightforward job description, 'teacher' will hold. But the rest—the Brahmin claptrap, the mystification, those stupid nostalgia-for-feudalism titles that we hide behind—none of that helps us teach; it gets in the way; it is to be outgrown. (Farber 277)

I understand that there are those who do not share this primary identity. That's certainly a stretch for me to imagine but I'm willing to do so, as long as I'm allowed my own bedrock. I understand how one *can* worry about the intrusion of the personal, the supposed lack of critical consciousness, or the reputed indulgent excesses of the writing classrooms of a previous century, which some fear continue to haunt the corridors of many old brick buildings, or even how one might argue that we need to brace up our students' moral infrastructures. Concerned about the ethics of students' personal writing, of students being encouraged to address the personal, Dan Morgan claims that:

> *Students' topics and concerns, and their life experiences and points of view, reflect what has been occurring in our society at large.* Our students write about violence and substance abuse and broken families because they're writing about what they have lived and witnessed firsthand, what they care most deeply about. Their crises, past or present, mirror the condition of our society, reflect what has become more and more ordinary. And writing about profoundly personal issues comes easily to our students because we live in a pervasive culture of public self-disclosure, as talk shows, tabloids, daily newspapers, books, and movies will attest. In our popular culture, private issues are no longer private, and public self-disclosure seems to have become a means toward personal validation. (92)

I collected this quote in August 2001, wondering how I would argue against its subtext of alarm. In September of the same year, the course of events made my argument for me. I don't believe writing about profoundly personal issues comes easily. I think emotional profundity and intellectual profundity go hand in hand and require scrupulous attention and hard work: We feel this in our fingers as we touch the keyboard, in our bodies as we push toward or away from desks, in our subconscious that suddenly becomes alert to the sounds of the city or the countryside around us. We have to question the overly tidy polarizations of public and private, emotion and intellect, student and teacher that have been guiding composition studies discussions. We have to because we have been forced to. We have to because we want to. Because the self-examined teaching life is well worth living.

As is each and every teaching moment. That teaching moment. This teaching moment. Instances and experiences from which we derive our theories and into which we plunge again, re-armed with deeper understanding. The personal is political. The private exists in relationship to the public.

As the epigraph to his collection *The Prehistory of The Far Side: A Tenth Anniversary Exhibit,* cartoonist Gary Larson shares this quote from comedian Mel Brooks: "Tragedy is when I cut my finger. Comedy is when you walk into an open sewer and die." Tragedy and comedy. We like and need our teaching stories. My friend Lynna Williams has long been tracking cut fingers and open sewers, here in her flash nonfiction "Scenes from the 'Teaching Moment' Lounge":

> It was simply a given that we would have these moments in our teaching lives. Epiphanies. Road-to-Damascus flashes of understanding. Lights coming on, flamenco dancers, ducks dropping from the ceiling: all of it. The only problem—and the reason we all thought the line was funny—was that every story we heard about a Teachable Moment seemed to involve a disaster of some kind in the classroom. Students who made out in the back row were a teachable moment, and students who thought grammar was a bourgeois plot were a teachable moment, and teachers who taught the hell out of Raymond Carver's "Fever" for 50 minutes—when the class had read Carver's "Feathers"—well, that was a teachable moment, too. After a while, none of us wanted to be anywhere near a T.M. unless we were holding an airline ticket to Buenos Aires and the offer of a job from a Fortune 500 Company. What didn't occur to us at the time was the fundamental truth behind the stories: that, when things go terribly wrong, somebody might as well learn something. (142)

To Lynna's observations, I'd add: We have the obligation to learn also from when something goes terribly right as actually is happening in uncounted writing classrooms across this country.

6 Education for Irrelevance? Or, Joining Our Colleagues in Lit Crit on the Sidelines of the Information Age

KURT SPELLMEYER

No one here needs to rehearse the history of poor composition. Overworked, underpaid, the academic proletariat, Susan Miller's now-archetypal "sad women in the basement"—these descriptions have marked indelibly the common sense of our field. Given this bleak image of our past, who can doubt the wisdom of the course we've pursued more or less unswervingly for the last fifteen years? To gain respect, including self-respect, we've set out to emulate the respected. If literary studies has a canon, so should we. If criticism has an august legacy reaching back to Aristotle's *Poetics,* rhetoric can show a counterlineage, starting with another founding text of Aristotle's and swelling across the centuries to fill editions closely matching in thickness and weight the volumes of lit crit. If literary doyens occupy titled chairs and teach once or twice a year, then we can hold endowed chairs of our own with commensurate exemptions from routine. If their feminists rush to Judith Butler's side like ingenues at a cotillion, we can run just as fast and with just as much wide-eyed credulity. If they have Fredric Jameson, we have Raymond Williams. If they have Michael Bérubé, we have Paulo Freire.

You may have noticed that I've left something out. The surest sign of our ascent, the jewel in our profession's crown, is the burgeoning of graduate programs granting PhDs in our various specializations. Nothing validates our rise more decisively than the distance we have put between ourselves and that dreadful freshman service course English 101. In contrast to the bad old days when we got stuck with the recently postpubescent, our full professors now sit alongside gray-haired British Chaucerians and Frenchified senior modernists, and they have votes on the committees that choose graduate directors and hammer out degree requirements. Not long ago, people widely thought and even said openly that "anybody can teach comp." Now, as many of us might be proud to observe, our job descriptions in the MLA listings are just as fussily parochial as the ones for "Feminist African Diaspora" and "Queer Eighteenth Century."

The institution of graduate studies is a curious thing. Simply by teaching graduate students we have become instantly more important, and by seeming more important now, we make it possible for those same students, in turn, to seem important when their time comes. As for what actually gets taught, it matters less than that instruction goes on. Here, too, the model of English studies has guided us. The truth is that any literate and moderately thoughtful adult can read, understand, and appreciate a poem, a play, or a novel. Although advanced study makes all kinds of sense in fields like microbiology or physics or pediatrics, our society and its literary arts could get along quite healthily without advanced study in the reading of literature, just as it has gotten along without advanced study in the watching of television, the eating of good food, and the enjoyment of sex. But English studies has managed, all the same, to sell itself as a discipline roughly on par with physics and all the others, simply by doing something called "research," which gets read almost exclusively by colleagues and by graduate students who aspire to become colleagues, who will, in turn, do research and turn out new graduate students, who will, etc., until the end of the world.

Who, I say, can doubt the wisdom of this strategy, when it has made a better life possible for us and probably for the generation coming up? New journals and new conferences get created every day. More than a few members of our profession have crossed the golden threshold of 100K. Some from our ranks have moved on to prestigious jobs as deans, provosts, and vice presidents. Some even chair the English departments that formerly looked down their noses at comp in much the same way as one used to look at one's poor, alcoholic uncle. Surely we *have* arrived. But I still find myself haunted by doubt: where exactly does *arrived* put us? The truth may be that we have fought our way out of steerage only to claim a chair on the deck of a sinking ship, while we are eagerly waving our young protegées into the chairs beside us.

Consider, for example, the fate of my own department. Twenty years ago, the English department at Rutgers housed nearly eighty tenure-track faculty. Since then, the ranks have contracted by 25 percent, and now, as colleagues retire or move on to better jobs, our institution seems unwilling to replace most of the dear departed. These events can hardly come as a surprise. In late 1999, an article in the *New York Review of Books,* surely a bastion of the old-guard literati, referred to English as the one department in the university that only needs to be mentioned at faculty meetings to elicit expressions of open ridicule (Delbanco 32). I believe this attitude to be quite widespread, both inside and outside the university. Every time I go to Barnes and Noble and see all the remaindered copies of *The Ar-*

chaeology of Knowledge, I keep thinking that lit crit has lost its bid, which seemed so promising not long ago, to establish itself as the physics of culture. The same is even more true for cultural studies, however well-intended its practitioners. I'm simply not convinced that the people who *live* culture feel the need to study it at the feet of our masters, nor do I believe that they would ever take to heart the sort of work that gets written about them, if they somehow happened to read it. The truth is that scholars in cultural studies write largely for one another, with no organic constituency outside their professional lives, and in this regard, they exemplify the predicament of English studies generally—and our predicament as well if we persist in taking our cues from that discipline.

Let's say that it's still 1999, and you've just finished watching a movie, and your outrage is so great that you set to work on a critique—an "intervention," as we say, in popular culture. In your critique, coyly entitled "Saving Ryan's Privates," you demonstrate that Steven Spielberg's seemingly anodyne film is in fact deeply complicit with the same patriarchal ideology that undergirded the Third Reich. Wasn't the point of soldiers' mission to rescue the Ryan family's sole surviving *son?* And isn't Ryan white and Northern European? Why didn't Spielberg call the film "Saving Private Gomez"? Or why not "Saving Ryan's Daughter," although that title would collide with a different film. But no matter—the point of your dazzling critique is that Spielberg and his writers may pass themselves off as good guys but they are really moral monsters, and you would then send the whole thing off to some journal that agreed to consider it. By the time your intervention rolls off the presses, something like two hundred million people will have seen Spielberg's film at least once. Now consider the impact of your response. For the journal that prints your article, even a prestigious journal like *Cultural Critique* or *Social Text,* the print run is about eight hundred copies, most of which lie moldering on library shelves until they get decently interred in microfiche. Assuming that most people don't read every article in every edition—and they don't, to say the least—then you can expect a readership of about a hundred or fewer.

The case of cultural studies exposes in a dramatic way the marginal character of English studies as a whole, a marginality quite unlike the one celebrated twenty years ago by Jacques Derrida and his followers. The interventions made by cultural critics are merely symbolic gestures that no one, or almost no one, ever witnesses, which makes them autistic gestures as well. The same holds true for the more conventional articles on John Milton and Oscar Wilde, except that few people outside academic English will actually ever read *Paradise Regained* or *The Portrait of Dorian Gray.* The marginality in that case is so extreme that it can pass forever unnoticed. Needless to say, millions of people read authors like Jane Smiley, Russell Banks, and Cormac McCarthy, but no one outside the academy runs to academic criticism to make sense of their works. Through sheer bravado,

English studies has survived this contradiction for the better part of a century, but I believe that its luck may running out. Job postings in comp are still burgeoning, but our luck may be running out as well, or it will if we persist in imagining that feminist recoveries of Hypatia or pragmatist rereadings of 1950s Marxists are somehow less autistic than Marxo-feminist unmaskings of *The Simpsons*. I suspect that our good fortune to date has much less to do with the quality of the scholarship we've turned out than it does with the widespread perception that print literacy is in trouble.

The obvious response to my argument so far is that we needn't try to win the public over when we already hold their children captive in our classes. Alas, I'm skeptical of this claim, too. The mere exposure of impressionable young minds to John Berger or Gloria Anzaldúa does not guarantee that students will leave the course ideologically reborn, whatever they might tell us in order to exit with a passing grade. To believe them when they start to talk our talk strikes me as the height of naivety. I still remember watching an interview on C-SPAN with the young conservative columnist Michelle Malkin, who was asked about the sources of her deeply conservative political commitments. "I got them at Oberlin," she told the interviewer, where the drumbeat of political correctness finally drove her in the opposite direction. Although English remains the largest humanities major, the power of numbers has failed to translate into the power to persuade. True, there was an article in *Time* long ago about the Yale deconstructionists, and more recently, Stanley Fish has been profiled in the page of *The New Yorker* (MacFarquhar). I suspect that these moments of public attention actually serve to showcase the bizarre and irrelevant character of our central concerns.

Does anyone really believe that we need a new theory of textual meaning based on, of all things, legal forensics—which is the argument that Fish goes around making these days? Milton is dead, so he can't really be put in the dock, and when critics like Fish put Milton's *poetry* in the dock and subject it to what they think of as cross-examination, I don't believe these leaders of the field come away looking more tough minded. They come away instead looking slightly mad, as one would have to be, in my view, to take such an enterprise seriously. Even our concern with the political has been utterly fanciful. In the three-plus decades since 1967, the year *Of Grammatology* first appeared in English, our society has drifted steadily rightward. When you stop to think about it, what politics could ever be derived from Michel Foucault's *Discipline and Punish,* long a staple of freshman English, thanks to its inclusion in *Ways of Reading*? What political changes have arisen from Derrida's writings on ethics or Judith Butler's critique of intentionality or even from Jürgen Habermas's theories of transparent communication? So far as I can see, a Grand Canyon divides our "political" discourses from real world politics in a place like Trenton, New Jersey, or Washington, D.C. I would bet that few recent PhDs in English could tell you much about operations of the Supreme Court or about the Democratic Party in the state where they live. In fact, most people in my own department seemed surprised when I pointed out at one faculty meeting that the highest level of elected official at our own university was the department chair and that at many institutions even chairs get appointed by higher-ups. These colleagues were the same people for whom *The Political Unconscious* has played the role that the Bible does among fundamentalists. Might the title express an unintended irony?

When compositionists emulate English studies, we are emulating irrelevance, world evasion, and failure, but why haven't we noticed what by now ought to be obvious? I suspect that we remain so thoroughly enclosed within the horizon of English studies because we keep aspiring to be embraced at last as "one of us." Personally, I don't believe that colleagues working literary studies will ever have much respect for comp, even if they have begun to recognize how dependent they are on us financially. For one thing, the idea that the writing of a first-year student is anything more than trivial exercise runs counter to the founding ideology of a discipline that has conceived of itself from the outset as the preserver and defender of true culture against the corrosive impact of democracy. There are other reasons why the history of contempt is unlikely to change. A discipline declining so dramatically needs a foil: Criticism may not be physics, but at least it's not comp.

We do an injustice to ourselves when we chase after literary studies, but we do an even greater injustice to our graduate students, who are not in a position to recognize that their training for a PhD in comp probably condemns them to a professional life even more hermetically sealed than the life of a medievalist or an expert on nineteenth-century feminist American prose. Foucault and English 101, Lacan and the scene of instruction, writing and difference, writing and counter hegemony—no parody could be more absurd than the reality of many dissertation topics I've seen. Do you really think that the Revolution will begin in developmental English? Isn't it more likely that we strike the rebel pose precisely when our own inconsequence begins to nag at us? In some ways, the obvious alternative to all this—a retreat from high theory into pedagogy—is even more constricting. Quite honestly, I don't believe that we ever need another classroom ethnography or another study of the writing process of some poor undergraduate. Surely this kind of intellectual exercise has no legs: no one will ever read it who is not actually compelled to, not even within our own field. At any rate, when we accept pedagogy as our natural concern, we allow ourselves to underwrite a division of intellectual labor that will always place us at the bottom, along with undergraduate education itself. Pleas to value teaching are bound to go unheard precisely because the structure of the university cannot dignify the social relations that the activity of teaching—real teaching—necessarily presupposes.

Don't misunderstand what I've argued so far. I do not hate literary study or the reading of literature. I am not against analysis or reflection, and I don't think that most of our colleagues are dupes or rogues, although some of them clearly are. My thesis instead is that all of us—compositionists and literary critics alike—have been held spellbound for the better part of a century by a vision of the humanities as the leader, the conscience, and the judge of the whole society. This vision, I want to argue, has become manifestly unachievable, but it remains so compelling internally that even intelligent and well-meaning people remain blind to its failure and unmindful of the alternative roles we might actually play if we gave up on the past. Even in their most radical expressions—as poststructuralism, critical theory, neo-Marxism, and so on—the forms of knowledge made by the humanities continue to assume our own leadership role as a given. We may ridicule Matthew Arnold, but we still believe that our task is to remain above the fray and to save the Philistines from themselves through acts of heroic interpretation.

No one, or almost no one, accepts the literary critic—or for that matter, the rhetor—as the arbiter of culture for society at large. I believe that graduate study in our field should begin with this cold fact as a point of departure. I'm not suggesting that students should now start writing dissertations on the rise and demise of the deconstructionists. Instead, I suggest that we all could benefit from asking how written knowledge actually gets made or fails to get made, how it circulates or fails to circulate, and how it enables or disables in all of the venues where writing takes place, from the newsroom and screenplay conference to the preparation of accident reports. The truth is that there is no central site of cultural production that holds the key to the whole system, as literature was once imagined to. Instead, we need to study writing in its endlessly varied manifestations as a form of social action. People educated in English departments have a terror of what the Frankfort school called *instrumentalism,* but the truth is that except for literary art, all writing—and indeed all communication—is inescapably instrumentalist. Of course, that principle will hold true as well for the research and writing we ourselves produce, and we have nothing to fear as a result. If we can fashion a knowledge that makes more visible the ways and means of writing, together with its contexts and its consequences, then we can offer something of genuine worth to people in many different walks of life.

As we pursue this course, however, we should take particular care to extricate ourselves as much as possible from the legacy of literary studies. In particular, we need to resist the temptation to start with the grand theory first, with Karl Marx or Antonio Gramsci or Jean Baudrillard or some other major figure of the critical canon, nor do I regard Aristotle, Quintilian, or Hypatia as better places to start. I suggest we conduct our investigations in an agnostic spirit, with a willingness to follow our primary evidence wherever it might lead. At the same time, we should make a serious effort to read—and to read along with graduate students— from history, anthropology, sociology, linguistics, all fields that probably played no role in our own graduate training.

Let me pause here to acknowledge what you may already have come to suspect. Obliquely, I'm suggesting that comp, in spite of its expressions of contentment, is still not much of a discipline. By this I mean that in some dark corner of our collective consciousness, we know how very little of the work we do ever travels outside the field. There are a few notable exceptions. Among them are Ann Ruggles Gere's *Intimate Practices: Literacy and Cultural Work in U.S. Women's Clubs, 1880–1920,* Deborah Brandt's *Literacy in American Lives,* Charles Bazerman's *The Languages of Edison's Light,* and Richard E. Miller's *As if Learning Mattered: Reforming Higher Education.* There are certainly other books I might have mentioned here, but these four are the ones I keep returning to recently, perhaps because all four have legs—all four are books that a historian or anthropologist or psychologist might actually read and find quite useful. Please notice also that these are not books that rely heavily on the intellectual paradigms bequeathed to us by literary studies. These books can't really be described as poststructuralist or neo-Marxist or even feminist in the sense of engaging with the recherché debates that preoccupy our feminists in English studies. In reading Gere or Miller, I get the distinct impression that they are citing Stuart Hall or Bruce Robbins only because some reader of their manuscript told the press that they had to. I would say, however, that their material and the observations they independently make far exceed the reach of the theoretical works they may have been compelled to draw upon. I see this a sign of their maturity and of their promise as guides to the future of our field.

Readers outside of English—and outside the university itself—might find these books useful for a number of reasons. It has become a truism that we now live in a knowledge society, where information has replaced goods and services. But the economy of information, so to speak, is very poorly understood even by those situated at the most valued sites of production. Clearly, genetics now enjoys greater influence than, say, social work or invertebrate biology because of the money to be made through innovations like biotech. Market forces by themselves, however, cannot explain the complex economy of knowledges. Many developers of biotech products, for example, have had a difficult time managing public perception, and their products have become synonymous with dangers to the health of consumers and the natural world. One lesson to be drawn from the public reaction against biotech, in many ways an irrational response, is that the making of knowledge by itself, no matter how careful or rigorous, cannot guarantee the survival of any field. The failure of high theory and the fall of English studies illustrate my point as well. Surely English professors could not have worked harder, explored ideas with greater courage, or presented those idea with more vigor and ingenuity, but their enterprise was doomed from the start because they lacked an adequate *systemic* understanding of how their knowledge fit within a larger constellation of knowledges, some rising in value and influence, some declining, some moving to the center, and some dropping to the periphery. What all four of the books I just mentioned have in common is their focus on these larger constellations, many still almost wholly unexplored. Some readers might say that the four books belong to what is called *the sociology of knowledge,* but given the work that sociologists now produce, that term strikes me as much too restrictive. Sociological in spirit, all four books are also richly historical and ethnographic, without the scientistic pretensions. I can't think of any other academic discipline that could have produced books like these, precisely because they synthesize in such creative ways many different traditions of inquiry.

This synthetic quality is not, in my view, simply an issue of style. It points to a larger problem with our hunger for the status of a discipline, whether our model happens to be English or any other field. It is worth acknowledging that English does not stand alone in its current malaise. To a greater or lesser degree, all the humanities and social sciences appear to be in crisis.[1] In 1991 at an international conference, two prominent anthropologists openly acknowledged the prospect that their field no longer served any purpose other than to perpetuate itself (Grimshaw and Hart). No discipline in the entire curriculum has fallen farther and faster than sociology, but a similar decline has begun to overtake the foreign languages. Economics, linguistics, and philosophy—within each of these fields the question of survival itself has been raised by some of each discipline's most creative figures. The problem is not simply that anthropologists and philosophers have turned their back on a public readership, although that is one part of the problem. There is also the question of the pertinence—the question what good one's research does—no matter how many readers one might reach. Do we really need another book on John Donne or Herman Melville? Does anyone seriously believe that ethicists writing on stem-cell research played any significant part at the events leading up to the announcement of President George Bush's policy? Can we credibly claim that work in academic religious studies has had a significant impact on American religious life? Can we say with any confidence that current scholarship in art history will help to shape in a salient way the future of the fine arts? I suspect that most of us would answer "no" to all of these questions.

In some ideal sense, the curriculum as we know it reaches back to ancient Greece, but it actually took shape about a hundred years ago with the decline of the liberal arts college and the rise of the modern university. The provenance of the research university is more recent—around the time of World War II. The problem with the current academic disciplines is precisely that they still bear the heavy imprint of life at the turn of the nineteenth century. This is true, at any rate, of the humanities. The sciences continue to refashion themselves at a furious pace, and science as practiced fifty years ago has been forced out of the academy. Some of the best naturalists today, for example, are amateurs who comb the last few jungles and deserts at their own expense. Much the same holds true for conventional astronomy.

Humanistic knowledge in the year 2003 looks very much like knowledge a century before, despite all the so-called revisions. In our department, when a medievalist retires, a new one takes his or her place. Needless to say, no division wants to close itself down to make room for something new, and consequently "innovation" occurs only as a series of ad hoc accretions—someone to deal with the Caribbean writers this year, a theory maven in 2005. It seems to me, by contrast, that the most pressing issues our society must now face are not only quite far from the purview of English studies but also more complex than any single academic discipline can do justice to. Consider, for example, the recent terrorist attacks on the World Trade Center, the Pentagon, and other places. An adequate response would demand a knowledge of the recent history of Saudi Arabia, Afghanistan, and the problem of Palestinian statelessness; some understanding of Islam; and some reading on the culture of the Middle East. No single department I know of could provide the comprehensive picture that people need to see the event with some clarity, and it strikes me that the same applies to genetic technology, the environmental crisis, globalization—all of which now pose for us potentially life-and-death questions.

I have long believed that writing courses offer the one place in entire curriculum where issues like these might be addressed in the synthetic way they require. To reimagine our undergraduate courses along these lines—as we have already done for some time now at my own institution—is to place composition, of all things, at the center of the undergraduate experience. In economics, students learn about markets; in biology class, they learn about natural systems; in political science, they learn about world politics. In their writing classes, they might have the chance to connect market forces with ecology, and both of these with global politics, and this is likely to make the lowly writing course the most-coherent educational experience the students will ever get. At my institution, we have even gone so far as to assign many of our writing-program teaching assistantships to applicants from disciplines other than English, including economics and physics. For the most part, these TAs have done an exemplary job.

Such changes imply a reversal of the logic now prevailing in the university, a logic that dictates that graduate study ought to shape the undergraduate major while assuming that courses for the major are the only courses that matter. Instead, the changes I propose we make in English 101 might enlarge and ennoble the graduate experience. After all, if we ask our comp-rhet TAs to teach across existing divisions of knowledge while addressing the most important issues our society now faces, their conception of themselves and their proper work might be profoundly changed. Changed for the better, I would say. We will never be successful in the effort to walk backward out of English studies, with our eyes still turned to our unlucky institutional origins; we really need to turn our eyes away. When we do, we might begin to recognize that the glorious empire of the text turns out to be a troubled, stifling little Balkan state. Beyond it is an entire world to which we might make some useful contribution.

Note

1. The *Digest of Educational Statistics, 2000* offers some surprising insights. Since 1960, the number of bachelor's degrees has tripled nationally, increasing from about 400,000 to more than 1.2 million. Since 1970, the number of BAs majoring in English has dropped from 64,342 (7 percent of all BAs) to 49,708 (4 percent). History and the social sciences, listed together in the *Digest,* have dropped by more than 20,000, from 18 percent to 10 percent of the total. Philosophy and religion, also aggregated, have never managed to rise to a single percent, but their fraction has been halved since the 1970s.

Within the humanities, the conventional wisdom is that the culture of commerce has stolen the students away, but the reality is far more complex. True, enrollments in business have risen to 100,000 more than thirty years ago, but that amounts to a jump from 13 percent to only 19 percent of total degrees. Other gainers include the health professions, up from 3 percent to 7 percent; psychology, from 4 percent to 6 percent, and communications, from 1 percent to 4 percent. None of these are fields that necessarily promote greed or vulgarity. Computer science, imagined by some humanists to be a juggernaut, now claims only 2 percent of total BAs. It is significant as well that the number of graduates majoring in the performing arts has increased by 20,000 (from 3 percent to 4 percent). General liberal arts study has also registered a modest gain, from less than 1 percent to 2 percent, and the same holds true for multidisciplinary and interdisciplinary studies, again rising from nearly zero to 2 percent. From these statistics I would infer that the problem is not with business but with the humanities themselves (National Center for Educational Statistics).

7 The Juggler

RESPONSE BY BRENDA JO BRUEGGEMANN

The word *juggling* derives from the Old French *jogler,* associated with *jester* and *jongleur,* the wandering minstrel, poet, or entertainer in medieval England and France. Those of us juggling within the disciplinary and budgetary tents of English studies know the part of wandering minstrel well. Contemporary feminism and women's studies have gone around with the juggling concept more than a few times, too. At the dawn of the 1990s, professor and psychologist Faye J. Crosby studied women's multiple roles and posits that "to juggle [multiple roles] is to diminish the risk of depression, anxiety, and unhappiness" and that "juggling produces both practical and psychological benefits" (91). Jane S. Gould's memoir, *Juggling: A Memoir of Work, Family, and Feminism* (1997), lays out some of these same ideas in an engaging narrative.

We WPAs are jugglers. I would like to demonstrate this with juxtaposing the remarks offered by Wendy Bishop and Kurt Spellmeyer at the 2001 WPA conference alongside my own sense of the sometimes cupboard-cleaning and yet depression-diminishing acts of being a WPA at a large state university and alongside the variously colored, textured, and sized remarks the audience offered on that late-Friday afternoon of a blustery early-October day in Oxford, Ohio. I don't claim that my claim is original. Juggling rarely is. I believe, though, that we have no shortage of realizations and additions in thinking about writing program administration these days. Even the publication in 2002 of what Gary A. Olson calls the first "bible of writing program administration," *The Allyn and Bacon Sourcebook for Writing Program Administrators,* would make that evident. I choose to frolic and juggle instead. Besides, might it not be the case that talent better serves a WPA over genius any day?

I had the opportunity to read a longer draft of the remarks that Bishop and Spellmeyer delivered at the 2001 WPA conference about two weeks before we convened. I read carefully and multiply as I searched for what I would say and listened on that day quite raptly (much like the fall-quarter freshman in my com-position class also usually do), for their talks came, to me at least, at a quite op-portune moment. An uncanny moment, in fact. Just as our fall quarter and aca-demic year were kicking in at Ohio State University, I found myself thrust into the position of first-year writing program director. The former director, Kay Hal-asek, was called up to the major leagues to become an associate vice-provost. She joins a startling number of our rhet-comp team, in only the past two years at OSU, to move into those prestigious positions that Spellmeyer mentioned early on in his talk—the positions that point to the sign of our having arrived. The 2002 publication of the *Sourcebook* also points to this having arrived, and several of the essays in it—by Geoffrey Chase, Douglas Hesse, Jeanne Gunner, and Charles Schuster chief among them—further chronicle the "here we are!" state we seem to be enjoying as witnessed by a flourishing job market for writing program ad-ministrators, strong alliances with numerous other professional organizations, the success of some of our journals and conferences, and the recognition of some of our policies.[1]

Yet, even though as a field and group of disciplinary professionals we might have located ourselves, a closer look at a place like Ohio State University will show that nearly everyone now in our twelve-member faculty has a two-, three-, or even four-course released teaching load a year (the standard is teaching five courses on a three-quarter system at OSU)—and rightfully so, of course—because of our administrative positions. Only the untenured (and those are only two) are truly teaching, teaching full loads, and teaching undergraduate students especially on a regular basis. Recently, we counted and discovered that we are down, due to our various administrative course releases, twenty-two courses each year. At an En-glish department average of thirty-five students per course over all the courses we offer, that comes out to be 770 students each year whom we don't come into contact with. What's more, that is 770 students a year—mostly undergraduates—who won't then get exposed to our field and the possibilities for themselves study-ing in rhetoric and composition.

So now we know that I can add and multiply, divide and subtract—that I can crunch the numbers. What does this all mean though? What's my point? Aside from this tally serving as a demonstration of my budding administrative skills, it might mean that although truly we might have arrived as a field, I find it ironic that this arrival has put us significantly out of touch with undergraduate students especially. I heard echoes of this troubling call in both of the essays I am respond-ing to. In general, we still aim mostly to maintain the *graduate* courses first when we are down in our teaching numbers. We do still train (and, thus, teach) the new graduate teaching assistants each year; we do still train (and, thus, teach) our writing-center tutors, we do still train (and, thus, again, teach) the graduate students who might take graduate administrative positions under (or rather alongside) us. We continue to develop exciting new graduate courses and to re-vision our older popular ones—the success of our field as a whole rides well, I think, on the coattails of our success working with these graduate students, training them, teaching them, sending them out for good jobs by and large. Our general success in and at the academic job market is yet another major marker of our having arrived. It is also, I suspect, a strong marker of some of our tensions and differences with our colleagues not just in English but in the humanities at large—colleagues we also remain quite similar to in critical archival, theoretical and pedagogical positions—as Spellmeyer has done well to point out. His keen remarks, I note, turn again and again to graduate students—even in the end of his remarks, when undergraduate education is taken up, it is under the familiar logic that troubles me, too, the one, as Spellmeyer says, "that dictates that graduate study ought to shape the undergraduate major."

Bishop was speaking about how "it is within these writing classrooms that we most often address the problems and pleasures of teaching and learning writing. It seems important, then, to return those sites, to reconsider pedagogical roots, to discuss anew both acts and actions, and to focus on teaching." Perhaps, as Bishop might be posing it, the undergraduate major is (or should be, at least) dictating graduate study? Actually, I hear both Bishop and Spellmeyer (especially in his ending) leaning that way—toward the teaching of undergraduate courses in writing as the pivot point.

Of course, I don't think it's as easy as just turning the tables between undergraduate and graduate studies in our field—and I don't think that's what Bishop and Spellmeyer, together or singly, are suggesting. I think they're offering us a significant challenge—and it's one, especially in my new position as a WPA, that I am very eager to take up. It's a juggler's challenge, so now you can imagine me with (at least) three balls that Bishop and Spellmeyer have kicked to me, hackey-sack style, and I'm going to set them in motion, juggler style, and then toss them on to you. The primary related questions I want to keep mind as we juggle these balls together are:

- How do we—how do *you*—negotiate these lively balls? (I'm not even going to pretend that some kind of true balance is possible.)
- How do we as a field—and perhaps you as an individual player in and on this field—negotiate, keep juggling, keep moving between these positions as we also stand and gaze out from the WPA overlook.

That is, how do we negotiate even and at least these first two balls: (1) our having arrived in numerous administrative and full university-citizen roles with (2) our work—whether teaching in the classroom or via administrative contacts—with graduate students in the multidisciplinary ways and interdisciplinary ways that Spellmeyer calls for so that we move them, and ourselves, into "a knowledge that makes more visible the ways and means of writing, together with its contexts and its consequences, . . . [in order to] offer something of genuine worth to people in many different walks of life."

Then, further and third, what do we do with this "poor composition" ball—the one that both Bishop and Spellmeyer evoke in their chapters—a commonplace most of us have, at one time or another, probably gone to in presenting our field, our work, our selves? Has it been balanced out by the first one I threw at you—by our having arrived? Or does it (and how does it) continue to enter into the juggling act?[2] How do we negotiate the disciplinary power we are coming to know (already do know?) with the history of what it took to come to that knowledge? One thing I know I do not want to see us doing is just tossing the "poor composition" ball onto our comrades who are the freeway fliers, the "sad women in the basement," the part-timers, the not-yet-running-on-the-tenure-track. I actually do think we need to keep this "poor" ball in play, keep it in the mix, yes, continue not just to rehearse it but to imagine other ways to play it.

Fourth—yes, there are four balls here—and this one really counts. It is the one that truly complicates things now for us—the one that puts our true skills to the test and really makes the juggling hard. This is the one about undergraduate education in rhetoric and composition. How can we truly turn back to teaching, to our classrooms—and especially, again, to undergraduates in our classrooms—and keep those other balls circling smoothly, too? What are we risking if we let this ball drop—or, too, I'd ask, if we just let it be only about freshman composition—and we don't start attending more to raising up students into our field instead of waiting for that magic conversion moment we've all loved so much when a graduate student in literature comes to "see the light" of our field and answer its calling. This conversion stuff is often messy, often even overzealous; perhaps paying better attention to the undergraduate ball might offer us more than a conversion narrative that has long dominated our field. (I started first in cognitive psychology, interested in studying the creative process there, and then found myself, long story, in Romantic literature. What about you?)

Now, a fifth ball—yes, a fifth—that I want to send your way. I had thought about not tossing this ball out. But I must. Because it really does matter. This is the ball that is about the other lives, roles we play, either in the academy or well off that playing field. Hockey Mom, Soccer Dad, Sorta Athlete, Afterschool Literacy Volunteer, Sunday School Teacher, Local Activist, etc. I know your hands are very full already now, and you are sweating a little just handling those other four balls. But here, you have to take this one, too. At this point, once you have those five balls all going successfully, you'll be happy to know, we can put the balls down.

Coda (Without Balls)

I took wild and rapid notes after Bishop's and Spellmeyer's talks as roughly nine table leaders came forward and reported briefly on what they and their table colleagues had talked about in their discussion period following the two talks. First, Bishop, Spellmeyer, and I sat back for some time and watched this Burkean parlor scene unfold. We chatted a little among ourselves up there in the big empty area toward the front of the ballroom while the discussion tables did their thing at the back of the ballroom. We took a bathroom break, got a cup of coffee or glass of water, returned to remark on the nasty weather outside, waited to see what they would say.

I had a real-time captioner (the deaf person's version of a court reporter) helping me "listen," and her hands fluttered and flew, pounded and performed, beside me, as she worked to take down everything. I watched her work scroll rapidly by on the laptop screen, taking notes on her notes, table by table, discussion leader by discussion leader. Conversational balls flying everywhere. In the last thirty seconds before it was my turn to respond, I took yet another round of notes on my notes of her notes and stood, took a deep breath, read from my prepared remarks, then added the key resonant chords of what the discussion tables had offered at my end.

While I talked, I threw real balls. Five of them. I had wanted the audience to begin juggling them, keeping them going back and forth across the room, all the time I talked. They couldn't do it. People kept getting hit in the head with a ball (I did choose soft, squishy, and small balls, the choice picks from my seven-year-old daughter's prize ball bin), people kept dropping them, the frustration level rose (and I could see and sense it), they said they couldn't listen to me and toss balls at the same time. I think there might be a moral to this story. For now I want to avoid moralizing and instead offer the highlights of what came from the various discussion tables following Bishop's and Spellmeyer's talks at the 2001 WPA conference:

Bishop spoke of focusing on our greatest success, the individual student. Spellmeyer offered critique as more than an academic exercise. They inspired us to think and talk about: how to value local and public together; not enough attention to K–12 education; the graduate student perspective in WPA circles; how and why to tell a teaching story; how much and why to focus on personal narrative; how to handle emerging technology; literacy across communities as it impacts our WPA work. Both addressed the question: What can composition offer the humanities as a field? Spellmeyer gave us cautionary tales about being in the humanities; Bishop offered hope for teaching at the heart of the humanities. Her talk gratified us; his is still bubbling about. We appreciated Bishop's nondefensive stance. She was doing what he was advocating. We wanted to talk more about the private-public split we thought they were addressing. We wanted to look more into practice—how what they were advocating plays out in practice. We thought they were expressing two radically different paradigms: Bishop centered on students and spoke as a teacher; Spellmeyer spoke as an administrator and addressed social action and big ideas. We are struggling to bring the two talks together. Bishop offers not a retreat to pedagogy but a movement toward it. We wondered: What in their talks has legs today?

What stuck for me in all this talk about talk, summary upon summary, were two primary notes being played again and again: first, the expression of a lot of *feelings* about the two talks and trying to put into one harmonious chord the different notes most had felt they heard Bishop and Spellmeyer playing. (I would invoke juggling again, but I've grown weary of the metaphor myself and have put the balls down for now.) Second, the interplay of the local classroom and specific institution and individual student with the global and public issues of disciplines and the academy also arose in waves, time and again, throughout the table-discussion summaries that followed their talks. What is uncanny yet meaningful, I think, about these two notes being played, riff-like, throughout the remarks that followed the two talks is how these notes appear, almost harmoniously, as two out of the three suggestions that Laura Micciche offers at the end of her *College English* essay, "More than a Feeling: Disappointment and WPA Work," six months later in March 2002. In the ending of her essay, Micciche foregrounds "several implications suggested by [her] study of the spirit-breaking nature of WPA work" and one of these is that "*we need to more fully describe the affective dimensions of our work through materialist analysis*" (451); another she presents is that "*we need to educate ourselves about the way work is organized in the university and to provide administrative mentoring and professional development to graduate students and junior faculty*" (453). It was almost as if Laura Micciche was there with us that day (perhaps she was?), juggling along with us, as we sought, with Bishop's and Spellmeyer's words, to keep our spirits from breaking, perhaps then following the ideas of psychologist Crosby when she contends that such juggling can affirm spirit, can "diminish the risk of depression, anxiety, and unhappiness" and also "produces both practical and psychological benefits." Let's juggle on, then.

Notes

1. One example in English studies of a significant movement that began primarily with attention to the staffing of composition courses was the earlier Wyoming Conference Resolution that morphed into the CCCC Statement of Principles and Standards for the Postsecondary Teaching of Writing and that even more recently the MLA is beginning to turn to as a model for a similar kind of statement they want to develop about standards for part-time teaching.

2. According to Laura Micciche in an essay that appeared in *College English,* six months following the 2001 Composition in the Twenty-First Century conference that the essays in this volume are all contextualized in, the current of "poor composition" runs deep and wide through a larger sea of "disappointment that characterizes English studies generally" (432.) She addresses the reasons and possible redresses for the "disappointed hope" that WPAs especially operate under in the current academy.

Part 3 Where Will Composition Be Taught and Who Will Teach It?

8 Reimagining the Landscape of Composition in the Twenty-First Century: Contingent Faculty and the Profession

ART YOUNG

In the twenty-first century, college composition is taught in a variety of locations: in traditional and computer classrooms; in wired and wireless spaces; at job sites, shopping malls, and prisons; in English, rhetoric, and engineering departments; in high schools; and in two-year and four-year colleges. Composition is taught at for-profit colleges and outsourced by public colleges to private learning centers. Composition is taught face-to-face and at a distance. This multiplicity of landscapes promises to increase. It may not be an exaggeration to say that composition in the future, like most other subjects, will be taught everywhere, all the time. Composition is taught by people all over the globe: by tenure-stream and non–tenure-track faculty, by regular and contingent faculty, by those credentialed and those not, by full- and part-time teachers, and, in this country, mostly by women.

Employment practices and the material and professional conditions for teaching writing are crucial issues for writing program administrators (WPAs) at the beginning of this millennium. We must establish a working professional community of teachers of composition, where the material conditions of employment for all teachers enable students to receive a quality education. We must seriously consider two-track faculties or multi-tier faculties, although they may be unpopular options. Our discussions in the next few years must lead to actions designed to change the culture of our campuses and the academy. To do nothing is to accept the status quo, and the status quo is an unacceptable place to inhabit in the twenty-first century, for the status quo devalues composition and mistreats many teachers of composition. As David Bartholomae points out in *PMLA*'s special millennium issue:

The growth of the professional status of composition as a field and the remarkable increase in the number of [tenure-track] jobs has had no significant effect on the problems of staffing or on the conditions of employment for the
vast majority of those who teach composition courses—that is part-time faculty members and full-time adjuncts. ("Composition" 1953)

The New Landscape

Most of us are familiar with the new landscape, the corporatization of the academy, the aggressive importing of staffing, and other policies and practices from
the business world to what has been popularly perceived as the isolated, protected,
ivory tower of higher education. One of these practices is often referred to as the
dejobbing of America, the loss of regular permanent jobs, as businesses have down-
sized over the past few decades and relied more on outsourcing and contract
workers. In his book, *JobShift: How to Prosper in a Workplace Without Jobs* (1994),
William Bridges describes the modern workplace:

> Throughout today's work world, we are witnessing a search for speed: faster
> product development, faster production, faster delivery, faster information
> processing, faster service, and faster implementation of all the changes neces-
> sary to keep up with the changes in the marketplace. We are seeing a switch to
> a fast-break, no-huddle style of doing business. And jobs are disappearing as
> a result. . . .
>
> Because conventional jobs inhibit flexibility and speedy response to the
> threats and opportunities of a rapidly changing market, many organizations
> are turning over even their most important tasks to temporary and contract
> workers or to external vendors. That way, when conditions change outside the
> organization, there is no turf guardian inside whose livelihood depends on not
> changing how things are done. (28–29)

Bridges's self-help book describes the work world that most of our students
are in now or will shortly enter, and he offers entrepreneurial advice on how to
survive and even prosper in such a world.

When we hear of important business tasks being given to "temporary and
contract workers or to external vendors," it suggests a comparison to higher education in which important educational tasks are distributed the same way, particularly in the field of composition. Certainly, the loss of jobs in industry is comparable to the loss of tenure-track jobs in the academy, and, just as certainly, many
public officials view tenured professors as inflexible turf guardians resistant to
change. Furthermore, the demand for temporary composition teachers across the

nation each fall semester the week school begins exemplifies delivering just-in-time education with a just-in-time workforce.

The job world that Bridges describes embodies the world of higher education for many of our itinerant colleagues. Bridges says that this dejobbing will continue to occur in the foreseeable future, so employees and job seekers might as well accept it and plan to be successful in the new job market. However, this strategy accepts alienation and isolation as inevitable and thereby works against community building, which is a main goal for most composition programs and, indeed, most college campuses. Nonetheless, this entrepreneurial approach is being adopted by some adjunct teachers, if numerous articles in the *Chronicle of Higher Education (CHE)* are any indication.

For example, in the August 3, 2001 issue of *CHE,* a front-page headline reads: "An Adjunct Calls for Less Whining and More Teaching." Scott Smallwood's article begins:

> FOR SALE: ONE CLASS. Covering Western-civilization from Plato to Marx. Taught by experienced Ph.D. with top-notch student evaluations. Slightly used. $2,500 or best offer.
> Yet another example of the corporatization of higher education? Exactly. Only this time it's not the administrators doing the hawking—it's the professor herself. Jill Carroll wants adjuncts to think about themselves as entrepreneurs selling a product to a client. (A12)

The article goes on to give tips for building your "teaching business" (A12), including opting, as Ms. Carroll does, to develop "courses like products" and to teach "'grunt'" courses (A13). (By the way, although she has a PhD from Rice in religious studies, the article refers to her as Ms. Carroll throughout). Ms. Carroll reportedly made $54,000 last year as a full-time part-timer at three institutions. What such articles as this do is suggest that all contingent faculty have similar opportunities, and if they do not act as Ms. Carroll does, it is not the system's fault but their own lack of entrepreneurial spirit. Such articles accept that higher education is a business like any other business.[1]

It is interesting to note that this same issue of *CHE* ran stories on unionization efforts by adjuncts and graduate students (A14), what colleges pay janitors (A27), and how the stock index of For-Profit Higher Education performed (A30). Stock in for-profit education, which includes the University of Phoenix Online among others, rose 27 percent in the second quarter compared to just 6 percent for the Standard and Poore's Index 500. All of these issues are connected, as Nicholas Tingle and Judy Kirscht, lecturers and union leaders at the University of California, Santa Barbara, recognize:

Unionization has taught us this hard lesson. Few of us started our academic careers believing that universities operated with values similar to those of Dow Chemical. Most of us yearned for the protected environments higher education seemed to afford. Working with the union, however, has shown us that for nontenurable faculty, the university has values no different from any other corporation. Lecturers enjoy less job security than researchers, than staff, than groundskeepers—all of these workers are considered more central to the mission of the university than those who teach writing, elementary math, or beginning foreign languages. (220)

CHE is the one newspaper that most of our upper-level administrators read and discuss, and the spin it puts on stories is undoubtedly influential in shaping public opinion. In an article on the "authenticity of adjuncts" by Bruce E. R. Thompson, the single pulled quote reads, "Adjunct professors walk the walk and practice what they preach in ways that regular faculty members cannot" (B16). Thompson argues that adjuncts by virtue of living in the "real" world offer students something ivory-towered professors cannot—and thus implies that employing a large number of adjuncts is beneficial to a student's education. On July 6, 2001, *CHE*'s Web site published two additional articles. One was entitled "Why I Like Being a Contract Faculty Member" by Nancy Fasnacht, a pseudonym, extolling the virtues, including academic freedom, of being a full-time, non–tenure-track faculty member. The second article, by Cathy Trower, a senior researcher (non–tenure-track) at the Project on Faculty Appointments at Harvard University, estimates "that 45 percent of all new hires in academe are on the non–tenure track, including 65 percent at research universities." This project's survey data of doctoral students reports that about 25 percent of doctoral students would accept a non–tenure-track offer over a tenure-track offer holding everything equal about the positions. Trower concludes, echoing Bridge's interpretation of contemporary business practices:

Full-time, non–tenure-track appointments are here to stay. And some institutions are making changes to overcome the negative aspects of these positions and to ensure that all scholars, whatever track they are on, feel fulfilled and motivated. After all, a happy faculty is a productive faculty.

For WPAs and compositionists, these reports about employment in higher education mean (1) that colleges more than ever are administered like businesses, (2) that the hiring of non–tenure-track faculty is increasing and will likely continue, and (3) that we must face these two realities and strive proactively to improve the working conditions of all teachers of writing.

The More Things Change . . .

Writing in *College Composition and Communication (CCC)* in 1971, Ray Kytle asked this question in his title: "Slaves, Serfs, or Colleagues—Who Shall Teach College Composition?" Kytle proposed that most courses at both two-year and four-year institutions be taught by full-time faculty on the tenure track who specialize in composition. Kytle reasoned, "[I]f the status of college composition is to change the status of those teaching composition must change" (340). Unfortunately, Kytle's question has been answered thirty years later in this way: Most first-year composition courses are taught by slaves (graduate students) and serfs (non–tenure-track faculty). What has changed, at least according to James Sledd, is the emergence of "boss compositionists," PhDs who specialize in composition and administer the slaves and serfs for the plantation owners ("Why the Wyoming"). Sledd's 1991 metaphor continues to unsettle many writing program administrators.

If we had an opportunity in 1971, when Kytle was writing, to develop a fully democratic community among tenure-stream, PhD equals, it is gone. We know it does not take a PhD in composition to teach first-year writing effectively, or any other general education course for that matter, and higher education administrators know that, too. One way we can ensure that composition is taught effectively is to enhance the working conditions of all who teach composition, even as we experiment and develop models for establishing collegial communities of professionally vigorous teachers and scholars. From one perspective, we have exceptional opportunities to reform higher education because of our commitment to democratic values in teaching first-year composition itself and because there are more teachers working nominally within our discipline teaching first-year composition than in any other discipline.

As many of us know, one of the obstacles that undermines efforts to improve working conditions for non–tenure-track teachers is our tenure-stream colleagues who, through apathy or turf protection or open hostility, contribute to the demeaning of fellow teachers and the important work they do—the teaching of most of the undergraduates in English departments.[2] Others have additional thoughtful objections. Some labor unions that represent tenure-stream faculty oppose the hiring of any full-time faculty members unless they are on the tenure track because a commitment to hire full-time faculty should be also a commitment to their academic freedom. Others are concerned that if administrators can hire full-time faculty on long-term contracts, why would they hire tenure-track faculty at all? Such faculty believe that to hire teachers on such appointments would further erode tenure and thereby the quality of education. Certainly, we need to resist the further erosion of tenure-track jobs and their replacement by non–tenure-track jobs. However, is the quality of education well served by the practices we now engage in? Pro-tenure arguments have legitimacy within certain contexts, but they often do not address today's economic realities, the unacknowledged multi-tier systems already in place, the quality of education under current conditions, and the ethical responsibility that all teachers of composition receive a fair wage and reasonable professional support.

Because in crucial ways the landscape of first-year composition is not the same as it was thirty years ago, we have a renewed challenge on our hands. A survey published in 2001 by Michael Moghtader, Alanna Cotch, and Kristen Hague illustrates the nature of this change. Comparing their data with a similar survey published in *CCC* in 1974, they found that the number of schools with a writing requirement has increased significantly; that the number of schools with two or more required writing courses has increased likewise; that the number of schools where composition is taught by only full-time faculty has declined; and that the number of schools employing part-time instructors to teach composition "has increased dramatically" (459). This situation is made all the more urgent because we could use many more teachers of composition than we have now—to serve growing enrollments, to reduce class sizes, and to reduce teaching loads at two- and four-year colleges.

If we needed more evidence for the dejobbing of the academy, an important survey sponsored by the Coalition on the Academic Workforce documents who teaches which courses and the benefits they receive. In freestanding composition programs, only 14.6 percent of the instructional staff are tenure-track, and in English departments, only 36.3 percent are tenure-track. Roughly a third (32.5 percent and 36.6 percent respectively) of all undergraduate courses from both groups are taught by *part-time,* non–tenure-track faculty. And 69.4 percent of English departments and 63.2 percent of freestanding composition programs offer no benefits to part-time faculty members paid by the course.

These statistics on the employment conditions of faculty in higher education should spur us to address issues of employment equity and educational quality. We need to acknowledge the economic reality that the academy is not going to authorize anytime soon the number of PhD, tenure-track jobs it would take to staff first-year composition.[3] Reflecting on the working conditions of adjunct faculty in *Academe,* Anne Cassebaum wonders how this situation has evolved.

> The class system in our profession now shapes us in capitalism's mold, exploiters or oppressed, and we are all colleagues second or not at all. . . . In thirty years, how have we come to be so accepting of this class rift with our own colleagues? Has a close embrace of capitalist ideology so affected our brains that we lack moral imagination? (41)

Cassebaum recommends that tenured teachers cross class lines, for just a month, and live and teach as the adjuncts at our institutions do—sit in their offices, teach their course loads, walk in their shoes, live on their salaries. Such empathy, in the moral imagination if not in practice, may be as good a place to begin as any.

You will recall that we have been down this road before in 1987 with "The Wyoming Conference Resolution" (Robertson, Crowley, and Lentricchia). However, as Jennifer Seibel Trainor and Amanda Godley reminded us eleven years later, we need to continue to walk this road and not to meander from it:

> As the part-time ranks swell, the obvious inference to be drawn by policy makers and the public is: If good teaching goes on for little remuneration in terms of salary, tenure, and benefits, why should we pay more? One clear response to this is to insist that teaching and learning suffer when working conditions are poor. *That is, we must disrupt the ideology that rationalizes, justifies, and even celebrates the current situation.* (180) (emphasis mine)

However, if the spate of articles in *CHE* may be said to "celebrate" the current situation, composition scholars are suggesting thoughtful alternatives.

Challenging the Status Quo

Michael Murphy, who taught part-time at two colleges, argues credibly for a "full-time teaching-intensive track in composition" (14), thereby formalizing an already existing two-track system but making it a productive and rewarding place for students, teachers, and researchers. He calls for a "formalization of the heterogeneity that now exists on most campuses" and creating a norm that "would involve some combination of traditional research-informed faculty and full-time tenurable teaching-intensive faculty—along with a smaller number of regular part-time faculty, and temporary faculty, including graduate assistants" (25). Murphy continues:

> I'm only arguing that we recognize as fact that *most* compositionists are not, have never been, and will not in the future be supported to do research; that the economic strictures on the field will always require that we be primarily a teaching discipline; and *that we work within those limits to professionalize faculty and instruction as thoroughly as possible.* What does it say about composition if we in the discipline *ourselves,* after making so much noise for so long about the importance of teaching, don't appear to believe that teaching undergraduate writing courses is intellectually rigorous and demanding enough to make a legitimate academic career of it? (32)

Murphy's vision is one alternative to the dejobbing of the academy. It complements Joseph Harris's essay in the same issue of *CCC* entitled "Meet the New Boss, Same as the Old Boss: Class Consciousness in Composition." Because first-year composition is a site for much good work, both Murphy and Harris urge us not to abandon the first-year composition requirement as Sharon Crowley and others propose we do but to strengthen it with a renewed commitment to the course and those who teach it.[4] Harris writes: "I am calling here for a new sort of class consciousness in composition, one that joins the interests of bosses and workers around the issue of good teaching for fair pay" ("Meet the Boss" 45). Harris goes on to say: "If compositionists have any chance to effect change in the academy—and I think we do—it is through identifying our interests with those of teachers of basic and first-year writing" and not with "the professoriate in English, especially with its graduate faculty" ("Meet the Boss" 64).

How WPAs go about identifying with the interests of part-time and adjunct faculty is, of course, complicated, both in terms of professional and local issues. For example, Sledd accuses Harris and Murphy of "buying in" to a corrupt system that "would maintain the sort of hierarchy" that he detests ("On Buying In" 147). Susan Naomi Bernstein, Ann E. Green, and Cecilia Ready believe that Murphy by not "addressing gender or acknowledging how the type of institution affects the lives of adjuncts, leaves out much of the complexity of the lived experiences of adjunct lives" (150). They suggest that by "working collaboratively with adjunct faculty, WPAs could learn much about the material conditions adjuncts work under" (151). This lively interchange with Harris and Murphy, however, also reinforces the common ground of all these writers and suggests the usefulness of critique if it leads WPAs to action.

Composition, as Harris says, is a teaching subject. We are different from other disciplines that focus on research disembodied from teaching. Our commitment to teaching as central to our discipline is our strength. We are uniquely qualified to answer the calls of those who want to reposition undergraduate teaching as the focus of most faculty members' professional lives, such as Ernest Boyer of the Carnegie Foundation. We must join Boyer in finding ways for the academy to recognize, value, and reward teachers for teaching, thus changing the culture of the academy (qtd. in Schell and Stock, Introduction 24–26). If teaching and learning become the center of the academic reward system and if the scholarship of teaching and learning is recognized and rewarded as an important contribution to knowledge, then composition could lead the way in reforming the entire academy. However, this transformation will happen only if we improve the working conditions for our colleagues who teach composition.

In their important book *Moving a Mountain: Transforming the Role of Contingent Faculty in Composition Studies and Higher Education* (2001), editors Eileen

E. Schell and Patricia Lambert Stock document current conditions for contingent faculty and suggest several courses of action. Among the points of this collection are these two: (1) that contingent faculty already play an active role in producing the scholarship of teaching and learning in composition, and (2) because of their vulnerable status that often requires them to teach what, where, and how administrators dictate, contingent faculty often lead the way as practitioners in innovative teaching, whether teaching with new media, service learning, or distance education. Therefore, it is essential that these teachers identify with the composition profession and participate fully in their campus collaborative of writing teachers. Otherwise, the further fragmentation of community and pedagogy by electronic technology recently decried by Chris M. Anson and by John Alberti may be prophetic about the location of composition: Teachers unconnected to either a campus or a professional community teaching in *virtual* isolation to students who need never leave their homes.[5] As Dànielle Nicole DeVoss, Dawn Hayden, Cynthia L. Selfe, and Richard J. Selfe suggest, because part-time and contingent faculty are more likely than regular faculty to play at the fast-break, no-huddle pace of information technology, they are most vulnerable to abuse as well (267).

Entrenched faculty are not as responsive to change—whether in employment practices or in teaching with technology—as contingent faculty and graduate teaching assistants, whose positions may hinge on their ability to change rapidly as technology continues to rearrange the landscape for teaching composition. We need to understand the best practices for these new learning spaces, and for this we will need the contribution of all teachers of writing, full- and part-time. There is an irony, noted by Schell and Stock, of "an academy turning to its least secure faculty to lead the way in innovative teaching with new technologies, and marginalized academics who are inventing a scholarship of teaching for which higher education's leaders are calling" (30–31). If we are going to see the expansion of distance education as an opportunity to enhance literacy education, we will need the knowledge and experience of contingent faculty.

Changing Practices Changing Culture

Some faculties and administrators, perhaps many, are changing the status quo at their institutions.

At the University of Louisville, for example, Deborah Journet reports on a new initiative in which all tenure-stream English faculty teach first-year composition annually: faculty in literature, faculty in composition, and departmental administrators. Faculty members cannot buy their way out of this responsibility. The goal is to invest the faculty in its most important course, as judged by numbers of students enrolled in it ("Rethinking").[6]

Southern Connecticut State University in New Haven is taking another approach and raising the status of composition on its campus. The English Department was authorized to hire nine new tenure-track lines in the field of composition and filled seven assistant-professor positions with specialization in composition for the academic-year 2000–2001. This "dream team," as Will Hochman likes to call it, has responsibility for developing a quality composition program and for staffing most of the sections. These faculty have four-four teaching loads, and they teach almost exclusively the first-year, two-course composition sequence, aided by thirty contingent faculty.

Cheryl Glenn reports:

The Pennsylvania State University–University Park English Department has already moved in the right direction: for our non–tenure track faculty, we provide good salaries, full benefits, varying teaching assignments, courses down in exchange for extra duties, phones, offices, renewable three-year contracts, voting rights, and opportunities for promotion to senior lecturer. (A14)

In summer 2001, Erika Lindemann posted "Guidelines for Employing Lecturers" in the English Department at the University of North Carolina–Chapel Hill on the WPA Listserv. These guidelines, similar to those at Penn State, included specific details about salary. Lecturers earn $6,000 per course, with a three-three course load, with full fringe benefits for those employed 75 percent or more. The intent is for all lecturers to meet the required minimum, although the department will consider individual preferences in determining teaching loads. The department recommends that future salaries be indexed to the salaries offered to beginning assistant professors. After a probationary period, lecturers are awarded three-year contracts, renewable indefinitely. Lindemann later reported that the Chapel Hill guidelines have been distributed to all the campuses in the UNC system "thanks to a favorable response to them from officials in the general administration ("Re: request"). One school that offers a longer renewable contract is the University of Wyoming, which after a six-year probationary period offers a six-year renewable contract to lecturers (Brumberger 93). Local context clearly influences the nature of such positions: at UNC, lecturer positions require a PhD, and at Wyoming, they require an MA. Perhaps tellingly, Clemson University and other schools award tenure after six years and then require tenured faculty to undergo posttenure reviews every six years, a process similar to Wyoming's six-year renewable contracts for non–tenure-track faculty.

In another lively discussion on the WPA listserv, Rolf Norgaard of the University of Colorado at Boulder announced the launching of a new program for writing and rhetoric with four tenure lines and several non–tenure-track composition instructors. With leadership from the upper administration, the Boulder campus instituted the "Instructor's Bill of Rights" that provides job security and improvements in working conditions. Instructors at UC–Boulder now teach a three-three load and have small class sizes (15–18), full benefits, salary about $35,000, access to travel funds, and "a significantly reduced load every few years that amounts to a quasi-sabbatical."

Bill Lalicker of West Chester University in Pennsylvania, responding to Norgaard's post, described what his campus and the other thirteen campuses in that State System of Higher Education are doing. The union contract provides a formula for the replacement of adjuncts "where they are clearly overused, with tenure-track positions." For his department, it means tenure-track faculty in composition studies have grown from five to ten with the planned hiring of five more this year and at least four more next year. In terms of departmental politics, university governance, and improvement in the quality of education, Lalicker reports: "It's revolutionary. And it's beautiful."

Susan H. McLeod of the University of California, Santa Barbara posted a job ad recently ("Job Opportunity") on the WPA listserv for an assistant professor or a lecturer. In response to a query, McLeod reported:

> The U. C. system has two tracks for permanent faculty: tenure track and a track called Lecturer with Potential for Security of Employment. . . . The first is a research track, the second rewards teaching. Salaries are comparable in both tracks. Members of both tracks are in the Faculty Senate, the body of all UC faculty eligible to vote on university governance matters. ("Re: job opening")

Even though these lecturer-instructor positions at Penn State, UNC, UC–Boulder, and UCSB do not carry tenure, it is important to note that they are renewable indefinitely and thus contractually permanent. If instructors or lecturers do not have such contracts on a particular campus, the WPA should work to institute them. It certainly hurts the quality of our programs when we must release teachers we know to be excellent and innovative after three, or four, or six years, and replace them with less-experienced teachers because of an irrational employment rule or the opposition of tenured faculty. Such employment practices directly and negatively impact the quality of the education that our students receive. According to Schell, the "bottom-line on educational quality is employment equity", and the true challenge in meeting this goal is "whether faculty of all ranks can work collectively across lines of difference to address contingent faculty's working conditions in light of issues of educational quality" (338).

Working conditions are changing at some two-year colleges as well, especially in California, where adjuncts at two-year colleges have organized for pay equity. According to Scott Oury, community college part-timers have been

> organizing the entire state, initiating legislation, accompanied by public rela-
> tions and media campaigns, protests, petition drives, and hearings; and last
> year 'A2K' (Action 2000 Coalition) State Equity Week, all of which shamed the
> governor to make a "down payment" of $62,000,000 on a three-year promise
> of $75,000,000 each year to bring adjuncts to equity. This has been a 20-year
> effort, intensive these last two years, by part-time faculty. (A6)

Oury further states: "Adjunct working conditions affect students as well. California ran its campaign on the theme that poor working conditions for adjuncts impact the quality of education students receive" (A7).[7]

The employment practices at these institutions suggest that working conditions for composition teachers are improving at various sites across the nation. WPAs should build on this momentum—to secure pay equity and improved professional and material conditions on our local campuses for all teachers of writing. We need to build consensus among our departmental or programmatic faculties. We need to tell our administrators what other colleges are now beginning to do. We need to build coalitions across our campuses, with other state colleges, and into the community. Because local conditions are complex, begin as circumstances permit: whether converting part-time positions to full-time, or non–tenure-track to tenure-track, or some other combinations of tracks and tiers; whether converting by-the-course contracts to annual contracts, or annual contracts to multiyear contracts renewable indefinitely; whether supporting the unionization of adjunct faculty or all faculty or not. We cannot afford to argue for an ideal solution (whatever that might be on our campuses) and if it fails, refuse to compromise and thereby support the status quo. We need to build viable alternatives to the corporate academy, where market forces allow some institutions to turn teaching first-year composition into a decades-long temporary job at barely minimum wage.

Composition sees itself as a change agent—empowering writers, students, and teachers—to make a difference. Imagine for a moment one possible scenario. If contractually permanent lecturers' salaries were indexed to regular faculty salaries, perhaps lecturers to assistant professors, and senior lecturers to associate and full professors, many prospective faculty, for a variety of reasons, might choose to pursue a teaching-intensive career path over a research-intensive one. If, eventually, tenure accrued to lecturers with promotion to senior lecturer, we would be on our way to establishing full-time, teaching-intensive tracks as described by Murphy. We might also imagine a day when some faculty members would go back and forth between teaching and research tracks as professional and personal circumstances dictate. Maybe they would even go back and forth between full-time and part-time employment, all without losing their tenure or job security and their professional and wage structuring. We might even imagine faculty on two parallel tracks—not two hierarchical tiers—doing the work of this teaching profession, respecting each other as peers. Such imaginings envision a tremendous cultural shift on local campuses and nationally, but the goal of changing campus culture, one step at a time, is our only viable one.

Notes

I would like to thank readers of a draft of this book chapter for their helpful feedback: Chris Benson, Ellen Cushman, Beth Daniell, Kathi Blake Yancey, and especially Donna Reiss.

1. The October 12, 2001 issue of *CHE* referenced an article by Ms. Carroll on "Being Professional in an Unprofessional Climate" that was on its *Career Network* Web site. In addition, *CHE* announced that she had been contracted to write a monthly column for *Career Network* on adjunct life and work. Ms. Carroll's approach to being an adjunct clearly resonated with the staff and readership of *CHE*.

2. Cheryl Glenn reports that "96 percent of first-year writing is currently being taught by graduate student instructors, part-time instructors, and full-time non–tenure-track faculty members. . . . Over 40 percent of all undergraduate instruction in English in four-year colleges and universities is now delivered by faculty who do not have permanent appointments" ("Last Good Job" A12). See also the National Center for Educational Statistics's "1999 National Study of Postsecondary Faculty" and subsequent years, the "Coalition on the Academic Workforce Report," *The Report of the ADE Ad Hoc Committee on Staffing,* and the *Final Report of the MLA Committee on Professional Employment.*

3. Richard E. Miller dramatically makes this point in "'Let's Do the Numbers': Comp Droids and the Prophets of Doom."

4. Crowley argues that teachers of freshman English "must remember that we inherit an oppressive institutional history and a repressive intellectual tradition" ("A Personal Essay" 164). The deplorable working conditions of most composition teachers are endemic to that repression. For a discussion of Crowley's article and the subsequent abolitionist debate, see Schell (*Gypsy Academics* 114–17).

5. See Anne Herrington and Charles Moran's "What Happens When Machines Read Our Students' Writing?" Computer programs, if they eventually can "evaluate" student writing as well as human readers, will further alienate students from

teachers and raise political, economic, and educational challenges for teachers and administrators of college composition.

6. For subsequent discussions about the conflicts created by this departmental decision at the University of Louisville, see Debra Journet ("Redefining") and Beth A. Boehm.

7. Equity Week has spread from California across the U.S. and Canada. One week each fall, many full- and part-time contingent faculty use the occasion to raise consciousness about their working conditions in their local communities. One popular event for activists is a showing of the Barbara Wolf's documentary about contingent faculty, "Degrees of Shame: Part-Time Faculty: Migrant Workers of the Information Economy."

9 Twenty-First-Century Composition: The Two-Year-College Perspective

MARK REYNOLDS

As has been the case for nearly three decades, the majority of composition has been taught and will continue to be taught in two-year colleges for the foreseeable future. That's an easy projection for anyone who looks at the statistics of college enrollments over the past decade and projections for the next one. The figures show that most of those entering college for the first time continue to select community colleges. Recent reports give a range of from 44 to 54 percent of all first-time entering students choosing two-year colleges (Doucette and Roueche; Phillipe). According to projections from the National Institutes of Education, that trend will continue at least through 2008.

Two-year colleges are a good place for most students to begin their composition instruction given the nature of the colleges' English departments. There the major work has always been the teaching of writing—all levels and all varieties. University English departments should follow the example of their two-year college colleagues and make writing the central focus of their instruction. The very survival of university departments of English may depend on such reform. In order not to have them go the way of departments of classics as Harold Bloom has suggested (17) or morph into departments of cultural studies as Michael Bérubé (address) and others have indicated may now be happening, a concerted effort to focus their work on the teaching of writing and to place composition at its center—as has always been the case in two-year colleges—could lead to significant reform of university English departments as we know them.

When I first entered the profession in the early 1970s, it seemed that most community colleges were aspiring to be more like universities. They were highly conscious of offering college-level courses deemed worthy of the universities to which their students would transfer. As the vast number of newly created two-year colleges from the 1970s gained maturity, their faculties grew into professionals, accomplished at teaching the first two college years. However, at the universities those teaching in the first two years have remained, for the most part, graduate students, mainly interested in their course work instead of teaching first-year writing courses. These students teach for a few years, at most, then move on. Even recent efforts at some universities to involve senior faculty in teaching first-year writing courses have met with mixed results, and those efforts have resulted only when the reward for that work has been some sort of trade-off such as more full-time faculty hires in exchange for senior faculty members agreeing to teach at the first-year level (Journet "Redefining"; Boehm).

As two-year colleges gained their maturity in the 1980s, they looked less and less to the universities and forged their own identities, so much so that most were becoming innovative leaders in higher education in their own right, especially in the fields of remediation, basic literacy, and work-force training. By the 1990s, it seemed, one could make a case that no small number of universities had begun to take notice of two-year colleges and even to imitate some of their programs and methods, especially attempts at more community involvement, more use of internships, more distance education and consumer-oriented delivery, and more efforts at work-force education. Witness only the proliferation of university conference centers and the growing continuing-education programs offering the kinds of activities that most two-year colleges have been engaged in for many years. So, the suggestion that university English departments might have something to learn from their two-year counterparts should not sound revolutionary in this new millennium nor should the suggestion that deliberate efforts to forge partnerships among two- and four-year English departments might go a long way toward strengthening programs in both.

Composition Focus

Comprehensive community colleges have always had a three-fold mission of remedial, transfer, and technical education. Each of those functions has traditionally required some writing courses as a component, and because community colleges offer only the first two years of collegiate programs or one- or two-year technical programs, they have been primarily concerned with the teaching of composition instead of literature—writing instruction in a variety of precollege, first-year, and second-year writing courses. Those include composition from remedial to advanced, from technical to creative, from life writing for area citizens to specialized writing courses created on demand for local businesses and industries and even writing taught to children in on-campus summer camps. Departmental literature offerings in two-year colleges make up the minority of courses. However, most faculty do teach one or more literature courses.

It is in the teaching of writing, however, that two-year faculty members specialize. They teach from one to four or more composition courses each term: several levels of basic writing, regular college composition, advanced composition, technical writing, creative writing, and often business communications, professional writing, or various applied-writing courses in technical areas such as nursing or office administration. Regardless of a teacher's load—and in community colleges those loads are notoriously heavy—whether three, four, five, or six classes a term, one may be a literature course but all others will be writing courses.

Because of such extensive teaching of composition, two-year faculty members become specialists in the teaching of writing. They become specialists through repeatedly teaching a variety of writing courses over a number of years; through extensive curriculum development within writing programs; through work with writing assessment programs; through reading and grading papers; through developing detailed course syllabi; through extensive conferencing with students about composing; through evaluating countless writing textbooks each year (because texts are most often departmentally adopted and thoroughly discussed in meetings of all department members); through developing numerous supplementary materials, exercises, and activities for writing courses; through developing courses for electronic delivery and course Web sites; through teaching composition using all forms of technology; through tutoring in writing labs or training tutors for those labs; through supervising writing centers; through selecting, training, and mentoring adjunct instructors of writing; through teaching specialized writing courses in continuing education programs or in training for business and industry programs; through attending local, state, regional, and national meetings on the teaching of writing; and some through giving conference presentations and publishing articles about teaching writing in professional journals. The vast majority of two-year faculty do all of these things and more.

Their teaching is to students who are for the most part first-generation college students, recent high-school graduates, dual-enrollment high-school students, adults who have been out of school for many years, area workers and professionals seeking career change or job advancements, recent immigrants, and community members seeking enrichment or social outlets. These students have complex lives beyond the classroom. Most commute to school, hold part-time jobs, and have major family responsibilities. Two-year faculty also teach writing to these students in all sorts of settings other than traditional classrooms: shopping malls, banks, hospitals, community centers, nursing homes, local industries, prisons, and others. Most have had to immerse themselves in distance education in all its forms, so they teach writing online, via television, through videotapes, and satellite downlinks.

Because two-year colleges are open-admissions institutions, they consider composition an essential foundation for students' future academic success. Entering students are generally placed in an appropriate composition course based on assessment that usually includes a writing sample. For those placing in developmental or basic writing, colleges have created several levels of such courses to incorporate a vast range of students. Normally, students can move through basic-writing courses at their own rate and into regular college composition, where they can achieve success both there and in other academic course work. Students who are persistent, attend regularly, and are motivated to succeed do so. Such success may not always occur in one or two terms. Depending on an entering student's ability and background, successful completion of basic-writing courses may take several attempts. However, studies continue to show that those with perseverance and determination can succeed, as Marilyn Sternglass's important longitudinal study has demonstrated and as community-college teachers' experiences readily validate.

Community colleges nationwide seem to have been designated, whether by design as some would have us believe (DeGenero; Shor qtd. in Tinberg) or by default, as society's primary locale for training the academically and economically disadvantaged. As more and more four-year colleges and entire university systems opt out of remedial education altogether, the community college appears the last public vestige of hope for training those without adequate language skills, whether they are recent high-school graduates, immigrants, or adults many years removed from formal education. In the future, this area of composition instruction alone—basic writing—will be the most significant and important area for composition instruction in the country. No other of society's institutions is equipped or prepared to handle the teaching of vast numbers of underprepared high-school graduates, those learning English for the first time, adults long out of school, and employees at all levels seeking to upgrade career skills. According to statistics, 41 percent of two-year-college students and 29 percent of all beginning college students are deficient in at least one basic skill, reading, writing, or mathematics (Sarah Taylor 6). Critics of the developmental function of two-year colleges are many, but one of the latest major studies of remedial education in community colleges indicates that "43 percent of remedial students successfully complete their developmental programs" and "those who finish go on to perform almost as well as non-remedial students." This study also states that most studies of remedial education report only on remedial students who continue in academic programs and not on those who continue in occupational programs or only take a remedial course to receive a job promotion or pay increase (Sarah Taylor 7). As more and more states like New York, California, and Louisiana relegate remedial education to community colleges, those institutions will continue to teach more basic writing and correspondingly more college composition as successful completers of remedial programs remain on two-year campuses for additional course work. Therefore, composition in all of its incarnations is at the center of two-year-college English departments, and it will remain there for some time.

Such diversity of students in both academic ability and demographics is what makes community-college teaching so challenging. For the field of composition, two-year-college-student diversity also offers a vast and potentially productive research opportunity. Marjorie Roemer, Lucille M. Schultz, and Russel K. Durst have made a strong case for "the richness of first-year writing as a site" for research and scholarship (386). As Ellen Andrews Knodt has pointed out, however, much composition research has been carried out in institutions with more homogeneous populations than those found on two-year campuses (131). Cynthia Lewiecki-Wilson and Jeff Sommers have argued convincingly that "the profession should see open admissions composition teaching not as a low-level site merely for the application of knowledge, but as an intellectually productive and transformative site of disciplinary practice" (459). Additional research is needed in the diverse arena of the two-year college. Opportunities exist for both two-year and four-year researchers to explore composition methodology, ethnographic studies, and pedagogical strategies on the great range of abilities represented on two-year campuses. Such research will undoubtedly prove valuable as student populations across all institutions only become more diverse.

Faculty Focus

Faculty members in two-year colleges are hired based on their ability first and foremost to teach composition. These faculty members have historically viewed themselves as generalists within the discipline of English, and most are the essence of generalist, teaching the entire range of English offerings in composition and literature during the first and second undergraduate years. All faculty hold master's degrees; many hold doctorates. Many have had high-school teaching experience or adjunct experience prior to community-college employment. Most PhDs employed in community colleges tend to be specialists in composition and rhetoric rather than literature. Even those with literature PhDs find themselves mainly teaching composition.

Individual faculty are themselves usually designated as instructors, because most two-year colleges do not have faculty rank. Two-year institutions avoid rank because of the strong emphasis placed on teaching and the value placed on the democratic spirit on which two-year institutions were founded. This lack of rank and view of all faculty as equals engaged and united for the purpose of teaching, aiding students, and serving the college community also contributes to the democratic nature of two-year institutions. The very designation most often given to these colleges, "community," also suggests a team working together for the good of all rather than the traditional image of professors in academe as solitary scholars engaged in specialized research, who can only communicate to a few other specialists who are not local and may well be a world away. More importantly, because all members of two-year English departments teach composition, all have a common bond that helps to build community. One seldom sees turf wars in such departments, and faculty always have familiar topics of conversation and common interests when all teach the same subject at the same level. Departments in four-year colleges and universities might learn much from studying such an arrangement. Indeed, in university departments where all faculty have recently taken on the teaching of composition, as Debra Journet has reported about the University of Louisville, the results have mostly been positive ("Redefining"). Indeed, the two-year-college response to the traditional university method of course assignments is quite simple: Why should the most experienced and highest-paid faculty members be the most removed from the largest number of students to pass through the department and those with the greatest needs?

Two-year-college teaching requires flexibility, adaptability, and stamina. The English instructor at a two-year college may find herself teaching Composition 101 to transfer students in a campus classroom building at 8 A.M., memo writing or technical report writing to industrial electronics students at 9 A.M., life writing to senior citizens in a retirement community at 11 A.M., and basic writing in a campus computer lab at 6 P.M. Such is the routine life of a two-year-college instructor, where diversity of teaching matches diversity of student body.

I have argued extensively in other places about the intellectual work that goes on in two-year-college English departments ("The Intellectual Work"), even quoting Nellie McKay about how much she learned from her contacts with two-year faculty at the English Coalition Conference (qtd. in Elbow *What* 1). Too often, those in other segments of higher education view two-year institutions as inferior, concerned only with remediating those unable to crack the restrictive admissions standards of many universities, and the faculty who teach there as only practitioners, uninterested in research or scholarly pursuits. Seven years of editing *Teaching English in the Two-Year College* demonstrated to me the erroneous nature of such a view. Professional articles in *TETYC* and other journals attest to the rigor of the intellectual pursuits of many two-year-college faculty members.

Because most are not required to publish to get a job or keep one, not as many publish as should. However, many have been active as authors, especially of textbooks in basic writing and first-year composition. Two-year faculty have also been at the forefront of developments in distance education and classroom computer applications. The widely known mediated-learning approach to composition entitled *Interactive English* pioneered by Academic Systems Corporation was authored by two, two-year-college faculty members, and many well-known compositionists have been involved with two-year-college English teacher Peter Berkow's pioneering video approach to teaching writing. Whether in-service learning or CD-ROM software, distance-education or writing-center innovations, critical literacy, or ESL pedagogy, two-year faculty have been and are active knowledge-makers and innovators.

Instructional Focus

If two-year institutions will continue to be major sites for composition instruction in the future and deserve more attention from universities, as I believe, what else might two-year colleges share with their four-year colleagues? To answer this question, I want to get personal.

My son was a good student in school and knew early on that he wanted to be a doctor. To that end, he chose to attend a private liberal-arts college with selective admissions because of the high acceptance rate of its graduates into professional schools and because he got a good scholarship. His first-year-composition experience included writing an initial narrative of personal-experience essay. His other papers were of two types: documented papers on subjects of his own choosing (and he invariably chose medical or scientific topics) and a few critical analyses of literature. Throughout his first year, he asked me to read only one draft of a paper he had to write, an assignment calling for him to trace a single theme through three Flannery O'Connor short stories. His concern was about the theme and not about the composing. His draft was adequate, and like a good parent, I praised it, offered a couple of suggestions about content, and provided the expected punctuation adjustments. He earned an *A-* on the paper and was perfectly content, glad to have that typical-English-teacher assignment over with so he could move on through the two required first-year composition courses and into the interesting courses of his biology major.

After that first year, my son asked for no more composition help from me throughout his undergraduate years. Then came the time for him to apply to medical schools and to write the application essay—all some variation on the subject of why he wanted to be a doctor. After some laboring and complaining, he finally sought help from me with content. What should he say, he asked. What should he put in the essays to explain why he wanted to go to medical school and become a doctor? His attempts were limp and feeble and disappointing because of their lack of specificity. He didn't seem to understand the need to provide examples from his personal experience to support his contention that he *really* wanted to be a doctor. I felt that somehow his education had failed him if this bright-enough twenty-one-year-old didn't know how to write a personal narrative that was concrete and example-laden enough to be convincing. So, it was parents to the rescue. My wife and I brainstormed about our son's growing up and those occasions we could remember that seemed to suggest he wanted to be a doctor. I then emailed him several examples that his mother and I thought would be good to include in his essay. Out of desperation, a looming deadline, and assurances from his girlfriend, an English major, that he did, indeed, need some concrete personal examples in his essay, he selected a couple from those I sent and managed to get his essay written and eventually gain acceptance to med school, no doubt more from his GPA and MCAT score than any brilliance displayed in his essay.

Move forward with me now to the end of my son's first course in medical school—twelve concentrated weeks of gross anatomy. I was sitting in my office one morning when the telephone rang and when I answered, unexpectedly heard, "Dad, what are you doing?" Trying not to show the normal panic any parent experiences momentarily when getting such an unexpected call from a child away at college, I mumbled something about some work I was doing, and trying to be calm, asked, "What's up, son?" My son said that he needed some help with a writing assignment. He had to write, he said, a thank-you letter to the family who had donated the cadaver he had been working on for the past twelve weeks. All the anatomy students had to write such a letter. The letters were then going to be collected into booklet form and given to the families of the cadavers at a memorial service to be held at the medical school. "I've done a draft," my son said. "Can I email it to you to see what you think? I really don't know what to say and I don't have time for this. I've got a test to study for." "Okay," I said, reluctantly. "Email it to me and I'll take a look." "Oh," I added, "when is it due?" "Tomorrow," came the answer over the phone.

My point in detailing these personal accounts is to point out that my son's expensive, elitist education didn't prepare him very well to feel confident enough to write either of these two assignments, one a personal-experience narrative whose purpose was persuasion, the other a thank-you letter, albeit an unusual one.

I thought at the time of each of these writing "crises" and even more since then that most of my two-year-college students would have been better prepared based on their composition courses for both of these assignments. In the composition program at my college and most others I know about, we stress the use of multiple examples from personal experiences to persuade in several essay assignments in the first composition course. We also use letter-writing assignments in composition as we try to bring real-world writing situations into the classroom to give students the tools that will serve them in good stead not only in future courses but also in the world at large. We do have students do some literary analyses because we value the critical-thinking skills such writing demands, but we work hard to make sure that we prepare our students for a variety of future writing experiences by providing an ample number of applied-writing activities. The research papers in English 102, for example, are always on topics that the students choose themselves, and they seldom select literary topics. They write about treating Alzheimer's because they have a grandfather with the disease, about ultrasound technology because they want to work with it in a hospital, about the construction of Hoover Dam because they want to become civil engineers, about laser-light shows because they want to be electricians, or about no-load mutual funds because they want careers as stockbrokers. We have also begun to require students to use some graphics in these papers because we know that most will have to include them in papers for future courses or in job-related writing. As Roemer, Schultz, and Durst have also pointed out, "we cannot educate our students solely to our purposes, ignoring their own" (382). Community-college students will not allow anyone to ignore their purposes. Most are practical, realistic, and determined that their education be relevant.

I would submit that such efforts at applied writing that I describe have value and will be even more valuable to all students in the future. Roemer, Schultz, and Durst go on to add:

> Advanced classes in esoteric specialities can't fill, highly educated PhDs in narrow fields can't get jobs. Everywhere that we look we see the demand for generalists, for people who can teach basic skills, communication skills, introductory courses, for educators who can make connections between the world's work and the university, and, specifically for people who can teach, not just research. (390)

This is a description of most two-year-college faculty members I know.

It is past time that four-year and two-year faculties join forces for the greater good of higher education. Together we must make the teaching of composition better and more relevant for all students in all institutions. Let university English departments look no further than their local community college to see how placing writing instruction at the center of all they do might well strengthen their work and produce stronger and more valuable departments. By involving all English faculty in the teaching of composition, by acknowledging its service function to the institution, by making its instruction of value to students both in their future course work and in their lives, and by collaborating more often with their two-year-college colleagues, the whole of higher education can be better served.

10 Vertical Writing Programs in Departments of Rhetoric and Writing

RESPONSE BY ELLEN CUSHMAN

The questions of where composition will be taught and who will teach it lend themselves to an answer that focuses on first-year composition, though composition and writing are not the same thing. Composition has an institutional history that has in part created the labor crisis that Art Young discusses and that has in part created the caste system, to which Mark Reynolds refers, between community colleges and universities. We have excellent histories that discuss the formation of composition as a first-year requirement and the labor and professional identity problems resulting from this formation (Harris, *Teaching Subject;* Crowley, Berlin, Susan Miller, and Thomas Miller). These works and Young's and Reynolds's essays lead me to ask: How can we change institutional structures that devalue the teaching of first-year composition, that exploit the teachers of first-year composition, and that underestimate the disciplinary knowledge in the field of rhetoric and composition?

Young asks us to work within the institutional structures to change them, and in that way, I believe he's practicing a savvy form of institutional critique that seeks to analyze, then flex, and, perhaps, alter the university structures while working within those structures. Reynolds asks us to learn from community-college colleagues who are teaching composition according to the "three-fold mission of remedial, transfer, and technical education." When Reynolds describes the teachers at community colleges, he does so by noting that teachers of community-college composition courses become specialists in the teaching of writing. The difference between composition and writing is that writing courses have a vertical curriculum attached to them. If *composition* is relegated to the remedial, the first-year, the disenfranchised, underemployed, and the exploitive, then *writing* opens up the possibilities of teaching courses about the literacies that various professional, community, and organizational members practice.

Sharon Crowley took a stab at this idea when she mentioned that the alternative to first-year composition would be "the vertical elective curriculum in composing, a curriculum that examines composing both in general and as it takes place in specific theoretical situations such as workplaces and community decision making" (*Composition in the University* 262). Such a curriculum seems to be precisely what Reynolds described as already in place in the community college. Developing a vertical writing curriculum could possibly enact the kind of institutional critique and cultural change that Young mentions as well.

So let me revise the questions: Where will *writing* be taught? and Who will teach it? James Porter, Patricia A. Sullivan, Jeffrey Grabill, Stuart Blythe, and Libby Miles (2000) ask similar questions: "Is our continued self-identity as *composition* teachers helping ensure our continued subordinate status? What would happen if we reconceived ourselves as 'writing experts' working in the public realm instead of 'composition teachers' working within the university?" (632; authors' emphasis). The authors offer three ways in which institutional critique can guide a sustained set of micro practices that when seen alone, change very little but when seen cumulatively, do move institutional structures.

How can we develop vertical writing curriculums at our institutions? How can we staff these? What would these look like?

My sense is that part of the problem in developing vertical writing programs is that the PhD programs in rhetoric and composition are simply not producing enough graduates for the number of positions available. For example, in 1997, 139 PhDs in rhetoric and composition were granted, but 161 jobs were listed and available (National Center for Educational Statistics 404). Computer-mediated communication and professional-writing positions have seen the most growth as an area in 1990–2000, according to the MLA spring newsletters, with over 100 percent growth in some years. With positions going unfilled, few departments can staff vertical writing programs.

Another problem might be that professors already in departments aren't doing their share, as Young points out, to teach first-year writing, let alone any vertical writing courses. Conference participants who were writing program administrators and seated at table leader Irwin Weiser's table noted: "having all faculty teach composition [or writing] presents [the] problem of how to bring about this transition, particularly if some faculty disdain teaching first-year composition. . . . We envision embattled WPAs facing resistance from faculty and complaints from students" (Weiser).

Still another problem that hinders the development of vertical writing programs is that composition is seen by most literature faculty as a contentless curriculum. Young writes: "If teaching and learning become the center of the academic reward system and if the scholarship of teaching and learning is recognized and rewarded as an important contribution to knowledge, then composition could lead the way in reforming the entire academy." These are some mighty big *ifs*. As many pointed out in their table discussions, professors in traditional English departments often do not value, appreciate, or understand composition studies; they see the field as empty. Specialization as an institutional structure has hindered Young's above two *if* clauses from coming to fruition. Research, in many universities, is still highly regarded, and research in composition and rhetoric has gone far beyond only including the first-year-comp class as a site for understanding—indeed, it had to for composition and rhetoric to establish itself as a respected discipline. But writing courses have no content, the argument still goes, and without a content, an area of specialization, we haven't a professional identity.

Writing will be taught in the vertical curriculum by fully enfranchised teachers only if our colleagues in literature understand and appreciate that writing, a practice, is also a knowledge base. A social capital. A profession. I don't hold out much hope for such a change in the value systems of literature professors because it hasn't come about yet. Though, if the number of jobs available in the field of composition can be read as an indication of administrators' values, then we have evidence that writing is valued at the university level. Administrators have in some cases given English departments new lines with the contingency that these lines be filled with composition and rhetoric scholars.

In order to develop vertical curriculums, composition and rhetoric scholars could tap into the cachet that writing has in many university administrations. One reason for writing's value at administrative levels stems from the value placed on writing by leading business, government, and community members. Perhaps we can help colleagues understand that writing is a content area if writing professors and instructors teach, write, and publish with community and business partners. Community members, organizational representatives, business representatives, government employees, health care workers, and military officials—all tend to appreciate the knowledge base of skilled writers. Many see writing influencing their chances for success, persuading decision makers, and making a stand. Community literacy projects, service-learning initiatives, business and technical writing all emphasize the connection between universities and communities and offer numerous sites for writing instruction beyond the first-year composition course.

Yes, let's continue to build our institutional cachet as knowledge producers, but let's not do this with those who have not valued writing, who are threatened by it, or who merely exploit its instruction. Isn't it time for composition and rhetoric scholars to break from English departments to form their own vertical writing programs within their own departments?

Would such a break change unfair labor practices? Vertical writing programs may not solve the labor issues the field faces. Even in community colleges, like the one where Reynolds teaches that has writing courses, systems of exploitation and rigid class structures exist. Carol Haviland (whose students who graduate with an MA in composition from California State University—San Bernardino often seek work at community colleges) pointed out that community colleges rely heavily on contingent, part-time labor to teach their writing courses. At the table led by Irene Ward, "positive experiences with unionization of faculty and adjuncts were discussed," which gives us hope that labor issues can be addressed. However, they also noted that "the interests of tenure-line faculty and adjunct faculty are often at odds in such negotiations" (qtd. from Ward's notes). Quoted in Young's essay, Eileen E. Schell and Patricia Lambert Stock's book on labor practices in the academy offers many insights into these issues.

Both Reynolds and Young offer interesting and timely suggestions for where writing will be taught and who will teach it. Although certainly attractive, their ideas may not be feasible if composition and rhetoric stays within English departments. I'm not advocating the teaching of writing in programs, though, that do not have department status with the tenure-track lines and institutional stability that department status offers. I taught for three years as a lecturer in the University Writing Program at the University of California–Berkeley, the type of program that Jennifer Trainor and Amanda Godley describe in their article "After Wyoming." The program relied heavily on part-time and graduate-student labor, had very little university status, and was housed in what students called "the shack" and "the outhouse" behind the grand humanities building. Similar programs exist at Duke University and Harvard University, and they are exactly what I do not want to advocate. Without department status and a mission to do so, vertical curriculums can not be developed in such programs, and tenure-track lines will never exist. These kinds of writing programs are merely service programs to the university, a place where remedial-writing problems and first-year composition are addressed.

I am also not arguing for BA writing programs to develop in English departments in which literature faculty only pay lip service, if that, to the value of writing as a field. I was fortunate enough to work at Colorado University, Denver for two years, where more than twenty-five years ago a Bachelor's Degree in Writing developed alongside the BA degree in Literature. It was a writing-teacher's dream: I could teach magazine writing, literary nonfiction, travel writing, multimedia writing, and more. However, though the range of writing courses existed on the books, the department chair could never staff them—the department employed one-third the number of writing professors as it did literature professors, and 80 percent of all the department's writing courses were taught by contingent labor.

While I lay no claim to knowing the departmental history that contributed to such imbalances, I can say that in the years I was there, the hiring priorities were set according to the demands students had for courses (this practice was unusual, apparently, and was facilitated by the retirement of a number of the literature professors). Thus, student demand was high enough that the writing program had two full-time positions and creative writing had one because these courses had the largest enrollments and overflow. The department also hired two full-time instructors to teach four writing courses each a semester, with a one-course reduction for administration work, positions that had full benefits though a barely livable wage. Had those literature professors not retired, the department's hiring priorities would likely have been different. These brief anecdotes, I hope, illustrate why I see the need for vertical writing programs to be taught in writing departments by fully enfranchised writing professors. We can no longer trust literature professors to do the right thing when deciding where composition will be taught and who will teach it.

Part 4 What Theories, Philosophies Will Undergird Our Research Paradigms? And What Will Those Paradigms Be?

11 Ethics and the Future of Composition Research

GESA E. KIRSCH

In this chapter, I examine current trends in composition research from both feminist and ethical perspectives. Specifically, I look at what I consider to be some of the most interesting, exciting, but also potentially problematic developments in qualitative research: (1) the way in which scholars attempt to make their interactions with participants more interactive, collaborative, reciprocal, and socially responsible, and (2) the increasingly diverse research sites scholars explore, sites that take them far beyond the academy and into community centers, corporate boardrooms, volunteer agencies, medical facilities, nonprofit organizations, government-sponsored programs, and beyond. I briefly describe these trends and then explore what they mean in terms of the future of composition studies, specifically in terms of research and theory building, and, most importantly, in terms of our ethical obligations. I argue that ethics will play an increasingly important role as scholars explore new research sites, work with increasingly diverse participants, and develop new approaches to research methodology. I conclude by proposing several ways of addressing the ethical concerns now emerging in composition studies.

Recent Trends in Composition Research

I begin with some predictions about the future of composition research, or, perhaps more accurately, I should say I begin with descriptions, because much of this work is already underway. First, I predict that composition scholars will engage in more qualitative, ethnographic, self-reflexive, dialogic, and auto-ethnographic research, work that grows out of social-activist, feminist, postcolonial, and postmodern traditions. Researchers who engage in this type of research usually follow a number of principles, such as

- asking questions relevant to participants' experiences
- collaborating with participants during all phases of research
- establishing relations that are mutually beneficial, interactive, and nonhierarchical
- including the voices of participants in publications and presentations
- using the results of research to benefit the community being studied
- taking social and ethical responsibility for the design and dissemination of the work

Second, I predict that research will take place in increasingly diverse settings, such as

- community centers (e.g., many service-learning projects bring students and researchers into community settings; see, for example, Ellen Cushman, "Rhetorician"; Thomas Deans, *Writing Partnerships*)
- cyberspace (e.g., the edited collections by Gail E. Hawisher and Cynthia L. Selfe, *Passions;* Kristine Blair and Pamela Takayoshi, *Feminist Cyberscapes*)
- church and other religious settings (e.g., Beverly Moss, "Creating a Community")
- youth centers (e.g., Jabari Mahiri's work on youth culture, *Shooting for Excellence;* Mary Sheridan-Rabideau's work on literacy of young girls in a feminist afterschool program, "The Stuff That Myths Are Made Of")
- workplaces, where scholars in technical and professional writing have long conducted research, but where scholars with an activist or feminist orientation might ask very different questions (e.g., about equity, access, power, gender, and politics)
- the streets (e.g., Paula Mathieu's work on street newspapers and literacy of the homeless, "'Not Your Mama's Bus Tour'")
- nursing homes (e.g., Ruth Ray's work on the uses of literacy among female nursing-home residents, *Beyond Nostalgia*)

Finally, I predict that these increasingly diverse settings will entail working with increasingly diverse participants. From the list of research sites described above, we can surmise that scholars will work with increasingly diverse participants, such as business executives, homeless people, nursing-home residents, members of religious congregations, government employees, and volunteer coordinators in nonprofit organizations. These populations are far removed from, and perhaps could not be more different than, the participants whom composition scholars have traditionally studied—writing students, writing teachers, and writing program administrators. Working with such a wide range of populations requires new, specialized knowledge on the part of researchers as well as a heightened concern for ethical responsibilities, a topic I address in detail in the last section of this chapter.

In short, I am observing a trend toward more interactive, reciprocal, collaborative, qualitative research that is conducted in a range of new settings with increasingly diverse populations.[1] Furthermore, much of this recent scholarship actively challenges the boundaries among theory, research, and practice. I sense great enthusiasm in our profession for work that connects classrooms with communities, teaching with research, community service with students, and that goes across disciplines and across campuses—an enthusiasm that is reinvigorating the field of writing studies. What I am describing, then, is nothing short of a redefinition, a reshaping, a transformation of our discipline.

To take but one example, I will look briefly at Cushman's work on the uses of literacy among inner-city residents. This work clearly reflects some of the trends I have depicted, and it seems to have caught the imagination as well as the respect of our profession. Cushman argues for the "rhetorician as an agent of social change" (also the title of her article) and describes how she negotiated the divide between campus and the inner city (reflecting composition scholars' concerns for social justice, or, as other, perhaps more cynically inclined members of our profession might note, scholars' guilt and anxiety about their class and race privileges). She also explains how she engaged in a dialogic relationship with participants by "establish[ing] networks of reciprocity with them, and creat[ing] solidarity with them" ("Rhetorician" 7), and how she attempted to make the project mutually beneficial for researcher and participants. In other words, Cushman was able to gather valuable information for her research project while the inner-city residents with whom she worked received support for their literacy activities, such as fighting eviction notices, negotiating legal contracts, and interacting with city and government agencies. What her work illustrates, Cushman observes, is that "authority to represent others does not come de facto from an academic position, but from the reciprocal and dialogic relations shared by scholars and community residents" (Cushman and Monberg 167).[2]

Cushman's work is particularly noteworthy because it won two Conference on College Composition and Communication awards in the same year. This feat is remarkable for several reasons: (1) the award committees work entirely independently of each other; (2) CCCC selects committee members in order to represent diversity in terms of scholars's research interests, theoretical perspectives, teaching philosophies, institutional affiliations, years of service in the profession, gender, generation, ethnicity, and many other factors; (3) the independent committees develop their own set of criteria (within the broader guidelines of the award);

and (4) they do not share their deliberations until all CCCC committees have completed their work and submitted a report to the CCCC chair.[3] Thus, when two committees independently of each other selected Cushman's work as winner of the CCCC Outstanding Dissertation Award and the CCCC Richard Braddock Award, I think it is fair to say that the work captured the spirit of a diverse group of composition scholars, perhaps even the zeitgeist of the composition community at the turn of the millennium.

However, I do not want to paint a picture of current trends in composition research with too broad a brush—there are, after all, other notable trends that do not reflect the picture I have drawn so far. For example, Deborah Brandt has recently suggested that she aims to "pulverize" ("Politics" 43) and disassemble the literacy narratives she collects for her research until they are no longer recognizable as individual stories. Brandt explains that although the stories of her participants are moving and powerful, they distract from the theories of literacy she is trying to develop, which is the main goal of her scholarship. Moreover, she notes that when she does not pulverize the literacy narratives she collects, they inevitably lead readers to analyze and psychologize research participants, in ways she considers very inappropriate. Brandt is quite aware that her work stands in stark contrast to trends in current scholarship: "Maybe you would say that I dehumanize the words people give me, but I think it would be more accurate to say that I try to depsychologize them. I try to empty them of their personal significance and understand their historical significance" ("Politics" 43–44). Thus, in contrast to most qualitative researchers in the field, who aim to capture the local, the specific, and the personal, Brandt works against the grain by segmenting, slicing, and disassembling the information she gathers from research participants.

Implications for Research and Theory

What does the trend I have sketched above mean in terms of our research paradigms and guiding theories? First, boundaries begin to blur among what constitutes theory, what constitutes methodology, and what constitutes practice. Many contributors to the edited collection *Under Construction: Working at the Intersections of Composition Theory, Research, and Practice*, for instance, illustrate the increasing interdependency and mutually informing relations among these three areas. The editors of the volume, Christine Farris and Chris M. Anson, note that "reluctant to assume a top-down, research-to-theory-to-practice relationship, compositionists increasingly claim to favor some sort of a dialectical relationship between theory and practice" (3). From my perspective, this new, scholarly orientation of seeing theory, research, and practice as mutually informing entities accounts for much of the innovative scholarship emerging in composition studies today.

Second, it means that we have indeed come face-to-face with what Stephen M. North calls "paradigm hope" ("Death" 194), the impossible, perhaps naive or nostalgic notion that our work in writing studies would evolve into a science of sorts, guided by a single research paradigm in which all knowledge accumulates slowly, gradually, in small increments, with each new addition being carefully tested and verified. North (in his usual fashion) dismantles the myth that our work moves smoothly along a single axis, and he casts a new light on the early work by Richard Braddock, Richard Lloyd-Jones, and Lowell Schoer. North exposes the hidden alliances, both financially and institutionally, which Braddock and his colleagues enjoyed, and debunks notions of paradigm building, of orderly progress, and of a gradually expanding knowledge-base in our field. Rather than lamenting this state of affairs (as he did in his earlier work *The Making of Knowledge in Composition: Portrait of an Emerging Field*), North celebrates these developments, predicting that research in writing studies will become more versatile, more varied, increasingly local, and closely intertwined with the needs and conditions of specific research sites.

On these points, I agree with North; he is correct to observe that we have evolved into a field that has "expand[ed] the range of [its] research interests"; that reports "on [a] wider range of issues in a wider variety of forms"; and has "develop[ed] a very different rhythm" ("Death" 203) of knowledge building and publication. North explains that "more inquirers working at a wider range of sites in a greater variety of forms—all less constrained by the cumulative weight of past inquiries—will produce a greater quantity of research and produce it faster" ("Death" 204).

Up to this point, North's description of developments in the field is on target, but he makes a final claim with which I disagree—that research will become "more disposable" ("Death" 205). Here, North seems to slip inadvertently into the assumptions about paradigm building, which he attempts to dismantle; he assumes that scholarship is more valuable (and less disposable) if it accumulates slowly, not fast; if it is generalizable, not tied to the local and specific. In contrast to North, I take the position that as scholarship in composition expands and diversifies, it becomes more insightful and more valuable. Such work might be put to different uses, addressing more diverse audiences and meeting different expectations and goals (when compared to traditional scholarship), but those factors, I suggest, make work in writing studies more significant, more meaningful, and more desirable—not less so.

Finally, I want to discuss the trend I have been describing (the trend of increasingly diverse, collaborative, interactive, socially responsible research) in light of some scholars' resistance to and critique of this trend, expressed in arguments for a return to a more scientific, empirical, generalizable research paradigm of the kind first suggested by Braddock, Lloyd-Jones, and Schoer. Scholars of this stripe are far and few between, but they are vocal nonetheless, perhaps serving as important voices of contrast, a necessary questioning of the new status quo in composition scholarship—the rise and dominance of qualitative research (e.g., Ellen Barton, "More Methodological Matters"; Davida Charney, "Empiricism"; Susan Peck MacDonald, "Voices").

A case in point is Susan Peck MacDonald's contribution to *Under Construction*. She reviews a decade's worth of composition scholarship and notes trends similar to what I have described—greater concern for including the voices of research participants, more efforts to collaborate with participants in studies, and more calls for producing multivocal texts. These trends provide MacDonald with cause for great alarm because they create "confusion about forums and purposes" (117) and distract composition studies from its most important goal—the "effort required to build a cumulative body of knowledge suited to our goals as students of rhetoric" (123). MacDonald explains:

> Compositionists' recent calls for more personal voices, more voices of our "subjects," more activist research, more subversion of dominant academic styles, and more empowerment of those whose writing we study in the end look like a form of disciplinary identity crisis or a form of anti-intellectualism long familiar in American society but now turned by the academy against itself. When we focus on goals like empowerment, activism, or social change, we implicitly deny the value of research or of a discipline which already may seem weak or pre-disciplinary to many academic colleagues. (123)

By setting up a binary opposition between "empowerment, activism, and social change" and the "value of research," MacDonald denies that goals like social change or empowerment can become value-added features of research, enhancing the knowledge and depth of our understanding. As I have argued elsewhere, by working closely with research participants, scholars are likely to ask questions that are more relevant to participants' lives and are more likely to have access to friends, family, and community members who can provide additional insights into the topic of research (*Ethical Dilemmas* 10–12).

What I am critical of in MacDonald's discussion is not the notion that the creation of knowledge, in the best of cases, is cumulative—I, too, find that research paradigm very appealing. Unfortunately, the work of North ("Death") and other scholars has convinced me that "paradigm hope" is just that—a hope always beyond reach. However, what troubles me about MacDonald's argument is her lack of concern, perhaps even her lack of respect for the voices, visions, and insights of research participants: "If our 'subjects' happen to be wrong or confused or resistant in what they are thinking, then adding their voices to our research may contribute little of importance to the knowledge developing in the field" ("Voices" 114). Here we get the sense of MacDonald's belief that researchers know best (because subjects can be confused, resistant, or simply wrong, something that is apparently beyond the pale of researchers).

What concerns me about MacDonald's paradigm hope is her lack of acknowledgment that the research methods of the past have often failed those who found themselves in vulnerable or subordinate positions, such as women, people of color, basic writers, adjunct teachers, and students. It is important to remember that historically, empirical researchers and their methods have produced "knowledge" that unfairly, inaccurately, or falsely represented those being studied.[4] Rather than acknowledging this troubled past of traditional research methods, however, MacDonald argues that researchers are misdirecting their energies when they aim to give voice to participants and listen to their insights and knowledge. She explains (in a rather cynical tone) that "another way to give voice to our 'subjects' would be to devote our research to the project of giving voice, but if that is our goal, we might do just as well to become newspaper reporters, tabloid TV hosts, social workers, or psychological counselors" ("Voices" 115). In sum, MacDonald's goal to resurrect paradigm hope, or, as Farris and Anson describe it, to "resuscitate empiricism" (6) is one thing (perhaps understandable in a world of chaos and unpredictability), but to ignore the history of empirical research, which, according to many contemporary scholars, is a history of failed research, that is another, more-troubling matter.

Along with North ("Death"), Susan H. McLeod (this volume), and Lynn Z. Bloom (this volume), I see the quest for a single research paradigm, or perhaps more accurately, the quest for a single body of knowledge, as misguided. What we need, instead, is room for multiple research methods, for flexible paradigms and theories that can help researchers adapt to changing circumstances, changing audiences, and changing needs of participants and the research community. Moreover, we need self-reflexivity, or perhaps more appropriately, what Cushman and Terese Guinsatao Monberg call "social reflexive scholarship . . . that does not assume authority in representing others but negotiates that authority" (166). In other words, collaborative, activist research, which attempts to create knowledge not only for the sake of knowledge but for the benefit of those being studied, is not a form of anti-intellectualism, as MacDonald contends, but a sign of a vigorous, growing field of study that is coming to terms with the legacy of empirical research and redesigning it for new purposes and new audiences.

Ethical Implications

As research becomes increasingly diverse, as researchers study communities far beyond the academy, and as the boundaries among research, theory, and practice blur, the ethical dimensions of our work will become increasingly important in at least three areas of our work. First, as researchers engage in more qualitative, collaborative, and socially responsible research, they are more likely to encounter ethical dilemmas in their interactions with participants and community members; second, as scholars examine theories and histories of composition studies, they are beginning to uncover omissions, gaps, and silenced voices; and third, as writing teachers assign more fieldwork and service-learning in their courses, they are creating new relations with community organizations and putting students into potentially vulnerable positions, both of which warrant a careful examination of our ethical obligations.

Implications for qualitative research. Research that is more qualitative, interactive, collaborative, and reciprocal in nature leads to more complex and intimate interactions among scholars, participants, and the community. These new relationships present both strengths and weaknesses. The strength lies in making research more alive, more responsive, more dynamic, and more empowering. At the same time, the potential for ethical dilemmas, for misunderstandings, for inappropriate, perhaps even exploitative interactions emerges. As I have explained elsewhere in greater detail *(Ethical Dilemmas),* it is perhaps ironic that

> Scholars are now discovering that the changes in research methodology proposed by feminists [and other qualitative scholars]—greater intimacy and increased collaboration among researchers and participants—may inadvertently reintroduce some of the ethical dilemmas they sought to avoid: potential disappointments, alienation, and exploitation of participants. (26)

As researchers and volunteers get to know each other, interact more frequently, establish trust, and develop friendships, they become vulnerable to misunderstandings, invaded privacy, and broken trust.

Consider, for example, this statement by a former research participant, Carole Deletiner. "The consent form guaranteed my anonymity and stated that I would be allowed to request to see any of the material that would be used in the final study. After the semester ended, I never saw the researcher again, nor did I ever read a single word of her writing" (2).[5] Later on, Deletiner learned that she had been the subject of a dissertation and went to read about herself:

> I remember going to the library and sitting in the sub-basement, reading the dissertation on microfiche. I felt physically ill. I was enraged and, more painfully, I was filled with guilt and shame. The study, which initially set out to examine how a "feminist" pedagogy can operate as a "liberatory" force in a writing workshop, became a critique of what happened in a class in which the teacher . . . turned out to be a neurotic and controlling martinet, one who ultimately silenced all of her students. (3)

As is evident from the description of her experience, Deletiner was troubled by several aspects of her relationship with the researcher: She felt disappointed, if not betrayed, because the researcher left abruptly and did not volunteer to show her the write-up of the research, and, more importantly, she was confronted with and clearly shocked by how she was portrayed in the researcher's dissertation. Deletiner narrates her chilling experience in response to Paul Anderson's article on ethical issues in person-based research ("Simple Gifts"), echoing his call for more protection and honesty in interactions with volunteers.[6]

Ethical dilemmas in relations with participants, then, can range from issues of broken trust to potential exploitation, abuse, and physical endangerment. I have examined many such examples in *Ethical Dilemmas* and do not want to revisit that topic here. Rather, I want to point out that as the field diversifies (including the participants we study, the methods we use, and the questions we ask), so, too, will the potential for ethical dilemmas, for contested research sites, for political controversy, and for conflict within the profession (all signs of a growing field, one that is increasing in importance and visibility).

Implications for theoretical and historical work. Composition scholars have also begun to call into question the ethics of creating historical narratives and constructing theories. For instance, almost all authors in the *CCC* fiftieth-anniversary issue invoke ethical concerns in their reflections on the field. Jacqueline Jones Royster and Jean C. Williams, for example, point to the inexcusable absence, omission, and neglect of African American scholars and educators in published histories of composition studies, and they urge scholars to assume ethical responsibility for telling more complete and socially responsible narratives about writing studies and writing students:

> The challenge then is to broaden the research base, the inquiry base, the knowledge base from which interpretive frameworks can be drawn, not simply to

say that we know that we don't know but to do the work of finding out. We need methodologies for seeing the gaps in our knowledge and for generating the research that can help us fill those gaps. (583)

Other authors in the same *CCC* anniversary issue who express concern for our ethical obligations as scholars and teachers are Marcy Taylor and Jennifer Holberg. In their article, "'Tales of Neglect and Sadism,'" they examine the ethics of representing graduates students in the professional literature and call for a closer analysis of what purposes these narratives serve, what representations of graduate students we create, and under which conditions we speak for them or invite them to speak for themselves. Concerns about ethics, then, are beginning to permeate the professional literature—in increasing numbers of conference sessions, journal articles, edited collections, and full-length books (e.g., Fontaine and Hunter; Porter; and Smith).

Implications for the teaching of writing. Ethical considerations are also taking on a new importance in the teaching of writing. Because of recent calls for experientially based approaches to teaching, such as service-learning and fieldwork-based courses, I want to suggest that there is a particular urgency to pay attention to potential ethical dilemmas. These innovative approaches to teaching typically introduce undergraduate students to fieldwork, ask them to conduct interviews and observations, analyze findings, and write about their learning experiences. Moreover, in service-learning courses, students and teachers interact closely with volunteer participants and community agencies. In other words, the activist research and teaching that are being advocated in the profession by scholars like Elizabeth Chiseri-Strater and Bonnie Stone Sunstein, *FieldWorking;* Cushman, "Rhetorician;" and others put undergraduates into community settings with all the potential for ethical dilemmas—as well as opportunities for learning and growth—that qualitative researchers face in the field but without the comparable training, guidelines, and professional oversight. That is, the fieldwork many instructors are beginning to require of their undergraduate students, often first-year students, mimics qualitative research, but unlike such research, it does not have a system of professional oversight in place (a system that is provided at the professional level, in part, by doctoral committees, peer-review processes, and federal guidelines as interpreted by Institutional Review Boards).

Like many other scholars, I find these innovative approaches to teaching promising, revitalizing, and exhilarating, and I recognize the many benefits that service-learning and fieldwork can provide. For example, such teaching can increase retention rates among students, can create conditions for serious learning, can help students commit to a major, and can build lasting connections between the university and the community. However, I do want to bring to the profession's attention the potential ethical dilemmas that students are likely to encounter and the resulting responsibilities their instructors assume when they assign service-learning or fieldwork as part of their courses. That is not to say that I want to discourage innovative, socially responsible forms of teaching or qualitative research—quite the opposite. I think we can learn from ethical dilemmas and work towards developing professional standards of ethics.

Towards developing professional standards of ethics. We can begin to develop guidelines for dealing with ethical dilemmas in a number of different ways. First, we can reflect on our research experiences, offer case studies, and narrate how we made difficult choices. We can exchange information about how we made decisions—which ones we would change and which ones we stand by—and what, if anything, we would do differently in future projects. Such contributions enrich the professional conversation, provide guidance for those embarking on research projects, and help first-time researchers develop realistic expectations about qualitative research. I have in mind such guidelines as suggested by Anderson ("Simple Gifts"), who proposes that we consider "renegotiating consent" with students at the end of teacher-research projects (so as to avoid any possibility of unintended coercion); the work by Thomas Newkirk ("Seduction and Betrayal"), who proposes a clear set of guidelines for the rights and responsibilities of researchers and participants; and my own work *(Ethical Dilemmas),* in which I offer some specific suggestions for addressing ethical dilemmas.

Second, we might consider ongoing education with a focus on ethics, both for new and veteran scholars. I can imagine professional-development seminars, summer institutes, workshops at conventions, collaboration among doctoral-degree-granting programs, and many other venues. Whatever form or shape, I think that as a burgeoning discipline (see Todd Taylor, this volume, for more details on the growth and current state of the profession), we need to make a commitment to ongoing professional development as a way to reimagine the field and meet new challenges. Professional seminars are not a novel idea; many disciplines regularly offer such opportunities. For instance, the Linguistic Society of America offers regular summer institutes, the Dartmouth School of Critical Theory addresses developments in cultural and literary theory during intensive summer seminars, and the National Writing Project offers annual professional-development summer workshops for writing teachers. In addition, it would be important to offer professional-development seminars at local and regional sites because not all composition instructors, especially those working in part-time or non–tenure-track positions, have the time and resources to attend national conferences or summer institutes. Some already existing local workshops can serve as models (and although they are not all focused on ethical issues, they do focus on professional development). For instance, the writing program and writing center at the University of Toledo offer a series of professional workshops for composition instructors, provide competitive grants for attendance at the CCCC convention, and have developed a mentoring program for new instructors (Mullin, personal correspondence). The Preparing Future Faculty program (PFF), a nationally funded program hosted by different colleges and universities across the country, offers a variety of workshops for graduate students to help them learn administrative tasks, institutional processes, and other skills needed to become successful members of the professoriate. The Center for Business Ethics at Bentley College offers annual workshops for faculty who wish to integrate a discussion of ethics, especially business ethics, into their courses.[7]

Finally, I propose that we consider developing a statement of professional ethics, or better yet, ask our professional organizations to take on this task (as many other disciplines already have done). CCCC has taken the first steps in this direction by publishing a statement, endorsed by the CCCC executive committee, on the use of student writing in our publications ("CCCC Guidelines for the Ethical Treatment of Students and Student Writing"). However, I am envisioning something more encompassing here, a statement like the American Political Science Association's "Guide to Professional Ethics" or the American Anthropological Association's "Statement on Ethics: Principles of Professional Responsibility."[8] My intent in developing such a statement would be in the spirit of fostering professional development and education, not to introduce additional hurdles or certification tools. As the field of composition studies continues to grow, as researchers explore new research sites and study literacy in increasingly diverse settings, as teachers ask students to engage in fieldwork and service-learning, as scholars make the case for activist, socially responsible work, I think we would do well to develop a guide to professional ethics in composition studies.

Notes

1. For a remarkably similar list of diverse scholarship and research, see Lynn Z. Bloom, this volume.

2. For an insightful, and more sobering, discussion of the limitations of collaborative research, see Paula Mathieu's notion of "radically insufficient" writing ("Not Your Mama's Bus Tour").

3. Having served as the NCTE Associate Executive Director for Higher Education for several years, I facilitated the work of CCCC committees and came to know their procedures well.

4. For a fuller discussion of how women, for instance, have been silenced, belittled, or ignored in past research in the social sciences and humanities, see my

discussion in *Ethical Dilemmas*, 8–10; see also Carol Tavris's book devoted to the topic, *The Mismeasure of Woman.*

5. Although it might seem simple and easy enough for researchers to promise to stay in touch, it is often a difficult promise to keep. Both participants and researchers move on with their lives, and time and circumstances may prevent future interactions. Subsequently, participants may be left feeling disappointed, misled, or exploited. Therefore, researchers engaging in collaborative work may want to be especially careful about any promises they make, setting up clear expectations about the nature and length of the ensuing relationship.

6. I have used this quotation on several occasions because it continues to haunt me. Carole Deletiner was severely affected—silenced—by her participation in the research; she experienced writers' block for several years before finally working through her traumatic experience by focusing her dissertation on this topic.

7. For further information on PFF, see <http://www.preparing-faculty.org/>. For information on the Center for Business Ethics at Bentley College, see <http://ecampus.bentley.edu/dept/cbe/>.

8. In 2001, the CCCC committee that developed the guidelines for the ethical treatment of students and student writing (see <http://www.ncte.org/cccc/positions/ethics.shtml>) was given an additional charge by the CCCC executive committee to

1. draft a set of guidelines for the ethical treatment in composition studies of persons who are not students. These guidelines would relate, for instance, to ethnographic studies that involve research participants who are composition instructors or employees in the nonacademic world, and 2. draft a document that aids CCCC members in working with the adopted guidelines. This document would include, among other things, practical suggestions for following the guidelines in various types of research designs. It could also suggest additional sources of information and ideas concerning research ethics. (Anderson, email)

Therefore, we can expect additional statements on ethics to be forthcoming from CCCC.

12 A Methodology of Our Own

TODD TAYLOR

The parallels between Virginia Woolf's essay "A Room of One's Own" and my chapter title are perhaps too painful, or too painfully obvious, to outline for those who serve as writing program administrators, but I'll do so anyway. Woolf observes that the intellectually illegitimate, in her case women writers and artists, are systematically denied simple, everyday material properties (in her case, a room in which to write and edit). Such properties consequently acquire immense symbolic and ideological weight. As Michel Foucault also observed (many years after Woolf) the disenfranchised lack an institutional space, a place to work, literally, metaphorically, politically. Compositionists often experience similar bias for a host of reasons including gender, pay, power, status, and job security. Today, however, I will focus on one dimension of our so-called institutional space within higher education, namely, our disciplinary methodology.

Simply put, does composition studies have a research paradigm of its own? If so, what is it? If not, does composition studies constitute a discipline? If we acknowledge that research in the hyphenated field of rhetoric-and-composition embraces multiple methodologies and a variety of topics, what defines our work? Thus, where is our research headed in the new millennium? My chapter will explore these difficult questions by examining, in particular, trends in composition dissertations and in the job market. I will argue that, on the one hand, composition studies has indeed enjoyed its own research paradigm, broadly defined. On the other hand, I identify important changes that are likely to disrupt whatever tentative methodological consensus we might have established to this point.

The Ancient Greeks often used the words μεν and δε in conjunction to mean "on the one hand" and "on the other," respectively. Here, I wish to explore both the μεν and the δε of the methodology question in composition studies. In other words, I will explore how, on the one hand, μεν, we might claim to have a methodology of our own, and, simultaneously, on the other hand, δε, we have no such security.

μεν: **All Is Well**

All is well, we have a central research paradigm, and it is this: We are interested primarily in better understanding the way nonfiction language works so that we can teach it more effectively. There are, at least, two important corollaries to this paradigm: (1) A vast majority of our research discusses the teaching of writing specifically, primarily at the college level; however, a significant minority of our work does not make specific reference to education, although such linkages are more often implicit rather than completely disconnected, and (2) Like a growing number of academic disciplines, we embrace a wide variety of methodologies in the purest sense of the term, meaning that researchers use a wide variety of strategies for gathering evidence and constructing their arguments.

What evidence is there that we can identify a cohesive research paradigm in our field? I would argue that a study of patterns of dissertations in rhetoric and composition can offer an effective profile of the current direction of our discipline. It is estimated that about 10 percent of the professionals in any field are responsible for publishing about 90 percent of the journal articles and book titles (Moxley 4). Thus, dissertations offer a much more democratic and accurate view of the interests of professionals in the field as a whole. *Dissertations Abstracts International* first created *rhetoric and composition* as a standard subject heading in 1996. At the time of my study in September 2001, 630 dissertation authors chose rhetoric and composition as one of the subject headings that describes their research. Because dissertation authors can and do select the rhetoric-and-composition subject heading somewhat by accident as opposed to trying to locate themselves consciously within the field, I eliminated from my study any dissertation that did not emerge from a PhD program that was included in *Rhetoric Review*'s most-recent listing of graduate programs in rhetoric and composition.

I found that an overwhelming majority of these dissertation abstracts, 73 percent, make explicit connections to the teaching of writing. Yet, a significant minority of these abstracts, 23 percent, examine discourse without explicit reference to teaching.

Initially, I tried to categorize the methodologies of these dissertations and calculate trends among them numerically. However, because these abstracts rarely declare a methodology per se, putting them into appropriate categories is difficult. If there *is* a pattern among the methodologies in these dissertations, it is that they defy placement in clear methodological categories. Consider, for example, the most recent abstract (number 630 on my list) published in *DAI* as of the time of my study:

> Writing Across the Curriculum at most institutions is a web of local knowledges and techniques "situated" within the historical and immediate contexts of aca-

demic departments, disciplines, and disciplinary cultures. Because of political and economic tensions existing within colleges and universities, and within academic disciplines themselves, WAC can become a "contact zone," where individuals and institutional structures struggle for power, influence, and in some cases, survival.

This dissertation uses the work of Anthony Giddens and Pierre Bourdieu to examine such a struggle as it occurred at the University of Missouri–St. Louis in the early 1980s. A WAC program was initiated there, but eventually failed as a result of political and economic influences. In the time since that failure, a growing emphasis on teaching and learning has helped create new potential for WAC at UMSL. Yet, to make it viable, WAC proponents there must recognize existing realities, attitudes, and conventions within each discipline or department, and develop new methods and approaches to writing and teaching that are relevant to that discipline or department. (Klein)

To see why these dissertations resist categorization according to methodologies, consider how difficult it is to locate William Dixon Klein's work within arguably the most-recognized taxonomy in the field: the one Stephen M. North describes in *The Making of Knowledge in Composition: Portrait of an Emerging Field.* Without knowing Klein or reading his dissertation in its complexity, I can deduce that he examines a program within which he is (or was) employed, making his work *practitioner*-based and somewhat *ethnographic.* He examines a program that no longer exists, making him also a *historian.* Klein refers to two philosophers and a canonical work in rhetoric and composition (Mary Louis Pratt, "Arts of the Contact Zone"), and in doing so, invokes both a *philosophical* and *critical* methodology, according to North. Klein conducts a case study of a particular writing program, making him a *clinician,* although he does not seem to be an *experimentalist* because he does not set controls. Klein does not appear to be a *formalist* in the strict sense that he diagrams a cognitive model like Linda Flower and John R. Hayes do ("Cognitive Process Theory" 370). Yet, he projects a political model when describes WAC programs as institutional contact zones. In short, Klein demonstrates elements that could locate his work within seven of eight of North's methodological categories. In other words, the dissertations in my study display a wide array of methodologies for gathering evidence, both within and amongst themselves.

Finally, according to the biannual survey of graduate program in rhetoric and composition in *Rhetoric Review,* the number of completed dissertations in the field is increasing—63 in 1994, 70 in 1996, 133 in 1998 (Stygall 383)—while the number of graduate programs in the field has declined slightly (Brown, Jackson, and Enos 235).

Why does this group of dissertations invoke an array of methodologies? Why are these dissertations concerned with pedagogy? And, most importantly, why is the number of dissertations increasing? I would argue that the material conditions of working in higher education today drive these trends, and that these conditions represent very good news for the relative status of composition studies in the contemporary university—they suggest that a room of our own is secure, at least for now.

North's *Making of Knowledge* certainly responded to the material conditions of its day. At the time, composition studies was gaining momentum as a discipline, but its place within the academy was less established. In that book, North worries that the field's methodological diversity and its need to sometimes embrace and sometimes reject a pedagogical focus threaten to pull it apart (364). Consider, however, that each new discipline at first seems like an abnormal amalgamation of its predecessors, but, in ways that Thomas S. Kuhn has described, the forces that bring a new area of inquiry to life arise from the very problems that traditional paradigms are unable to address *(Structure)*. In other words, if research in composition studies *did* fit neatly into established notions of a discipline, and it *could* claim a methodological integrity of the kind North found lacking in 1987, not only would the field be indistinguishable from others but also there would be no energy to promote its growth. Unless composition studies is *different* from other disciplines, until it has a room of its own that is unlike others, it is either a subdiscipline or a nondiscipline.

What problems did our predecessors fail to solve that gave rise to composition studies? They were unable to teach writing effectively to the new population that continues to redefine higher education after the GI Bill. How is research in composition studies different than other disciplines? Teaching is often but not exclusively its object of study. Is our discipline weak because our catalogue of research embraces a wide array of methodologies? It may be more the case that the health of today's academic disciplines actually *requires* methodological diversity and interdisciplinarity rather than rigidity and insularity—much like a wide gene pool promotes immunity.

Let me be more specific about what I mean when I claim that material conditions of working in higher education today are good news for composition studies. Institutions of higher education are under increasing pressure to articulate their value. Simultaneously, colleges and universities face the task of educating an increasingly heterogeneous population with vast differences in educational and cultural backgrounds.

Consequently, to survive, academic departments and programs, as the institutional houses for disciplines and fields, must now demonstrate the following:

1. a commitment to teaching effectively,

2. the ability to relate to a new generation of students,

3. the ability to connect their research agendas with undergraduate
   teaching.

For traditional disciplines with elitist values, these new imperatives can undermine their primary research paradigms and, thus, the disciplines themselves. Consider, for example, that, until the year 2000, the *MLA International Bibliography*
had a policy that specifically excluded the subject of teaching from its contents.
This meant that MLA bibliographers would search through an issue of *JAC: A
Journal of Composition Theory* and would index the interview with Stanley Fish
or bell hooks, but they would exclude everything else in the journal because it
was pedagogical. Why the change of heart? I suspect that the MLA administration, as the keepers of the *MLA Job Information List,* publishers of *Profession,* parents of the Association of Departments of English, and lobbyists for education
know better than perhaps anyone where their potential future membership will
reside and what these members will be paid to do. These new imperatives—to
value teaching, to embrace diversity, and to connect teaching and research—*favor*
composition studies, even as North defined the field back in 1987.

Admittedly, the status of compositionists in relation to other professors in the
humanities, as well as the status of the humanities in relation to the sciences, suggests that perhaps our future is not so bright. Compositionists continue to be paid
less and to enjoy less prestige than their colleagues in just about every discipline.
The title of Kenneth Oliver's essay "The One-legged, Wingless Bird of Freshman
English" from the first volume of *College Composition and Communication* in 1950
indicates that the legacy of poor working conditions for compositionists has defined our field since its inception.

On the other hand, composition studies has gained enormous ground since
1950. We now have large conferences and organizations, established journals and
publishers, thriving graduate programs, a growing first generation of full and
endowed professors, and increasing political sway on our campuses. But perhaps
the most relevant indicator of the future of our discipline is this one: A committed graduate student in composition studies can almost universally secure a tenure-track job, which is not the case in other areas of the humanities. According
to the spring 2001 *MLA Newsletter,* 26 percent of all advertised positions in English studies in the 2000 *MLA Job Information List* were for specialists in rhetoric
and composition, compared to 24 percent for British literature and 9 percent for
American literature—the two next-largest categories (Franklin 4). As of the late-
1990s, the number of tenure-track jobs for specialists in rhetoric and composi-

tion continues to outpace significantly the number of newly minted PhDs produced each year in the field (see table 12.1). Conversely, the number of PhDs produced each year in all of English studies continues to outpace significantly the
number of tenure-track jobs (see table 12.2).

Table 12.1

Deficit of Rhetoric and Composition PhDs Produced Annually

	1994	1996	1998
Dissertations completed	63	70	133
Rhet/comp positions	197	153	191
Deficit of rhet/comp PhDs	134	83	58

Source: Data from Gail Stygall, "At the Century's End: The Job Market in
Rhetoric and Composition." *Rhetoric Review* 28 (2000): 375–89.

Table 12.2

Surplus of PhDs in English Produced Annually

	1994	1996	1998
Dissertations completed	943	1,013	1,077
English positions	249	299	459
Surplus of English PhDs	694	714	618

Source: Data from Phyllis Franklin, "October 2000 Employment Trends." *MLA
Newsletter* 33.1 (2001): 4-7.

Thus, to return to the issue of whether or not the field enjoys a central research
paradigm, loosely defined, one answer may be that it doesn't really matter. It might
not really matter from a materialist standpoint because as long as tenure-track
compositionists continue to grow in numbers, they eventually gain the power and
authority to define what a discipline is or is not, what constitutes a central paradigm or not. In other words, we can decorate our room any way we like because
it is *our room.* That's our duty: to redefine what it means to be a discipline in
today's academy. I think our answer on this account is clear and makes good sense
in today's climate: Composition studies is a discipline that embraces a wide variety of research methodologies that are generally but not exclusively aimed at
improving the teaching of writing.

   Thus, when North announced the "death" of hope for a central paradigm at
the last Composition Studies in the Twenty-First Century conference, he was both

right and wrong. He was right—the urge to establish "methodological unity" or locate a "central research paradigm" within the field does not jibe well with our current sensibilities. Consequently, composition researchers can stop feeling guilty about their lack of paradigm; they can stop worrying so much about having a room of their own because no one believes paradigms can hold up anymore within the postmodern landscape. However, we also might consider the possibility that the term *discipline* is being redefined by emergent disciplines *like* composition studies. Within such new formations, our research paradigm literally becomes whatever we do in composition studies, whatever we want it to be—as justified by the fact that we now occupy space within academic institutions. We have now taken up a position within the new academy, thanks to favorable material conditions, and thanks to our sheer numbers, and thanks to the attrition of more traditional disciplines that are unable to respond to the current conditions. Sure, we're paid less than others. Of course, the fact that we're paid does not absolve us of our complicity in sustaining the troubled institution of literacy instruction. Sure, there is still much work to be done. We do not look or act like traditional disciplines, but we may not want to do so. Relative to other so-called disciplines in the humanities, our future is bright. Sure, composition researchers may occupy the basement, but the penthouse is not looking so attractive at the moment.

δε: Losing Our Religion

So far, I have argued that metatrajectory of research in composition studies will be shaped by the changing material conditions of the higher education. In short, the prospects for our collective research are relatively bright because we will continue to get paid because we solve problems for the academy.

But what will we study specifically? How will we study it? And why? Our work will continue to explore conflicts emerging from the postmodern condition, broadly conceived, including, most prominently, issues of race, class, gender, culture, disability, sexual orientation, religion, ecology, technology, media, and (most recently) geopolitics. Most of our arguments will be theoretical, again in the broadest sense of the term, because a theoretical methodology allows us to move comfortably from an examination of specific classroom practices to generalizable principles about literacy and then back to a discussion of classroom practice. However, our research, like the research in disciplines that aim to adapt to the contemporary academy, will also be categorically interdisciplinary. For instance, even though compositionists once flirted with but then soundly rejected the idea of aligning the field with cognitive psychology, we are now more likely to return comfortably to cognitive psychology and mine it for what it has to offer. Philosophical, theoretical methodologies offer a natural fit with such inter-disciplinarity because they enable researchers to work more eclectically. Such in-terdisciplinarity also increases our tolerance for variety of approach in our work, including nontheoretical research. Why will we behave in these ways? Because we will be paid to do so, because this approach, this so-called research paradigm responds to the material conditions of higher education today.

However, if we define ourselves so externally, by what others need us and pay us to do, are we not in danger of losing our internal vision and perhaps the iden-tity that enables us to solve problems? If we immerse our research paradigm into the heteroglossia of the postmodern condition, do we risk being pulled apart into fragments? In September 2001, the WPA-L discussion list featured a debate about the need to offer regional versions of CCCC because the national conference may have grown too large, too intimidating, too expensive, too impersonal, too *pro-fessional.* Will the very real, material, nontheoretical postmodern reality of ter-rorism fragment the CCCC whose conventions will increasingly require travel to large cities like Chicago and New York?

Although I just argued that all roads in composition studies lead back to the writing classroom in constructive ways, it seems we are in danger of lacking a common focus and a common language once we get there. For some, the writ-ing classroom is largely a gendered space. For others, the purpose of writing in-struction is to prepare students for professional careers. For still others, the terms *writing* and *classroom* seem irrelevant in an increasingly multimedia, networked world. Although we may very well be positioned as an ideal discipline for the new university of the new century, might we also simultaneously be the agents of our own demise? Because it seems that our discipline is being pulled (perhaps apart) in many directions, it is obviously difficult to discuss concretely many of these (potential) tensions at once. Instead, I'll consider a long-standing issue: the sta-tus of the academic essay in composition studies.

The title and chorus of R.E.M.'s hit song "Losing My Religion" uses an old Southern colloquialism to express the anxiety of an unrequited lover. The phrase is roughly equal to the contemporary sayings "losing control," "losing my mind," or the truncated "losing it," all of which suggest an acute sense of distress and disorientation. "Losing my religion" is especially evocative considering its origins within the bible-belt South: To lose one's religion is to lose touch with the ideas, principles, and beliefs upon which all others seem to rest—to lose that which seems foundational, fundamental.

What happens when writing courses begin to abandon, for example, the re-search paper, essay, and other familiar formats in favor of emerging alternatives, such as multimedia student compositions incorporating audio, video, photographs, and graphics? What happens when students no longer compose exclusively or primarily through written words? Dozens of scholars and researchers have speculated about this moment, but no one has yet articulated a specific pedagogy of multimedia composition. As we begin to do so, one of the most pressing questions we face is "Are writing teachers equipped to teach photographic, audio, and video composition?" On the one hand, we might adapt successfully because we can identify some unifying perspectives on composition across media and disciplines. For example, many contemporary art critics emphasize how not just aesthetics but also the very act of seeing is socially and rhetorically constructed. The term *composition* itself certainly translates well across media. On the other hand, the professional divide between writing teachers and speech instructors, for instance, suggests that compositionists may have difficulty converting to a new religion, even one that at first seems as closely allied as speech communication. More importantly, in terms of my materialist argument, if we turn our backs on teaching writing exclusively, will we be evicted from our institutional space because we are no longer helping to solve the problem for which we are being paid?

Writing instructors are currently consumed with text, whether it resides on paper or (more lately) on screen. Text is their religion. What happens when they lose this religion? Johndan Johnson-Eilola aptly describes the experience of reading and writing in the new media as a combination of vertigo and euphoria. Likewise, I argue that a pedagogy of multimedia composition promises to disorient writing instructors, so much so that they risk their very identity. At the same time, multimedia composition, because it greatly broadens our notions of composition, might redefine the field in productive ways.

It seems that every significant move we might make locally within our own programs or more generally within our disciplinary structures has the potential to move us (individually and collectively) into an even better room of our own or, perhaps, into the streets. Would it be best to move your writing program into a free-standing unit? Should you aim to eliminate first-year composition courses in favor of a holistic approach to writing instruction across the curriculum? If you embrace prototypical, electronically mediated approaches to writing instruction, will you seem eccentric? Is it logistically feasible, ethically responsible, and legally possible to send one hundred sections of first-year writing students per term into the community to pursue service-learning? It's our responsibility to interrogate such questions. Such interrogation is our central research paradigm. However, at what point might we go too far? At what point might the continued critical examination of the institution of literacy instruction lead to the collapse of the institution as we know it? And, should it collapse, will composition studies be left standing?

13 Celebrating Diversity (in Methodology)

RESPONSE BY SUSAN H. MCLEOD

The topic of research paradigms in composition studies is rich indeed, one that resulted in a lively discussion at this session of the Composition Studies in the Twenty-First Century conference. Table leaders summarized a wide range of reactions, from a worry that somehow our field has become fragmented to confusion about what actually constituted a research paradigm. Many researchers in our field (see Farris and Anson) have discussed the issue of research paradigms in composition and rhetoric at length. Some, in particular Gary A. Olson ("Death of Composition"), have offered spirited analyses and defenses of theory in our field. I recommend these resources to readers who are interested in more extended discussions of the topic. What I would like to offer here as a response to Gesa E. Kirsch and Todd Taylor and to the reactions of the audience at the session is not an attempt to answer the question nor a synthesis of opposing views (because Kirsch and Taylor are not really opposed, and those in the room were more bemused than opposed); I offer instead a somewhat different way of looking at the subject. In order to think about the future of research in composition studies, I would have us look at our past—at what theories and philosophies have informed our research so far. In looking at the roots of what we do, at our origins, I think we can better examine and categorize the branches, the flowers, and the fruit. This look to our past will also provide a somewhat different taxonomy from Stephen M. North's (discussed in Taylor's paper), another way of sorting out what we do.

As Patrick W. Thompson points out (in a discussion of differing research paradigms in another discipline), any research is carried out from the perspective of a "world view," a particular way of looking at phenomena (148); "each researcher . . . takes (often unwittingly) an epistemological stance concerning the nature and genesis of . . . knowledge," and "this stance exerts a strong influence on what he or she takes as acceptable research" (157). As a field, composition studies has grown out of two different research paradigms, each of them with different world views, both of them originating in our parent field, English studies. The first paradigm, from the humanities (literary studies, rhetoric, philosophy), is hermeneutic. In the humanities, we look at text and interpret it, tell stories about it. Because so many of us in composition have come out of or still have our homes in English departments,[1] this is a tradition that feels comfortable, familiar, somehow natural and right. Many of our flagship journals (*College English,* for example) publish research in the hermeneutic tradition.

The second research paradigm comes from the social sciences, which in turn was adapted from the hard sciences. The social-science paradigm was embraced by educational research, a model that informed some of the earliest studies of written composition (see Braddock, Lloyd-Jones, and Schoer); those who use the social-science paradigm in composition studies now also borrow it directly from other disciplines—psychology, anthropology, and most recently, sociology. This is the empirical, quantitative approach, focusing on data and working with numbers to make meaning. Because so many of us in composition studies come out of the humanities tradition, we tend to find the social-science world view an alien one—we like and do words, not numbers. Some of us, myself included, chose the humanities precisely because of what we might term "data discomfort." Witness our enthusiasm for the qualitative approach in the social sciences—it seems more familiar to us, closer to interpretation and narrative than quantitative approaches, and it doesn't require an extensive knowledge of statistics. Witness also the agonies voiced on the writing program administrators' listserv when we have to generate data to convince administrators that our writing programs are functioning well or that we need more resources to do the job right. Nevertheless, the social-science paradigm was and continues to be part of our research tradition; *Research in the Teaching of English* publishes work that uses this approach.

I want to join Kirsch in urging us to continue our pluralistic approach to research and theory building. I have been distressed by the tendency in our profession to dismiss empirical research as based on positivist assumptions and therefore at best not contributing anything worthwhile, at worst something evil to be avoided. (I am thinking in particular of the attacks on the methodology used by Linda Flower and John R. Hayes, refuted in Flower's defense in "Cognition, Context, and Theory Building" of what she calls "observation-based theory building" and some of the discussions of George Hillocks's *Research on Written Composition* that did not evidence an understanding of metanalysis as a standard statistical technique). My sense is that this dismissal of one of our traditional-research paradigms stems at least in part from our own insecurity as a new field. It is easy for those of us in the humanities to scorn a world view that we do not understand, to seize on the limitations of a particular approach instead of noting its contributions to our understanding of particular phenomena, its way of looking at things from another angle. This dismissal of the social-science paradigm is all the more puzzling because we as a field are now focusing on issues of diversity and celebrating difference. If we really celebrate diversity, we should extend that to our research paradigms; we should try to understand that which seems different from the way we do things, try on a world view that is the "other."

Let me be clear. I am not advocating a wide-eyed acceptance of all that is written in either research tradition. There is much to critique in studies using each paradigm. Nor am I advocating that all of us trained up in the humanities need to learn to do research in the social-science tradition or that every one of us needs to attend meetings of the American Educational Research Association as well as the Conference on College Composition and Communication. Although a few of our colleagues have become paradigmatically ambidextrous—I am thinking of Richard Haswell, who does elegant work in both paradigms—most of us are more comfortable in one or the other. I also want to acknowledge that I do know we are living in a postmodern era, that in our research we do need to acknowledge the indeterminacy of meaning, that even in the "hard" sciences, the notion of objectivity in the search for new knowledge is breaking down (or perhaps expanding). However, in this postmodern, postpositivist era, it does seem to me that there are some phenomena that we can document over time or show as occurring among most individuals or in all cases. We can still seek after new knowledge in the social-science sense if we define knowledge not as something true and universal because objectively proven but as a socially justified belief that is a good approximation of observable phenomena. I call for an ethic of respect for various research methods, for a stance that is not uncritical but that acknowledges that a research paradigm different from the one we use ourselves might also be one from which we can learn. We should not let ideology trump methodology.

As I mentioned at the outset, there was one group of discussants at the session who voiced concern about our research field becoming fragmented. Fragmentation implies that something was once whole, perhaps a longing for that golden age in which everything was as it should be. However, our research paradigms have from the beginning been varied. A discipline is not always defined by its research approach; historians, for example, define themselves variously as in the humanities or in social science, depending on the kind of research they do. Another field provides us with a possible future model for our research (and perhaps also our institutional structures although that is a different discussion)—the field of women's studies. The most common structure for women's studies in the university is the interdisciplinary program, a unit with a few tenured or tenure-track faculty with degrees in women's studies and affiliate faculty in other disciplines who teach in their own departments as well as in the women's studies program. In one institution I know, the affiliate faculty are from English, psychology, biology, sociology, history, and philosophy. They use the research paradigms of their different disciplines to examine related phenomena. Composition studies began and should continue as an interdisciplinary field of study. I encourage us as a community of researchers focusing on the same phenomena to continue to use—indeed, to celebrate—our varied paradigms and methodologies.

Note

1. The overwhelming majority of PhDs in composition and rhetoric still come out of English departments (see *Rhetoric Review* 18 [spring 2000]). I would venture a guess that many of us who identify ourselves as being in the field of composition studies have PhDs in literature; at the conference I asked how many at this particular session had degrees in literature, and about two-thirds of those present raised their hands. That this will continue to be the situation, at least for awhile, is suggested by Taylor's data on the gap between the number of jobs in composition and rhetoric and the number of comp-rhet PhDs produced each year.

Part 5 How Will New Technologies Change Composition Studies?

14 Under the Radar of Composition Programs: Glimpsing the Future Through Case Studies of Literacy in Electronic Contexts

DÀNIELLE NICOLE DEVOSS, JOSEPH JOHANSEN,
CYNTHIA L. SELFE, AND JOHN C. WILLIAMS JR.

What new understandings of terms such as *text* and *composing* will students bring with them to the college classroom in the next decade—especially those students habituated to reading and composing the kinds of new-media texts that have come to characterize contemporary computer-based environments?[1]

Are teachers of English composition—grounded by their education and values in the environment and history of print—prepared to work with these understandings in productive ways? To help graduates develop new understandings of text and composing that extend beyond those associated with print? Are writing programs prepared to modify current curricula to accommodate the practices and values of new-media bricoleurs who create compositions not only from words arranged on a page but also from digitized bits of video, sound, still images, and animations that communicate across conventional linguistic, cultural, and geopolitical borders?

This chapter offers short case studies of three individuals—a White woman and White man, both 28; and a Black man of 52—each of whom brings an unusual understanding of what it means to compose texts in electronic environments and to exchange them with the other people populating such spaces. Their values and talents and skills—indicative in some important ways of those held by the populations of students now eligible to enter college classrooms—may test the resolve of faculty who were professionally prepared in the age of print.

How does (and how will) our profession respond to such challenges? In this chapter, we introduce readers to a portion of our collective future by presenting these three case studies—our aim here is to let the subjects' experiences speak for themselves. Our analysis of these case studies focuses on the changing influence of composition studies on the ways literacy is taught and understood.

Dànielle Nicole DeVoss

Dànielle Nicole DeVoss, born August 8, 1973, was the first of two children in her middle-class, Midwestern family. DeVoss's parents pursued their own advanced educations early in their marriage and were committed to the literacy development of their children. As DeVoss noted:

> They encouraged my brother and I to read. I was involved in summer reading programs as young as I can remember.... [Around the house, there were] daily newspapers, all sorts of magazines (sports, home improvement, news, politics), books, and novels. My mother prefer[red] historical, cultural, and religious ... books. My father prefer[red] fiction paperbacks.... My mother took us regularly to the library and to used bookstores when we got older.[2]

DeVoss's parents were also responsible, at least indirectly, for the computer-based literacies[3] she began to acquire relative early in life:

> I first came in contact with computers when my parents bought a computer ... when my brother and I were fairly young. I think I was maybe ten. The computer quickly became his domain, but I eventually learned how to use it by looking over his shoulder, and as we got older, we fought for time on the computer. I used the computer as a social space, accessing computer bulletin-board systems by phone.

> I learned pretty much by looking over my brother's shoulder and then jumping on the computer when he and his friends were gone. He did eventually teach me a few things, but most of my initial learning was on my own.... My brother primarily used the computer for the same reason I did—games and bulletin-board systems.

> Between all the bulletin board systems we called, my brother and I wound up logging about 250 calls a month (I know this thanks to the per-call fees from the local phone company when I was growing up).

As DeVoss progressed through secondary school, her mother made every effort to direct her daughter's interest in computers toward more conventional, academic pursuits, but DeVoss continued to enjoy gaming and bulletin-board–

chat-room exchanges. In these gaming environments, she became adept at reading and interpreting imaginary scenarios and composing the exchanges between characters of various types and abilities. She learned, as well, to create elaborate descriptions of her own characters and to respond to the complex situations that other players' characters generated. Her literacy in these electronic environments, DeVoss remembers, had a great deal to do with her increasing confidence as a reader and writer offline, as well: The exchanges in games and chatrooms, for instance, were especially instructive to her growing sense of rhetorical awareness because they so often resulted in social consequences that she felt keenly:

> Chat rooms and bulletin-board systems are complicated spaces where missteps or inappropriate talk can pretty much exclude you from a conversation, or make you the target of venomous textual assaults.

DeVoss also learned other literacy skills and values in the online gaming environments she frequented—those based as much in the visual, kinesthetic, and interactive components of gaming as in the alphabetic. These practices, moreover, diverged dramatically from the conventional, literacy instruction she received in school, where, as she got older, writing instruction was increasingly limited to the alphabetic and to the two-dimensional representational space of the page. Although she certainly did well on such conventional tasks, DeVoss's real attention remained focused on composing the interactive scenarios and exchanges of gaming situations; learning to read and predict the rule-based movements of characters in time and space; visualizing, mapping, and navigating her own way through the multidimensional compositional space of games:

> Trying to create mental maps of the text-only games I played taught me a lot about mapping out textual spaces and trying to think of them in terms of "real" space. The text-only games required a heck of a lot of imagination, too—often, the games weren't that well written, and it was your interaction with the games that really made the difference.

> You had to create complex mental maps. I remember when I first started playing games in these realms and being lost. I'd wander in circles, and wasn't able to return to particular areas within the game. It was frustrating, so I became much more adept at creating mental maps of where I was and where I wanted to go. I started by paying attention to short distances—mapping how I was moving during one stint of playing. As I did this, I was able to create larger maps and form a stronger sense of the realm in which I was playing in.

Most of these new-media literacy skills and understandings, we should add, DeVoss acquired on her own, without a great deal of systematic help or guidance from others. Few of her teachers—their own understanding of literacy tuned into the relatively narrow bandwidth of the alphabetic—knew enough about computers to take her literacy development in electronic contexts seriously; none considered the games and chat rooms in which she participated to be an appropriate context for instruction in literacy.

For the next decade, DeVoss continued her online gaming, and as computers offered increasingly sophisticated environments for both gaming and composing, she developed considerable skill in designing Web sites using HTML code. She also became familiar with Adobe *Photoshop;* Macromedia *Dreamweaver* and a variety of other HTML editors; Microsoft *Word, PowerPoint,* and *Excel;* Corel *WordPerfect* and *Presentations; QuarkXpress;* Aldus *PageMaker;* and several kinds of bibliographic software. DeVoss enjoyed composing Web texts, in part, because these activities resonated with the earlier literacies she practiced in gaming environments. Both kinds of composition allowed her to combine alphabetic and visual elements; to organize texts along temporal and spatial axes; and to explore the structure of large bodies of complicated material. To compose both kinds of texts, DeVoss relied on her ability to predict the movements of readers, to organize and arrange materials according to these predictions, and to navigate space-time creations.

Readers can see an artifact of DeVoss's Web literacy in the main organizational interface of the site she created while working on her PhD at Michigan Technological University <http://www.hu.mtu.edu/~dndevoss>. The site opens with a retro-style collage crafted from pictures and texts that DeVoss scanned from popular magazines of the 1930s and 1940s. With these pictures—and borrowing from the layout and design of these historical two-dimensional, print-based texts—DeVoss composed a three-dimensional text in a new-media environment. On top of these images, DeVoss superimposed banner headlines—to remind readers of an older style of magazine cover—and made these alphabetic bits into electronic links that led to other areas of her new-media text. In exploring this site—rather than flipping through pages on which the full text of an article appears—readers click instead on a headline to access additional new-media compositions: hypertextual syllabi, an online photography exhibit, and an email connection. In this activity, readers are encouraged to rethink their magazine literacy in terms of the new-media literacies structuring the site itself. Through this design, unlike many of her composition teachers, DeVoss sought to connect online literacies with print-based literacies:

Part of what I want readers to feel when they navigate the site is that hypertext isn't a new concept. The ability to read a magazine requires a sophisticated sense of navigation, flipping, moving, and browsing. Creating a collage of images from old magazines and linking them was a move I wanted to make toward disrupting the belief that hypertext is an entirely new technology.

Joseph Johansen

Joseph Johansen, born on July 14, 1973, in Provo, Utah, is the second of eleven children. His family, members of the Church of Jesus Christ of Latter-day Saints, fostered a strong, intergenerational tradition of literacy. Johansen described his family's history:

I think a good place to begin would be with my grandfather. I attribute a great deal of my parents' emphasis on education to him. My grandpa grew up on a farm. As a young man all he wanted to be was a sheepherder. He loved to write poetry, read religious and historical books, and to experience nature. Sheep herding gave him ample opportunity to do this. Well, a few years after he got married, I believe he had either 4 or 5 children at the time, he was injured to the extent that he couldn't continue working on the farm and tending the sheep. So he decided to go back to school with a family and no job. He worked his way through school and ended up with a Doctorate in Microbiology. I believe he was the first in his family with any college education. He spent the rest of his career teaching Microbiology in various universities. As a result of my grandfather's legacy, each of his seven sons went on to get advanced degrees in Engineering, Medicine, or Computer-related fields.

Although Johansen carried his parents' love of reading into formal schooling contexts, his relationship with writing was not always as positive:

Writing . . . [was] a little different. I know that my parents value[d] communication and understood that writing was important for good communication, but honestly I didn't enjoy writing until my senior year in high school or later. I never did well in English courses as a younger child. I would pull a C maybe an occasional B but usually nothing more.

It was through writing, however, that Johansen first encountered computers. He was involved in a course where students were encouraged to learn and then write about a variety of topics including computers. Johansen then began programming with BASIC programming language and learned how to create banners and graphics files on computers, getting his first glimpse of the machine's potential as an emerging medium for visual composition. Such a focus fit well with Johansen's longstanding interest in art—a focus encouraged by his parents, if not by his teachers:

> My father is an art teacher. He exposed me to visual literacy at a very young age through art lessons and insights into the way he saw things. He has always encouraged me to develop visual literacies.

> For a while I was into comic book art so I would collect comic books and the character cards that went with them. I would try to recreate the characters I saw and make my own. I became interested in airbrush art in high school. I used to make tee shirts and even painted a mural on my bedroom wall (I am sure my Mom hated that but she never said anything).

> My teachers . . . convinced me that there was no money in it [the love of art]. My Dad certainly wasn't making a lot of money and he was a great artist. [And so] I had decided to become a Computer Engineer. That way I could make money and continue doing artwork as a hobby.

When Johansen finished high school and completed his missionary work in France, however, he discovered graphic design—a field highly dependent on computer-based communications and networked environments, and one that valued, in addition, his interest in visual arts. By the time Johansen finished his bachelor's degree, worked as a graphic designer, and enrolled in a masters-level program in professional communication, much of his composition work had taken place in new-media environments that involved computer-based graphic design, Web design, photo editing, word processing, and multimedia design. In his words, Johansen loved

> designing visual media . . . web sites, chat rooms (ironic since I don't really use them), multimedia movies, animations, 3D imagery and animations, streaming video, flash movies and CD-ROMs.

In undertaking these new-media projects, Johansen taught himself how to use *Office, Photoshop, Illustrator, Image Ready, Freehand, Fireworks, Dreamweaver, Director, Flash, Bryce, Poser, QuarkXpress,* and *Streamline*—with the help of books and CDs he purchased and by engaging in discussions with expert users in chatrooms, discussion boards, and listservs. Although he was enrolled in a graduate-level communication program at a well-regarded university, his teachers—like DeVoss's—had been able to provide Johansen relatively little systematic help in pursuing his visual literacy interests:

> Unfortunately, none of the schools that I have been to are very strong in the visual-computer area. . . . Both schools have great art programs and great computer programs, but neither of them integrated the two very well. I know some schools do but I can't afford them.

> So I have had to tailor what the schools did offer to meet my needs. This has meant a lot of work outside of class researching topics that dealt with the merging of art and computers.

Despite these challenges, Johansen continued to focus on visual literacy, recognizing the culture's increasing dependence on reading, understanding, and composing texts in which meaning is communicated through the visual elements of still photographs, video, animated images, graphics, and charts—a move Gunther Kress in 1990 described as the "turn to the visual" (66). Like DeVoss, Johansen also appreciated the intertextual applications of the new-media literacies:

> Working in a variety of media from text to illustration, to video has given me a fairly deep arsenal that I can pull from in composing. It allows me to create "textured" works, which I find interesting.

The visual essay *Robojo* represents an example of Johansen's new-media compositions, which can be seen at <http://www.clemson.edu/~njoseph>. Johansen created this flash movie in a graduate seminar he took in the spring semester of 2001—responding to an assignment that asked him to explore the relationship between humans and technology. His goal was to create a totally visual argument that would make a meaningful comment on this topic. *Robojo* opens on a foregrounded representation of a triangular cybernetic face glowing blue against a pale-gray background of whirling gears and pulsing circuit boards. Superimposed over this representation is a dynamic gunsight grid calibrated along x and y axes. The grid follows any mouse movements made by readers exploring this page. Through this interface, Johansen argues that technology—represented by the moving gunsight, the turning gears, and the circuit board—has come to both under- and overwrite the human body—portrayed by the cybernetic face. This technological revision that Johansen maintains in an accompanying commentary on this visual essay has turned our muscles, the actuators of motion, into moving gears; our heart and nervous systems, the body's energy sources, into pulsing circuits; and human brain into a central processing unit, represented by a disk-input slot in the cybernetic face.

Links from the main screen of this visual essay—three yin-yang symbols of varying complexity—lead to three more specific stories about technology, each of which was explored in the seminar that Johansen took. The first—and simplest—link takes readers from the splash page to a sequence of moving images depicting the most common, and most reductive, perspective that humans adopt in relation to technology: Technology is either a great good or it is a terrible evil. This story, appropriately, Johansen has composed entirely of shapes that recall the most primitive of machines: the wedge, the pulley, the lever, and the screw. The second—and more elaborate—link off the splash page complicates this initial narrative. Johansen juxtaposes images in different combinations to indicate that technology's effects may be both good and bad in varying degrees. A symbol of atomic energy, an artificial heart, and an airplane come together in the middle of the viewer's screen and then separate; a caduceus and a death's head appear and then fade; a light bulb, a sailing vessel, and an early airship approach each other and then retreat. The third—and most elaborate—link on the splash page leads to a series of images in which Johansen identifies the increasingly complex ways in which computers—represented by strings of binary code—have shaped the human experience. In this sequence, he uses a transmitting radio tower to indicate how computers have increased the global reach of our communication efforts; a clock to represent how computer technology has altered our understanding of time; a grasping fist, full of money, to suggest how computer networks have supported the spread of multinational capitalism; and a robot to indicate how computers have changed our understanding of intelligence. In this last argument, Johansen suggests that the imaginary line separating good and bad technologies has disappeared as the boundaries separating the human and the technological have also blurred.

John Calvin Williams Jr.

John Calvin Williams Jr., born on September 5, 1949, was raised by his parents in a state that did not complete the integration of public schools until well into the 1960s. As a result, Williams attended all-Black elementary and secondary schools until his senior year in high school in the same small town where he now works.

Williams learned to read, in part, from looking at "comic strips in the newspaper" and from studying the Bible. He didn't remember his parents—both of whom attended high school—teaching him how to read:

I learned to read and I learned to draw. Draw pictures out of the Bible. I was curious. I would read stories about David and Goliath and things like that. . . . I have always been a very curious person and . . . very detailed.

Although Williams was not a consistently outstanding student, he did well enough to be accepted into medical school on his graduation from high school. Neither his mother nor father, however, was supportive of this option, and so, in 1968, he enrolled, instead, in the Army, and was posted in Germany and at Fort Hood, Texas, until 1977. That same year, after Williams first met his future wife on a Greyhound bus, he proposed, married, and began a family. Both Williams and his wife considered education to be extremely important, and they have continued to work diligently over the years to make sure their two children, a son and a daughter, would succeed in school and be able to graduate from college. It was Williams's son who first brought a computer into his parents' house. Williams said he learned how to be comfortable around computers as he watched his wife and son work with that original machine and try to fix it when it crashed.

From 1977 to 2001, Williams's literacy activities and values remained focused almost exclusively around the Bible and reflected his own deep and enduring religious faith. Although he worked for sixteen years in a textile plant near his hometown, he considered the time he spent there important only in as far as it prepared him for the larger project that God ultimately wanted him to undertake.

In 1993, what God specifically directed Williams to do was to write a book—in particular a book informed by Biblical scholarship and focused on the relationship between faith and grace, or, as Williams put it in Greek, the relationship between *pistis* and *charis*.

To accomplish the task that God had set out for him, Williams found a job as a building custodian at a well-known university near his hometown. In this position, Williams figured, he could work the third shift—from 11:00 at night until 7:00 in the morning—and still have time to write his book. As he explained his schedule:

I work through my breaks at night and I try to finish up my work by 4:30 or 5:00. . . . Then I get me a cup of coffee, and I go up to the room where you see me spread everything out, and study.

The university job also provided Williams the electronic resources he needed for tackling his book project. When he became an employee, Williams learned how to request access to the university's computer system and eventually received a password and user-identification number. Although the university provided no specialized computer training for its janitorial employees, Williams began frequenting the twenty-four-hour computer labs on campus during his break and lunch times. There, he carefully observed what the students were doing as they typed their papers for classes, and he tried things out for himself. When he got stuck, he would ask the lab consultants on duty for assistance. Through this process—observing, asking discrete questions, trying things out, seldom bothering the same person twice to avoid drawing attention to himself—Williams learned how to create, store, and manage files, how to navigate the university's complex Novell network (the largest such network in the world, according to the university administration), and how to use several kinds of word-processing packages.

With this knowledge in hand and a bit of time to write, Williams began his book. He taught himself how to use email so that he could get in touch with other individuals around the world who studied the Bible in the way he wanted to, and he went out on the Web so that he could find and use free Biblical concordances and other scholarly tools. He also invented his own specialized system of color-coded note-taking and located a Web site that provided translations of key Biblical terms in English, Greek, and Hebrew, as well as the audio pronunciations of these terms. As Williams noted, this was how he learned to read and speak the Greek and Hebrew he needed to continue with his book.

Although it was clear that Williams was a devout man, it was the story he told about how God taught him to use this particular translation Web site that best demonstrated the intimate level on which his religious beliefs and experiences shaped his literacy practices and values. He recounted this narrative:[4]

> When I first started using the Web site, I didn't know how to use it. I would look up the translation for a word, read the passage on the screen, and then type it into the word-processing file for my book.
>
> One night, I was doing this, God said, "John, what are you doing?" And I said, "I'm writing the book, God." And I kept on reading and then writing.
>
> A half an hour later, God said, "John, what are you doing?" And I said, "God, I'm writing the book you told me to write." And I went back to translating and typing the passages.
>
> Finally, God said, "John, what are you doing?" And I said, "God, I am writing that book! What do you want me to do?" And God said, "Cut and paste, John; cut and paste."

This important link between Williams's religious beliefs and his literacy practices is expressed graphically on the title page of his book manuscript (see fig. 14.1).

**Understanding God's Amazing Grace
and the Faith That Receives It**

Written by:

John Calvin Williams Jr.

P.O. Box 1401

Clemson, SC 29633-1401

Prepared by:

The Holy Spirit

Most Holy Place. Heaven

Figure 14.1 The title page of John C. Williams Jr.'s book manuscript. Copyright © 2003 John Calvin Williams Jr.

What These Three Cases Can Teach Us

Although these cases suggest a range of lessons about literacy, power, race, and class as these intersecting formations shape—and are shaped by—our country's educational system, we will use the remainder of this chapter to focus on the insights the cases provide about the future of composition studies. In particular, we can identify three important lessons to which composition teachers may want to attend.

Lesson 1. Literacies have life spans linked to the cultural ecology of a specific time and place. Depending on a complex of circumstances, literacies emerge, accumulate, compete, and fade at varying rates. English-composition teachers and programs need to acknowledge, understand, and respond to this dynamic.

These three cases—especially when they are considered within the context of work done by contemporary literacy scholars such as Brian V. Street *(Social Literacies: Critical Approaches to Literacy in Development, Ethnography, and Education),* John Gee *(Social Linguistics and Literacies: Ideology in Discourses),* H. J. Graff *(Legacy of Literacy: Continuities and Contradictions in Western Culture and Society),* and Deborah Brandt *(Literacy in American Lives)*—serve to remind teachers of English composition that we can understand literacy as a set of practices and values *only* when we properly situate these within the context of a particular historical period, a particular cultural milieu, and a specific cluster of material conditions. We call this interrelated set of contexts the *cultural ecology* of literacy.[5] Within any particular cultural ecology, various forms of literacy have their own particular life spans—they emerge, accumulate, and compete with other literacies, and fade, according to what Ronald J. Deibert might call their general "fitness" (31) with other key social, cultural, and historical phenomena. As Brandt ("Accumulating") and Miles Myers in *(Changing Our Minds: Negotiating English and Literacy)* have pointed out in historical studies, literacies accumulate faster and sometimes compete when cultures undergo periods of particularly dramatic or radical transition.

Increasingly, the literacies practiced by individuals who communicate primarily in online environments exist within a dynamic cultural ecology influenced by expanding global markets and computer networks that stretch across language barriers, cultural groupings, and geopolitical borders. Within this ecology, as the New London Group and Kress have explained, new-media literacies—which rely as much on images, video clips, animation, sound, and still-photography as on words—have begun to emerge and compete vigorously with more traditional alphabetic print texts for readers' attention.

In this dynamic context, DeVoss's gaming and Web-based literacies, Johansen's visually based literacies, and Williams's self-taught electronic literacies assume a new kind of currency. To communicate effectively within globally extended computer networks, individuals and groups increasingly are teaching themselves to design and use texts that have visual, aural, and kinesthetic elements as well as alphabetic components. To increase the effectiveness of their communications, they are also learning to design and use texts that are interactive, hypertextual, and complexly mapped in time as well as space. In addition, individuals are creating compositions that are highly intertextual in terms of their resonance across media boundaries as Diana George and Diane Shoos ("Dropping Bread Crumbs") have maintained. These things are true even though many English-composition programs continue to focus instruction almost exclusively on conventional alphabetic texts.

Lesson 2. English-composition teachers and programs must be willing to address an increasingly broad range of literacies—emerging, competing, and fading—if they want their instruction to remain relevant to students' changing communication needs and experiences within the contemporary cultural ecology.

These three cases also suggest—to us, at least—something about the new responsibilities English-composition teachers and programs have toward emerging, competing, and fading literacies at a time when the cultural ecology of literacy is changing so rapidly.

At the beginning of the twenty-first century, as Manuel Castells *(Information Age: Economy, Society, and Culture)* explains in his three-volume series, the rapid growth of transnational mass media and computer networks requires new kinds of texts that can effectively cross national borders, time zones, language groups, and geographic distances. Such texts, to be successful, often use "new and emerging discourses" (New London Group 67) expressed in a rich mix of video, audio, graphics, animation, and alphabetic elements to resist the limitations of a single symbolic system and its attendant conventions.

The new-media texts that grow out of these contexts differ so radically from those print texts with which we are familiar, Kress notes, that a conventional "emphasis on language alone simply will no longer do" (67) to adequately or accurately represent how meaning is generated:

> The focus on language alone has meant a neglect, an overlooking, even suppression of the potentials of representational and communicational modes in particular cultures; an often repressive and always systematic neglect of human potentials in many of these areas; and a neglect equally, as a consequence, of the development of theoretical understandings of such modes.... [T]o put it provocatively: the single, exclusive and intensive focus on written language has dampened the full development of all kinds of human potentials, through all the sensorial possibilities of human bodies, in all kinds of respects, cognitively and affectively, in two and three dimensional representation. (85)

DeVoss's, Johansen's, and Williams's stories, for us, corroborate Kress's claim; they indicate, moreover, that if we continue to define literacy in terms of *alphabetic practices only,* in ways that ignore, exclude, or devalue new-media texts, we not only abdicate a professional responsibility to describe accurately and robustly the ways in which humans are now communicating and making meaning but we also run the risk of our curriculum holding declining relevance for students who are communicating in increasingly expansive, networked environments.

Lesson 3. English-composition teachers and programs need to start with the literacies that students bring to the table and in which students are invested, but they can't stop there.

Literacy scholars Graff, Street, and J. Elspeth Stuckey *(Violence of Literacy),* among many others, remind us of the dangers we face when we cling too tightly to one single official version of literacy—like Standard English or alphabetic literacy, or even, we would suggest, new-media literacies. Thinking only in terms of one official way of composing, one way of reading, Street notes, not only fails to acknowledge and respect the complexities of literacy as situated historically, culturally, economically, and politically, it also supports "patronizing assumptions about what it means to have difficulties with reading and writing in contemporary society" (17).

Further, because students from different culture, races, and backgrounds bring different literacies and different experiences with literacy to the classroom, focusing so single-mindedly on only one privileged form of literacy encourages a continuation of the literate-illiterate divide that does so much violence to students (Graff; Street; Stuckey) and functions in a conservative, and reproductive, fashion to favor existing class-based systems and support intergenerational cycles of literacy—especially among families in poverty and families of color.

Thus, composition faculty and programs adhering to a narrow understanding of alphabetic literacy—or those that recognize the activities we call composing or reading only when they occur in conventional contexts—contribute to a situation in which individuals consider themselves (and, worse, others) more or less literate or illiterate depending on their facility within that small range of action. It should not be news to us, then, that English-composition teachers and programs need to understand, value, and work actively with the multiple literacies that students bring with them to our classrooms and programs, literacies in which they have—like Williams, DeVoss, or Johansen—considerable and deeply sedimented personal and cultural investments as well as significant skills.

So what will the future of composition programs look like? Better yet, what should it look like as we prepare our curricula to meet the needs of students like DeVoss, Johansen, and Williams? We suspect that at least two possible paths lie in front of us.

One path looks much like the one that many composition programs have claimed for themselves. If we take this route, we will continue to shape literacy curricula in our own image, to define composition primarily, or only, in terms of written alphabetic texts. Like many literature programs that have gone before us, our instruction will become increasingly far removed from the ideological values and material practices of the new kinds of students who attend our schools and communicate within the electronic contexts that involve the exchange of information on a global scale.

The second path looks a bit different. Traveling on it, we take the opportunity to expand our professional, curricular, and instructional understanding of literacy beyond our own narrow understanding of the alphabetic; we cultivate the habit of reading and creating visual, aural, and mixed-media compositions both within and outside of electronic contexts. On this path, we learn to recognize, value, and make instructional use of the multiple literacies students bring to our classrooms, thus, expanding the bandwidth of literacy and taking advantage of its dynamic nature within changing cultural ecologies. To us, the future of composition programs looks quite a bit more interesting and much more fun on this second path, and we hope that the profession of composition studies thinks so as well.

Notes

This project is funded in part by generous support from the National Council of Teachers of English, the Society for Technical Communication, Michigan Technological University, and the University of Illinois at Urbana-Champaign.

1. The initial phrase of this title we gratefully attribute to a song "Under the Radar," written by Bill Payne of the band Little Feat and recorded by that talented group on a CD of the same name. Both the phrase and the song are richly suggestive of all those phenomena that exist and flourish outside the relatively narrow range of our conscious minds—in this case, our teacherly consciousness. In particular, we refer to those things teachers know about literacy at some forgotten level of personal pleasure and practice (that is, how much fun it is to compose a story from pictures cut out of old magazines, create plays populated by fictional characters who interact in meaningful ways, read comics without even looking at the dialogue)—but to which we seldom pay attention when designing composition instruction at the collegiate level. That's why English teachers should listen to rock and roll more often than they do.

2. The responses of Dànielle Nicole DeVoss and Joseph Johansen were excerpted by Cynthia L. Selfe from the written responses that both subjects gave to a standard series of questions formulated in close collaboration with Gail E. Hawisher.

The responses of John C. Williams Jr. were excerpted primarily from an audiotaped interview conducted on February 28, 2001. One story recounted by Williams was not taped but was reconstructed from notes taken at the conclusion of that session (see endnote 5). Williams's audiotaped interview was tran-

scribed with the expert help of Teresa Bertram at the University of Illinois, Urbana-Champaign.

Quoted portions of these interviews were excerpted to provide a chronological structure to the narratives. Ellipses mark the removal of interview material
such as conversational markers, repetitions due to interruptions, family asides,
and interviewer comments. Brackets indicate explanatory additions by the research team and changes of capitalization. The primary effort has been to preserve both the tone and content of subjects' remarks while preserving their privacy and making their stories available to readers. All subjects were sent drafts of
the portions of this paper that featured their interviews.

3. By literacy, we refer not only to skills needed to read and understand texts
and compose texts but also, as Brandt, Gee, Graff, Street, and Barton and Hamilton
suggest, to the cultural values, understandings, and formations associated with
such tasks in a particular time and place, under specific sets of material, ideological, political, and technological circumstances. In this paper and in others, Hawisher and I refer to *literacies* because we think—like Kress and Theo Van Leeuwen
and the New London Group—that humans use multiple systems for reading and
composing texts.

We use *print literacy* broadly to refer to reading and composing efforts that take
place in print contexts (e.g., books, magazines, journals) and to the cultural values and understandings associated with these efforts. We use *alphabetic literacy*
in much the same way to refer to the reading and writing efforts that take place
primarily in alphabetic systems and to the cultural values and understandings
adhering to these efforts.

We use *new-media literacy* broadly as well to refer to the reading-viewing interacting and the composing-designing efforts that occur primarily in digital
environments as well as to the cultural values and understandings associated with
these efforts. New-media texts are often composed in multiple media (e.g., film,
video, audio, computer, among others) and designed for presentation and exchange in digital environments. These texts often place a heavy emphasis on visual elements (both still photography and moving photography, images, graphics, drawings, renderings, and animations) and sound; and they often involve
some level of interactivity. Although such texts often include some alphabetic
features, they also typically resist containment by alphabetic systems, demanding the multiple literacies of seeing, listening, and manipulating as well as those
of writing and reading. Because new-media texts often resist conventions of traditional fiction or nonfiction genres, they may appear unfamiliar to individuals
raised on print texts and invested in the cultural systems of print literacy.

We use terms such as *gaming literacy, Web literacy,* and *visual literacy* more
specifically to refer to particular subsets of new-media literacy. Some of the skills,
understandings, and values associated with a specific subset may be related to
those of another subset, and they may even overlap these in part (e.g., gaming literacy and Web literacy, both of which I consider a subset of new-media literacy),
but they are not exactly the same.

We should also note that we consider literacy to be the primary focus of composition programs.

4. This story was reconstructed from the handwritten notes Cynthia L. Selfe took when interviewing Williams; it does not represent an audiotaped excerpt. The emphasis here is the interviewer's attempt to represent the Williams's original rendition of this story. Williams is a coauthor of this paper.

5. Our understanding of cultural ecologies is based on a long history of work by fine scholars who have come at the phenomenon from different directions, but we will mention here only three of the most salient figures in our own readings. In 1986, Marilyn Cooper helped us understand that language and literacy practices are "essentially social activities, dependent on social structures and processes not only in their interpretive but also in their constructive phases" (366). In 1997, Deibert enriched our understanding of mediated communication with a discussion of "ecological holism" (37–94) that brought additional dimension to our study of computer-based literacies. In 1998, Bertram Bruce and Maureen P. Hogan reminded us that computer technologies and the literacy activities that they mediate are best understood through a study of the social systems and settings within which machines and the humans who use them exist.

15 The Challenge of the Multimedia Essay

LESTER FAIGLEY

Close to my house in Austin, Texas, are vacant tinted-window office buildings with empty parking lots that at the end of the 1990s were occupied by some of the brightest stars of the new economy—companies like Agillion that could afford to buy advertising spots on the 2000 National Football League Super Bowl telecast and hold a companywide retreat at the Baja resort Cabo San Lucas. By the 2001 Super Bowl, Agillion, along with many other Internet startups, had turned into a dot-bomb, with all employees shortly out of jobs and the Herman Miller chairs, mahogany tables, and the coffee maker that dispensed thirteen different varieties auctioned off on July 19, 2001, to pay creditors a few pennies on the dollar.

The meteoric rise and fall of Agillion is emblematic not only of the much-ballyhooed dot-coms that soared in the late 1990s and plummeted in the new millennium but also the representation of the Internet in the popular media. For most of the public, the Internet has become synonymous with the World Wide Web, which few people had heard of before 1994. The early newspaper articles about the Web printed before August 10, 1995, typically described it as a virtual library. After August 10, the library was gone, and metaphors for the Web became ones of apocalyptic transformation—everything is changed forever. On that day, Netscape made its initial public offering, and by day's end, the founders of Netscape realized profits on paper that exceeded the gross national product of many nations. The NASDAQ-stock-market frenzy had begun, sending the index from 1000 to over 5000 within five years, but when the stock prices dropped, so, too, did the hype. At the beginning of the new millennium, it became fashionable to say that the Internet changes nothing.

In the midst of the Internet gloom, one prominent contrarian emerged to answer to the dismissal, "All the Internet does is speed up information." Michael Lewis writes in the recently published *Next: The Future Just Happened* that it's as if "some crusty old baron who had been blasted out of his castle and was finally having a look at his first cannon had said, 'All it does is speed up balls'" (14). Lewis claims that while the profit-making potential of the Internet was overrated, the social effects were not. He sees the Internet demolishing old castles of expertise along with many traditional relationships based on that expertise. His primary evidence is three case studies of teenagers living in unremarkable places who gained notoriety by their activities on the Internet.

In the commuter suburb of Cedar Grove, New Jersey, Jonathan Lebed at age fourteen made $800,000 in six months by buying small, obscure stocks and then hyping them on Yahoo finance message boards with postings typed in all caps followed by lots of exclamation points. In the desert California town of Perris, south of Los Angeles, Marcus Arnold, who had never read a law book but watched court shows on television, became at age fifteen the top-ranked online legal expert on AskMe.com, beating over a hundred licensed attorneys. In the drab, working-class town of Oldham, England, Daniel Sheldon became a prominent player in the post-Napster, copyleft world of file sharing, even though Sheldon cannot download at home the rewards of his labor on his slow modem connection. For Lewis, these teens are the result of faster-is-always-better capitalism, which has eroded authority based on access to knowledge. The information that experts used to horde is now available to all but not all are able to exploit it. Lewis finds that children are the best equipped to adapt to this new social order because they are the quintessential amateurs with no commitments to old institutions and old ways of thinking.

My argument is neither to attack nor defend Lewis's thesis although it is worth pausing to speculate how his claim applies to our academic castle of expertise. Instead, I'm much more interested in the circumstances and form of the book's publication. *Next* began as a documentary commissioned by the BBC in spring 2000. Lewis was an obvious choice because of his strong track record as an insightful reader of trends in *Liar's Poker: Rising Through the Wreckage on Wall Street* (about high-rolling bond traders at Salomon Brothers) and *The Next New Thing: A Silicon Valley Story* (about Jim Clark, one of the founders of Netscape). Lewis began his research for *Next* in May 2000 and started writing in November, with the first results appearing in an eighty-five hundred-word article about Lebed in the *New York Times Magazine* in February 2001, which was simultaneously published on the *New York Times* Web site. In July 2001, Lewis published "Faking It," another long article in the *New York Times Magazine* taken from the about-to-be-released *Next*. The four-part television documentary aired on the BBC at the end of July 2001 and on the A&E Television Network in the United States at the beginning of August.

The book was reviewed by most major newspapers during late-summer 2001, and many also reviewed the documentary. The reviews run the gamut. The favorable ones praise Lewis's witty style and penetrating analysis; the unfavorable ones accuse him of extrapolating wildly from the particular to the general and of continuing binary thinking about the Internet as either paranoid alarms or gee-whiz optimism. What no reviewer found strange, however, was that Lewis published *Next* in three genres using four media almost simultaneously: newspaper feature, online feature, nonfiction book, and television documentary. Almost no one contrasted Lewis the writer with Lewis the television interviewer. Although most of the reviews of the book mention that substantial chunks were published in advance in the *New York Times,* none mentions the difference in form.

I doubt that Lewis realized the degree his book was scooped not just by the prepublication of key chapters but also by the pictures of Lebed and Arnold that appeared in the articles but not in the book. Here is the physical introduction of Arnold in both "Faking It" and *Next:* "Marcus himself was firmly earthbound, a great big bear of a boy. He was six feet tall and weighted maybe two hundred pounds. He did not walk but lumbered from the computer to the front door, then back again" (90). "Faking It" included two images of Arnold, one with his mother and twin brother. While Arnold appears indeed as a large boy, we also see that he is a person of color, which is not mentioned in the prose. In the television documentary, we see Arnold smiling broadly as he says he "just knows" when asked about the source of his legal expertise—words that are quoted directly and without comment in the book. The grin suggests that Marcus may be having a little fun with his too-serious interviewer. (A 105-second video clip is available on "The Future Just Happened.")

Perhaps no reviewer commented directly on the publication of *Next* in different genres and media because the practice is now common in both popular and high culture (think of films with books and major art exhibitions with elaborate catalogs and curator audio tours). But the multimedia publication of *Next* unknowingly raises issues about medium and genre because *Next* claims to be a look into the future. To start with the most obvious, the presence or absence of images affects how we read the prose. The strong genre constraints of what is considered serious nonfiction either rule out the inclusion of images or else severely constrain them for most subject matters. Histories and biographies often tip in a few pages of photographs, but books that use images to make an argument remain exceptional.

The collaboration of Marshall McLuhan and designer Quentin Fiore to produce *The Medium Is the Massage* in 1967 and *War and Peace in the Global Village* in 1968 stands out over three decades later as a remarkable effort to combine images and text. In *The Medium Is the Massage,* Fiore adapted ideas from McLuhan's previous publications to a format that visually drew from advertising and deliberately destabilized the relationship of image and text (see fig. 15.1). Even though

McLuhan's fame was at its apex in the late 1960s and the book would eventually sell nearly a million copies worldwide, seventeen publishers rejected it before Bantam agreed to a run of thirty-five thousand copies (Lupton and Miller 92). In an interview in 1992, Fiore recalls that the publishing industry "demanded words, lots of words—all set on good, gray pages" (Lupton and Miller 92). Then as now, publishers of serious books saw images in books as manipulative.

Figure 15.1 Excerpt from *The Medium Is the Massage* by Marshall McLuhan and Quentin Fiore, produced by Jerome Agel, originally published in 1967 by Bantam Books and Random House, 74–75. *Photo:* Peter Moore.

Yet, for most people and especially for younger people, the exclusion of readily available images from a text seems unnatural. Like Lewis, I became interested in the remarkable abilities adolescents displayed on the World Wide Web when it first became widely available in 1994, but I was especially struck by their design talent ("Material Literacy and Visual Design"). Since then, I've come to realize that I was witnessing a few exceptional individuals and that this talent was far from universal. The majority of students I teach do not enter with notable abilities in design. They do, however, display a sensibility in their use of images that differs from earlier generations if for no other reason than that the present generation possesses tools for incorporating images that earlier generations did not.

The Web site for a proposal argument created by Beth Weaver, a student in an elective, lower-division, special-topics writing course at the University of Texas during fall 2000, is representative. Weaver wrote a critique of the gender models in professional wrestling presented to an audience that includes a substantial segment of preteen children. Although the World Wrestling Federation claims its target audience is aged eighteen to thirty-four, Weaver documents that nearly 40 percent of the advertising is directed to young children. Weaver proposes moving wrestling to later time slots and labeling it for mature audiences. She also urges that parents watch wrestling with children and discuss its relationship to reality.

Weaver's argument is better developed than most, but the design is unremarkable. The pages use minimal paragraphing and do not control line width, making the text harder to read that it should be. Nevertheless, Weaver uses a rhetorical strategy that I find increasingly frequent. She not only uses images to support her argument but also to make a parallel argument that we see most clearly in wrestlers like Chyna and Kurt Angle—who with steroids and implants have assumed the shapes of cartoon superheroes—juxtaposed against the cartoon advertising for Rugrats and fast-food-brand icons. This parallel argument demonstrates Weaver's awareness of how images circulate and are reproduced in many different contexts in our culture and how media feed off each other, which McLuhan observed in *Understanding Media*. A key principle for McLuhan is that "the 'content' of any medium is always another medium" (7).

Web publishing was introduced to writing teachers in the scholarly literature as a hypertext, which has no necessary beginning, middle, or end. As we have grown more accustomed to the Web, the organization of Web sites does not seem quite so radical. There is always the potential for adding more text and graphics, but that potential has long existed in print through footnotes. Likewise, the links to other texts have long been represented in print as references. What is different is the multimedia capability that nearly all students who have access to a computer now possess even if they do not use and, more significant, their awareness of how to use images to make meaning. Even without the Web, cheap color printers allow us to place images besides text on paper. Furthermore, many students now routinely publish animations, audio, and video clips along with images on Web sites. Even though these students remain a minority, the power to produce and reproduce images and sounds using computers that cost in the hundreds and not thousands of dollars is staggering in comparison to what was available at the low end just a decade ago.

One option for writing teachers is simply to deny students the use of these capabilities, but that option is problematic for the field as a whole. A core assumption of composition studies is that the short-term goals of bringing students up to speed so they can fulfill the writing tasks required in their undergraduate curricula and in the workplace are in the long term aimed at empowering students to become active citizens in a participatory democracy. Herein lies the rub. I can think of no scenario for the revival of public discourse that does not involve digital media. The technical barriers are quickly diminishing. Web-page editors can now perform what used to require a team of designers and production staff in print media.

Even if the tools are increasingly simple for students to use (and of course not all of them are), many questions about design remain to be addressed when students make Web pages. Issues of outdated equipment and inadequate access have not been resolved for many students and teachers alike. Only a tiny percentage of writing teachers have had any training in graphic design. Although a large body of useful work in professional and technical writing and document design over the past twenty years is now beginning to find its way into mainstream composition textbooks, few writing teachers have any sense of how to sequence a curriculum that would include some instruction in design. Furthermore, writing teachers in general find their courses already overburdened without adding additional demands.

In spite of these difficulties, student work will be increasingly in multimedia forms. Employers, administrators, and even accrediting agencies want more technology-intensive courses, not to mention the growing percentage of students who believe that their ability to communicate using new media will be critical to their futures. Even from the perspective of a text-based writing teacher, I find that there are pedagogical reasons for at least considering Web publishing as an option for students. The ability to compose multimedia documents gives students an awareness of the advantages of text over other media. Many ideas cannot be translated well into other media, and the key moves in the practice of dialogic rhetoric, such as summarizing another point of view in a way that is acceptable to people who hold that point of view, are verbal.

The importance of text is not likely to diminish anytime soon, but we are already in an era where a great deal of reading is done on the screen and where text is often found in new environments. The Web has exposed the absence of a theory-based conception of multimedia texts in rhetoric and composition and in literacy studies in general. It's not just being at square one; I'm not sure we've even figured out where square one is or what the project might involve. If composition studies is to become an important player among liberal arts disciplines, it will have to take leadership in this larger project.

Indicative of the present confusion is the use of the term *visual literacy,* which has become a way for writing teachers to acknowledge the ease of putting images and text on the same page but at the same time a way of avoiding what is at stake. As Paul Messaris points out, visual literacy can mean many things ranging from limited claims about aesthetic appreciation and the need for a skeptical attitude toward the manipulative aspects of media to strong claims about the prerequisites for interpreting pictures and the cognitive consequences on spatial perception of viewing images. Perhaps I should not make a fuss because *literacy* is used casually in all sorts of ways: computer literacy, math literacy, economic literacy, mechanical literacy, geographic literacy, cultural literacy, and so on. However, I will argue that the term must be used more precisely if it is to be used at all and if those interested in the teaching and study of writing are to go beyond merely passing along received advice about document design. (See Wysocki and Johnson-Eilola for another critique of this term.)

A critical underlying question is to what, if any, extent visual literacy resembles reading and writing. This question has been debated since the 1920s when art historian Erwin Panofsky published *Perspective as Symbolic Form,* in which he challenged the prevailing view that the Renaissance system of linear visual perspective directly reflects reality. Instead, he maintained that linear perspective is an arbitrary style that does not correspond to what people actually see. In the strong versions of theories of visual literacy, knowledge of arbitrary conventions is assumed requisite for visual understanding and visual literacy, knowledge thought to be acquired by repeated exposure to images. One of the most influential proponents of this argument was E. H. Gombrich, who maintained in an often-cited 1960 book *Art and Illusion* that an adult who had never before seen a black-and-white photograph or an outline drawing might not be able to interpret it as an image of something in the real world. Gombrich and others pointed to a priori difficulties—that when three dimensions are collapsed into two dimensions, important perceptual cues such as color and shadow are often absent, and certain styles such as stick figures exclude nearly all detail.

Many experiments have tested this hypothesis with pictorially inexperienced viewers and even animals, with the overall results tending to undercut the claims of strong theories of visual literacy. They suggest that understanding two-dimensional pictures and drawings is not so very different from vision in everyday life. Other experiments have been conducted to determine the extent that the quick transitions in time and space frequent in television and film would be unintelligible to naive viewers. Again, the results of experiments have been similar; experiences of daily life appear to prepare people adequately to understand instantaneous time and space shifts on film, even if they have no familiarity with the medium.

My point is not that we should avoid visual instruction because visual perception is apparently part of our birthright, but that we should attempt to be clearer about the goals of instruction and scholarship and to be more forthright about the difficulties of understanding how images create meaning. W. J. T. Mitchell cautions us that in spite of living in a world saturated with images, "We still do not know exactly what pictures are, what their relation to language is, how they operate on observers and on the world, how their history is to be understood, and what is to be done with or about them" (13). He argues that pictures are a complex interplay among visual registers, media, institutions, bodies and spectatorship, and privileged ways of representing the world. Because these elements are not in a causal or sequential determination, the unity in a picture is necessarily temporary and highly contingent.

Although we can point to certain sets of images as arbitrarily defined such as international road signs, most images take on meaning though particular uses in particular genres at particular times for particular audiences in particular viewing positions. In short, they are highly rhetorical. What concerns me most in the gradual but evident movement of basic composition courses toward multimedia production and the Web is that the tools are becoming so easy to use that we'll simply teach students to do what the tools allow. The rhetorical dimension of putting images together with text is being lost in the interface.

Much recent work in composition studies (e.g., Kaufer and Butler) and in related fields (e.g., Brummett) has aimed at expanding theories of rhetoric to include nonverbal media. Furthermore, since the 1970s, there has been a series of noteworthy efforts to introduce visual texts into first-year composition courses (reviewed in Diana George, "From Image"). However, as a disciplinary project within composition studies, the study of nonverbal media suffers serious limitations from medium- and genre-based assumptions. When the Web enters a writing course, old assumptions about media and genre are disrupted. As Bolter and Grusin have pointed out, the Web is an intersection of several technologies that draw on each other. My larger argument made more fully elsewhere is that, contrary to claims that the Internet is the most transformative invention since the discovery of fire, the Internet represents a consolidation stage in the 160-year development of electronic communication technologies and the thirty-five-hundred-year history of writing technologies ("Material Literacy and Visual Design"). That the Web has expanded so rapidly suggests that it is not so new, because people immediately recognize its uses. By contrast, a relatively new technology like the telegraph can take decades for some of its primary effects to be realized; for example, standard time zones were not made official by law until 1918, over seventy years after the development of the telegraph. The Internet and the Web are more comparable to the spread of television in the United States from one million sets in 1949 to over fifty million by 1959. The saturation of television occurred rapidly because many of the critical political, economic, and content issues had been prepared by radio, including the government's decision to regulate the airwaves to protect commercial interests and the formation of networks to provide mass-media programming.

The Web began in 1990 as relatively uncomplicated technology to distribute working papers among scientists connected with CERN, the European Laboratory for Particle Physics based in Geneva, Switzerland. Because the Web is independent of particular computer platforms, it didn't take long for its advantages to be recognized. The Web didn't take off, though, until 1993 when the browser Mosaic allowed images to appear on the screen along with text. Certainly the ubiquitousness of television during the past half-century explains part of the desire to see images on a computer screen but only part.

Scholars of the history of literacy have not known quite what to make of the Web, which reflects a lack of knowledge of the history of genres that combine images and text. Images and text appear together as early as 1370 B.C.E. on Egyptian papyrus rolls, notably the Book of the Dead. From Roman times onward, there is a continuous history of illustrated texts in the West that by the time of Johannes Gutenberg in the mid-fifteenth century had emerged from a monastic tradition that focused on religious subjects to a wide range of secular subject matters produced in lay workshops. During the first seventy-five years of printing, printed books competed directly with manuscripts, and to a large extent the books were based on their design. Early printed books were often hybrids, with decoration, illustrations, and colored rubrics added by hand after the book was printed. By the middle of the sixteenth century, relatively few books were using hand coloring, and books remained almost uniformly monochrome for three hundred years. The unity of text and image production that had developed in the manuscript tradition was now divided. Different technologies were used to produce text and images, making books that combined text and images very expensive to produce.

In 1800, printing was still practiced much as it has been in the days of Gutenberg. Presses remained screw-type hand presses, type was still cast by hand and inked by leather-covered ink balls, and paper was still made a sheet at a time. By middle of the century, advances in paper production and steam-driven presses made possible the mass circulation of newspapers and periodicals, developments that historians and literary scholars have long appreciated. Less understood are the impacts of image technologies, which also were transformed during the first half of the nineteenth century. Accounts of the rapid development typically focus on the technology. In England during the last half of the eighteenth century, the technique of wood engraving was rediscovered. Wood engraving involves incising the end of a wood block with a cutting tool called a burin. The foremost practitioner was the printmaker Thomas Bewick, who demonstrated the potential of the technique in illustrations in natural history books, especially *A History of British Birds* published in 1797. Wood engraving allowed wider range of tones and shading than was possible for the prevailing steel- and copper-plate methods.

Wood engraving soon proved to have another major advantage over metal engraving. By the 1830s, steam-driven presses could produce newspapers and publications in numbers unimaginable in comparison to what had been possible with hand presses. Copper engravings, however, could not be printed on a letterpress and were good for only a few thousand impressions before wearing out. Steel engravings were much more durable, but they also were very time-consuming to produce because of the hardness of the material. Wood engravings by contrast could yield two- to three-hundred thousand impressions and were much cheaper to produce than metal engravings (Knight 253–56). In the 1830s, wood engravings began to be frequently used in magazines and occasionally in newspapers.

Herbert Ingram, a printer who lived in Nottingham, had noticed that issues of newspapers that included illustrations sold more copies. With his brother-in-law, he moved to London in 1842 to make his fortune by publishing the *Illustrated London News*, a weekly that began with sixteen pages of letterpress and thirty-two wood engravings with the goal of illustrating the news. The first issue sold an extraordinary twenty-six thousand copies. Ingram first used well-known artists but often the images were not taken from life. Soon, he was sending artists to the scene to cover current news on a weekly basis. One of the young artists was Henry Carter, who used the pen name "Frank Leslie" and brought the genre of the illustrated newspaper and the successful business model to the United States in the 1850s. That's more or less the standard account of the rise of illustrated newspapers.

If we look at the historical context of the early illustrated periodicals aimed at mass consumption, we get a different perspective. As I mentioned earlier, instant popularity should make us suspect that the demand preexisted the appearance of the *Illustrated London News.* Indeed, it comes after not only a decade of illustrated periodicals but in the wake of a seventy-five-year debate over the value of art in national culture. In 1769, Sir Joshua Reynolds issued the first of a series of eloquent defenses of painting against charges that it was mere imitation and inferior to poetry. He argued that there is an intimate connection between the nation's wealth and trade and its art and that the artist could raise the overall intellectual excellence of England and distinguish it from barbarous nations. This connection of art, trade, and national greatness became the central theme for reformers who would raise public taste through exhibitions and education. They immediately saw the potential of wood engraving to make the works of the old masters available even to the poor.

Charles Knight, publisher for the Society for the Diffusion of Useful Knowledge, in 1832 introduced the weekly *Penny Magazine,* the first periodical to combine rapid printing with high-quality wood engravings. Knight wrapped the magazine in the cause of propagating virtue through art, but his magazine also celebrated the advance of distribution technologies. The preface to volume 1 notes the ease of obtaining a copy of *Penny Magazine* throughout England:

> When unthinking people therefore ask, what is the benefit of steam-engines, and canals, and fine roads to the poor man, they may be answered by this example alone. In this, and in all other cases, ready and cheap communication breaks down the obstacles of time and space, and thus, bringing all ends of a great kingdom as it were together, greatly reduces the inequalities of fortune and situation, by equalizing the price of commodities and to that extent making them accessible to all.

The Internet was hardly the first communications medium to be hyped for promoting equality.

In the first issue of the *Illustrated London News* in May 1842, Ingram also paraded out the clichés about the moral value of art and its benefits for the national soul. In case anyone wondered what enduring qualities of great art had to do with the illustrated record of passing events, Ingram had the answer in the preface. Illustrations aided "Art and Literature, as well as the Christian policy, and Concentrated General Intelligence, and Universal History" (preface 1). The first issue contained images of a costume ball given by Queen Victoria, although the artist was not present and had to rely on second-hand accounts. Close to press time, news of a major fire in Hamburg, Germany, reached the paper, so an artist was sent to the British Museum to find drawings of the city to which a halo of flames could be added (see fig. 15.2 for an example of a front page of *The Illustrated London News*). When staff artist Frank Leslie moved to New York in 1848 determined to start his own illustrated newspaper, he brought the knowledge of how to build the sales. Leslie, too, paid lip service to the moral mission of art, but when circulation lagged, he knew there was nothing like a sensational murder case to increase readership.

The rise of illustrated newspapers in the first half of the nineteenth century demonstrates how the means of reproduction led to the proliferation of media long before the digital era. The example also illustrates how new technologies that gain wide appeal are shaped as much or more by users than by their inventors. Indeed, the desire for images quickly transformed old genres and by the end of the century led to new ones including the comic strip. New information technologies typically have a high-minded goal of disseminating a specific content at the outset, which becomes relatively insignificant or lost altogether when other uses

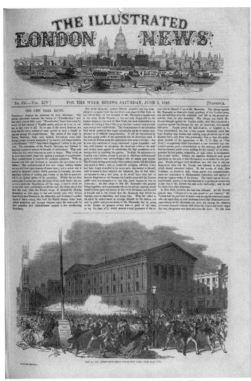

Figure 15.2 Coverage of the New York theater riots in *The Illustrated London News,* 2 June 1849. Harry Ransom Humanities Research Center, University of Texas at Austin.

are recognized. For example, the telephone was imagined by Alexander Graham Bell to serve to broadcast concerts, a function later fulfilled by radio.

We have some sense today of how new technologies bend old genres. One of the most frequent examples is the graphic design of *USA Today,* which transformed the conservative newspaper genre to resemble television in print. *USA Today*'s four-color photographs and attention-grabbing graphics are now typical of most newspapers, even the sober *New York Times.* Now, the color weather map seems normal presentation, where temperature ranges follow the spectrum. The color weather map is recognized widely as one of the clearest influences of television on newspapers. Yet, few have thought about how television drew on print representations of weather (see fig. 15.3) or how digital representations of weather evolved from earlier electronic forms. Newspapers had reported weather like other news throughout the nineteenth century and well into the twentieth. Maps that included weather information began to appear in the 1870s and were

Figure 15.3 An early U.S. Army Signal Service weather map, 1 September 1872. National Weather Service Photo Library <http://www.photolib.noaa.gov/historic/nws/wea01800.htm>.

well established by the turn of the century; thus, television's adaptation of the weather map was built upon a newspaper tradition.

This brief example suggests how little we understand the genealogy of some of the most familiar print forms today. These forms have not so much fallen through the disciplinary cracks as they have occupied a vast and largely unexplored territory, a territory that many people now enter through digital technologies. If Lewis's claim that the future just happened applies broadly to literate practices, its potency lies less in our ability to download music, day trade, and play games on the Internet and more in our capability to produce what required a team of designers and production staff, not to mention a recording and film studio, just a few years ago. The question for composition studies is what are we going to do with this capability.

Much scholarship in composition studies during the disciplinary period has argued for a place in the university beyond the limited conception of college writing that dominated for most of the past century. Yet, an attitude that Diana George and John Trimbur describe as a longstanding "counterposition of composition and communication" results in a polarization of the verbal and the visual. This polarization denies the materiality of writing as one means of visual communication alongside others, and it follows the bias of the humanities to distrust images not considered high art. Until quite recently, the field has enforced this distinction in writing courses by confining instruction in design, images, and graphics to technical writing. A neat and unproblematic compartmentalization of genre, however, is no longer possible.

The point is not that we have to abandon teaching the traditional essay in writing classes. I am confident that essays will continue to be written long into the future just as short stories are today, even though the readership has vanished. However, we do not have to restrict our definition of the essay to what we have come to know as a school form. Doug Hesse ("Saving a Place for Essayist Literacy") has argued that, unlike the school tradition of the essay that aspires to finality, the classic tradition of the essay from Montaigne onward does not strive for closure but instead emphasizes the provisional and contingent. Hesse describes the primary characteristic of the contemporary essay as "the attempt to cast the widest net of associations possible, then struggle to bring the gathered ideas into some meaningful relation" (36). If we grant Hesse's characterization, then it is not such a great leap to include visual ideas in addition to verbal ones in essays. The addition, in turn, allows us to think about rhetoric in much broader terms. We have no justification aside from disciplinary baggage to restrict our conception of rhetoric to words alone. More important, this expansion is necessary if we are to make good on our claims of preparing students to engage in public discourse.

16 Multimedia Literacy: Confessions of a Nonmajor

RESPONSE BY CHRISTINE M. NEUWIRTH

In "Seeking a Disciplinary Reformation," a response paper in the 1996 *Composition in the Twenty-First Century: Crisis and Change,* Charles I. Schuster appeals to the 1987 English Coalition Conference and its placement of reading, writing, speaking, and listening as the central business of English studies as a basis for his vision for our discipline's ideal form. In response to the question "How will new technologies change composition studies?" in this volume, both the paper by Dànielle Nicole DeVoss, Joseph Johansen, Cynthia L. Selfe, and John C. Williams Jr. and the paper by Lester Faigley challenge this vision of ourselves. DeVoss, Johansen, Selfe, and Williams use three case studies to document the new types of text—texts that include still images, sound, animations, and video—that have begun to emerge and argue that English composition teachers and programs must address an increasing broad range of literacies if we are to avoid declining relevance of our curricula for our students and abdicating our professional responsibility to describe the ways in which people are now communicating and making meaning. These authors call for us to expand out professional, curricular, and instructional activities to include interpreting and creating multimedia compositions, both within and outside of electronic contexts. Faigley similarly notes that many students now routinely publish animations, audio, and video clips along with images on Web sites, and he uses the historical developments of printing technology and the changes it brought about in the relationships of texts and images to project future increases in multimedia forms. He argues that we risk not fulfilling our disciplinary mission if we do not empower students to theorize multimedia and produce it, despite the difficulties of access, training, and finding room for it in an already overburdened curriculum.

Discussion-group responses at the writing program administrators' conference to the idea of teaching multimedia reminded me of the responses we are used to hearing at Writing-Across-the-Curriculum (WAC) meetings when we ask faculty in other disciplines to teach writing. There was widespread agreement among meeting participants that it should be taught but reservations about whether *we* should teach it (it's another discipline's responsibility), whether we *could* teach it, even if we wanted to (we don't know how to do it ourselves, and we don't know how to teach it, and we wouldn't know how to assess it), and *where* it would fit in the curriculum (we don't see how it fits into our curricular goals, and we already have too much subject matter to cover). One interesting difference between WAC and WPA responses concerned labor issues: The vast burden of work for WPAs involved in broadening what we teach would fall to brand-new graduate students and adjuncts.

What would that burden be? Enter the confessions of a nonmajor: In an attempt to increase my own visual literacy, I enrolled in an introductory design course for nonmajors, Communication Design Fundamentals, offered in our School of Design. This course is equivalent to our first-year writing courses for nonmajors. (Majors in our School of Design are admitted on the basis of portfolios and take a different introductory course; in addition, they take advanced courses in typography, drawing, photography, color, the design process, history of design, sound, motion, etc.). Interestingly, the theory in the course seemed familiar: We analyzed purpose and audience and discussed example designs in terms of how well the designs met communication needs; we learned about theories of how people read the visual; and we learned about the process of invention and revision. The execution, however, was totally unfamiliar. When an assignment required me to look *at* text rather than *through* it, I experienced something akin to looking at those ambiguous figures from the psychology of perception (*two faces* versus a *vase*), and it was only with great difficulty that I could *see* the text, and then only for brief moments. When for an assignment I was asked to emphasize a particular visual element, I laboriously rehearsed my novice grammar of the visual: "Hmmm. Let's see. I could use size, shape, contrast . . . I'm forgetting something. Let's see. Oh, symmetry-asymmetry. What else?" Somewhat annoyingly, the instructor insisted that we engage in inventional explorations, so we not only had to turn in our final draft but also sketches of all our explorations of alternative concepts (we were *required* to have alternative concepts, and I would find myself racking my brains for them), as well as explorations of and revisions to the concept that eventually resulted in our final draft. We also had to be prepared to talk about those in relationship to purpose and audience in class. When I thought that my design was final and could not be more perfect, I would be surprised when my instructor was able to point out "things to think about" that my novice eyes had missed and would lead to marked improvements during the revision process. These activities took hour upon hour, and, even though I started early, I would find myself working well past midnight on evenings before an assignment was due (and we were only dealing with static pictures, not animation, which is even more time-consuming to produce). At the end of the semester, we not only had to turn in a final project but also a portfolio of all our work from the semester. Sound familiar? Faced with grading final papers and portfolios in the courses I was teaching, I took an incomplete.

This experience leads me to want to stick to my expertise in language and to pose the question, "Are there alternative models to the long, arduous road of becoming designers (not to mention learning how to teach it)?" One alternative is to ask our colleagues in design to teach our students (or for institutions without design to hire designers in their own departments or programs); another is to teach interdisciplinary courses; another is to have interdisciplinary majors. My own institution engages in all three practices. For example, our School of Design provides the course I took, the Fundamentals of Communication Design, for our professional writing majors, who are required to take it (and, in return, we provide a course, Language in Design) for their majors. Some courses are designed as interdisciplinary courses, with students in majors such as computer science, design, English, and human-computer interaction enrolled. As a teacher of one such course, On-line Information Design, I cannot represent myself as an expert in areas outside my expertise but must think of ways in which students are able to respect and learn from each other's disciplinary expertises. We also have interdisciplinary majors. For example, in our Masters of Design in Communication Planning and Information Design, student applications are reviewed by faculty in both the English Department and the School of Design, and students are admitted to both units and study with faculty in both. Other alternatives, such as team-teaching, are possible, though at my own institution are not as pervasive for reasons such as credit loads, scheduling, and so forth. There are exceptions. For example, Documenting the Visual is a course that is team-taught with a professor of photography in the School of Design and a professor of journalism in the English department.

The shape that our teaching takes will depend on a complex of circumstances that emerge, historically accumulate and compete, both in our own institutions and in the various academic fields concerned with communication. New technologies represent one set of circumstances that challenge us to rethink our practices. How will new technologies change composition studies? That's a project for us to complete.

Part 6 What Languages Will Our Students Write, and What Will They Write About?

17 Composition's Word Work: Deliberating How to Do Language

MIN-ZHAN LU

In recent years, many in composition have worked to highlight the link among language, power, subjectivity, and knowledge. This body of scholarship critiques the assumptions of essentialist notions of language and functionalist approaches to literacy, including a tendency to reify the living process of language into sets of fixed and discrete entities, imagined as preexisting tools, and a tendency to cast students solely in the role of passive consumers of these supposedly fossilized linguistic forms. Treating language as a dynamic process involving competing ways of seeing, thinking, and talking, this body of scholarship often marks writing as a form of "word work" with the potential to build a more sustainable world for all (Morrison), that is, a world less organized by axes of domination along lines of race, gender, class, sex, age, technology, education, and so on.

I begin with a brief mapping of this scholarship. I then explore its implications for how we reread past debate over students' language needs and how we rewrite the work of composition studies in the twenty-first century. I focus my discussion on two topics in academic and public debates on students' language needs: debates over how to best help students learn the standardized conventions of a written English and debates over how to best prepare students for the so-called information age or global economy. I choose these focal points because both are pivotal to whether and how individual institutions deliver on their current catalogue promises to enhance diversity, interdisciplinarity, and active learning, issues in which composition studies has been highly invested from its inception. I argue that composition studies in the twenty-first century needs to foreground students' right to deliberate over how they do language. By doing language, I have in mind the work students perform in both reproducing and reshaping standardized rules of language in the process of using them; retooling the tools one is given to achieve one's ends; and more specifically, retooling the tools according to not only one's sense of what the world is but also what the world ought to be.

The Question of How to Do Language When Writing

Composition scholars in recent years have challenged essentialist notions of language and functionalist approaches to literacy in one of four ways. First, they have argued that the so-called tools of language—whether labeled *standard, written,* or *Edited American English*—are not neutral means for accessing the real or transmitting preexisting truth. Language tools are material forces that mediate how we see, think of, talk about, and live in the world. Secondly, although the standardized rules guarding the formation of a language tool are usually marketed as objective information on how actual people read and write, that information, like all knowledge, is a partial and situated interpretation of differences across language practices. Thirdly, all users of language are its makers and therefore accountable for its formation and transformation. In acting as passive consumers of fossilized language rules, we turn language from a living process, as Toni Morrison puts it, into a "dead," "unyielding language" that is "ruthless in its policing duties" (13–14). The vitality of language depends on how we exercise our ethical responsibilities when using—working with and on—its standardized rules. Fourth, how we do language informs and is informed by how we do—that is, how we construct—ourselves, others, and the world we live in. How we do language has material consequences for the life-span and shape of existing structures and relations of asymmetrical power, for no system of domination or language tool could survive without our word work.

Scholarship taking these critical turns has accordingly centered attention on questions such as the following: Are only certain rules valued in individual academic or social sites? Who within each site is and who is not authorized to standardize the rules of language? Why? Which forms of language practices are delegitimized by each standardized rule? How? Finally, how else might we do language besides passively reproducing standardized rules? These questions have pushed to the front the issues of ethical responsibility and revision: What kind of world do we envision our word work to build: a world more organized or less organized along axes of domination promoting individualism, anthropocentrism, patriarchy, cultural imperialism, mechanization, economism, consumerism, nationalism, and militarism (on ecological sustainability versus technological sustainability, see Orr 24)? Why do we consider certain visions of the world more sustainable than others? What might be the discrepancies between how we envision the world and how we do language? These questions motivate us to deliberate over which of the standardized rules of language to reinforce and which to reject or alter so that our words might indeed work to build the more sustainable world we envision.

In actual classrooms, these questions might lead us to examine, for example, not only the ways in which the protocols of a particular sportswear exposition constrain how we produce information on the quality, performance, or afford-ability of Nike shoes but also the ways in which such information occludes at-tention to global relations of production and thus mutes the voices of third-world sweatshop laborers whose existence is at stake but not taken into account by that information. We might then experiment with ways of producing and circulating information on Nike shoes that incorporate the previously suppressed issues, perspectives, and voices, or we might examine the ways in which geological sur-veys of oil in Alaska or sociological studies of the Alaskan labor market risk com-puting that world into information on so-called natural and human resources, thus delegitimizing human practices that acknowledge the agency of natural pro-cesses and treat humans and nature as interdependent agents.

In such classrooms, students would tinker with standardized rules of academic discourses by trying out voices and visions that the rules have rendered irrelevant, peripheral, even erroneous.[1] At the same time, they would perceive their efforts as taking place inside various regimes of knowledge and therefore as neither easy nor unproblematic. They would recognize that the connections opened up by such efforts are partial and the subject positionings at best provisional and "im-perfectly stitched" together (Haraway 193). Nevertheless, they would understand that how hard they try matters. Their efforts can have real consequences on the future of language, the world, and the lives of others as well as themselves. Writ-ing is one of the sites where one might wrestle with the potential discrepancies between the world one envisions through values such as social justice or world peace and the kind of world one's word work is likely to build.

To summarize, a significant number of composition teachers and researchers have been steadily calling attention to the question of how our students will do language and why. They have come up with pedagogies that encourage students to deliberate over how one uses—works with and on—the standardized rules of language about which one has explicitly come to college to learn. These pedagogies emphasize students' needs to explore ways of doing language according to not only one's sense of what the world is but also of what the world ought to be for others as well as one's self, so that one's words indeed work to build the world one envi-sions. In the next section, I examine the implications of this critical turn for how composition studies might participate in academic and public debates over how to best teach students to tackle "errors" in their writing.

"Error" and Deliberative Uses of Standardized Rules

The academy has traditionally taken a top-down approach to student composi-tion, marking as "error" any sign of deviation from the rules standardized by those in positions to assess the writings of others. The top-down approach assigns student writers the role of passive consumers of fossilized rules. It focuses energy on standardizing the rules students should know and follow. All signs of deviation in student writing are automatically taken as indicating the students' lack of information on or motivation and capability to learn the correct rules (Horner and Lu, "Expectations" 44). However, if we bring in the question of how individual students are doing language when producing a specific error, then it is not enough to merely consider what this student knows or does not know about a standardized rule. We need to also consider how this student is working on as well as with that rule and why. For instance, we might consider the ways in which acting as a passive consumer of a particular standardized rule confines the purpose and contexts of writing; we might take into account the student's effort to use this rule for purposes and in contexts traditionally dismissed by pedagogies that assign students the role of passive consumers of standardized rules.

Let me quickly illustrate how this type of deliberation might proceed in actual course work. In first-year writing classes I've taught, native-speaking students try to interpret the logic of an "error"—the verb construction *can able to*—in a student paper. Students take into account the critique put forward in the rest of the paper, which questions the tendency in mainstream U.S. culture to use both verb forms—*can* and *be able to*—to foreground individual capacity and willpower while erasing attention to the material conditions enabling or disabling the capacity and will of differently located historical agents. They subsequently consider the implications idiomatic uses of *can* and *be able to* in mainstream U.S. culture might have on how its users construct relations with peoples living in historical and social conditions significantly different from their own and if the relations they thus enact are in keeping with the kind of self and world they aspire their word work to build. They also try to come up with diverse revisions of the construction *can be able to* so that their sense of the limitations of idiomatic uses of *can* and *be able to* in mainstream U.S. culture are exposed rather than perpetuated (Lu, "Professing Multiculturalism").

When composing analytical essays on a short story by Leslie Marmon Silko titled "Storyteller," one student in my advanced critical theory class paused over the following sentence she had composed: "By listening to the sound of the ice under her feet, the girl led the storeman who is chasing after her to his death by falling through a crack his weight had caused on a thin spot of the ice." When revising, this student writer considered the extent to which the sentence she had composed was in keeping with her goal as a reader, which was to "respect and learn from marginalized ways of life." She wondered whether her sentence structure risked presenting as subordinate the action that is discussed in her subordinate clause. She also considered the way in which the subordinate clause and the phrase *a hole his weight caused in the ice* might have denied the agency of nature, contrary to Silko's depiction of the main character's understanding of nature's agency. Then, this student tried out different sentence structures to bend the standardized rules for packaging ideas into subordinate and main clauses and for choosing passive and active voices. She also reflected on the ways in which Edited American English constrains our relationship with nature and with cultures and peoples who contest our anthropocentrism.

In foregrounding the question of how one does language, I am arguing that we also teach students to engage in deliberative uses of standardized rules. I am therefore not arguing that we stop teaching students to grasp and use the standardized rules of written English in the ways they are commonly expected to by the gatekeepers of institutional sites. Rather, I am arguing that we encourage students to see the top-down approach as only one way of using a standardized rule and as effective (only) for writing purposes and contexts standardized by functional approaches to education and literacy. We should ask students to deliberate over what the top-down use of standardized rules can and cannot do, given the specific contexts and purposes of individual students' learning and writing. This would mean that we also acknowledge the potential aspiration of individual students to use writing in contexts and for purposes that are meaningful to their day-to-day existence or their vision of what the world ought to become even though these contexts and purposes have been implicitly dismissed by the top-down approach. We also need to encourage students to experiment with ways of using that standardized rule that acknowledges the complex and often contradictory motivations, aspirations, and purposes of their writing and learning. Furthermore, instead of expecting students to first prove their ability to act as passive consumers of standardized rules and then, only afterwards, learn to deliberate over whether they should confine their work to the top-down approach of using these rules and how to come up with alternative ways of using these rules, we need to encourage students to proceed along both directions simultaneously.

Contrary to conventional wisdom, such pedagogical moves are possible and necessary because deliberation over how to work with and on the standardized rules of language is often one of the most effective ways of helping students gain knowledge of and experience in using these rules in the way endorsed by the top-down approach. This is the case because such deliberation centers attention on the differences and intersections across languages. It helps students to learn written English by examining what its rules can and cannot do in a variety of contexts and for a variety of purposes. It acknowledges that our students are adult learners who face complex social and historical conditions and who have complex motivations, aspirations, and purposes as well as sophisticated knowledge and expertise using a variety of languages, Englishes or otherwise (Canagarajah). Teaching them to act merely as passive consumers of standardized rules of language is, in essence, to ask these adult learners and writers to simplify the contexts and purposes of their learning and writing. At best, such teaching can merely help them to produce "correct" prose in standardized contexts and purposes while leaving them on their own to figure out how to make use of these language rules for other(ed) purposes and contexts meaningful to their individual life plans. At worst, students lose interest in learning and confidence in their ability to learn merely because they refuse to leave by the classroom door those motivations, aspirations, purposes, knowledge, and expertise critical to their day-to-day existence.

Approaching the "errors" students at all levels of their college education produce from the perspective of how individual students are doing language can help the academy reach its most motivated, ambitious, and innovative students. This is the case because, to go by the mission statements in current college catalogues, "diversity," "interdisciplinarity," and "student-centered learning" are among the most publicized goals of higher education. In theory, this could mean that the academy encourages students to develop styles of thinking and writing that challenge the divisions across academic fields as well as cultures and social groups. Furthermore, the academy expects students to act as active producers rather than the passive receivers of established knowledge.

Yet, as many in composition have argued, when students take seriously the academy's promise to advance diversity, interdisciplinarity, and active learning; when they try to examine the strengths and limitations of one academic language tool from the perspective of a variety of disciplines and cultures; and when they refuse to take an either-or approach to competing ways of thinking and using language, they often have difficulty acting as passive consumers of a single set of standardized rules (Bartholomae, "Inventing"; Shaughnessy). Many in composition have also argued that a significant number of student writers at all levels—basic as well as intermediate and advanced—have the intellectual capability, material necessity, and political motivation to tinker with the language tools they have explicitly come to college to acquire (see, among others, Gavaskar; Herzberg; Horner, "Mapping"; Lu, "Professing"; and Lynch, George, and Cooper).

Faculty who subscribe to the top-down approach to error often inadvertently reinforce the logic of essentialism and functional literacy by labeling as "underprepared" or "indifferent" those students reluctant to act merely as passive consumers of standardized rules of language. As a result, they doom these students to the fate author Gloria Anzaldúa recalls facing during her own undergraduate days: except for one course she took with composition scholar James Sledd, she was regularly punished—graded down—for trying to hybridize standardized visions and voices in ways she was later to earn critical acclaim for in her book *Borderlands/La Frontera* (Lunsford). To ensure that the academy reaches those students most motivated to take seriously its current catalogue promises to promote diversity, interdisciplinarity, and active learning, we need to get more faculty and students across the curriculum to join us in problematizing the top-down approach to error. This is particularly the case for faculty and students in courses offered under such rubrics as cultural studies, environmental studies, ethnic studies, multicultural studies, postcolonial studies, and women's studies, where students are regularly assigned texts by writers such as Anzaldúa.

In these classrooms, insufficient attention to how student writers are trying to do language can be perilous. To begin with, we leave them to sink or swim on their own, as Anzaldúa had to decades ago. Secondly, the discrepancy in how we approach the work of published writers and the work of student writers might make these students distrust our ability to teach what we preach. Furthermore, the grades and comments we produce with the top-down approach to error may lead students to conclude that neither the texts they've been assigned to read nor the programs housing these courses are viable for them. As a result, these programs might fail to recruit or retain those students who are most likely to become the kind of active learners such programs ostensibly are attempting to draw. Finally, for faculty in interdisciplinary programs who take "errors" in student writing to be a distressing sign of the students' inability to do the real work they are eager to teach, combating the top-down approach to "errors" can help them recognize the energy and sophistication some students have brought to their learning. This can in turn boost the vitality of faculty members (Horner and Lu, "Expectations" 49). Attention to students' need to deliberate over how they do language can also enhance exchange between faculty assigned to support spaces of the institution—writing programs and writing centers—and faculty occupying the institution's mainstay spaces.

To argue for deliberative uses of standardized rules in college classrooms, we need to also call attention to the specific material conditions of our and our students' work (Horner, *Terms*). For instance, what kinds of institutional support—class size, teaching load, etc.—or student access to time, work space, technologies of writing, etc. are implied by accounts of pedagogical experimentation such as the ones I offer in this paper? Are such work conditions for teachers and students readily available across campuses and for teachers and students assigned different departmental or program status? How might teaching and learning practices aimed at deliberative uses of standardized rules proceed, given the different, specific conditions in which individual faculty and student work? How might we more deliberatively and effectively link our efforts to problematize the top-down approach to error with our effort to problematize the existing conditions of work facing differently situated faculty and students? These are urgent questions for composition studies in the twenty-first century.

A Situated Reading of Representations of Student Needs

It is not by coincidence that catalogue commitments to diversity, interdisciplinarity, and active learning are most often couched in terms of not only the projected diversity of the incoming student body but also the academy's charge to provide the students with the projected skills they need to succeed in the so-called global economy or the age of information (Giroux, "Cultural Studies"; Berlin, "English Studies"). To combat essentialist notions of language and functionalist approaches to literacy, we need to be more vigilant towards how we approach statements that posit a common language that all members of a nation, an academy, or a discipline supposedly need. We need to involve more faculty and students across the curriculum in treating the question of how our students will do language as an integral part of academic and public debate over students' language needs and rights in the twenty-first century.

Let me make my case by turning to two previous attempts made by the Conference on College Composition and Communication to advance students' language rights, first in a 1974 resolution, "Students' Right to Their Own Language," and then in a 1989 National Policy Statement. In "CCCC's Role in the Struggle for Language Rights," Geneva Smitherman, who served on both committees charged to draw up the two statements, recalls the complex, diverse, and often conflicting concerns and positions that members charged to draft both documents initially brought to the committee discussion. Smitherman's account of the composition of both documents suggests that the published documents do not fully represent all the concerns and positions voiced by the committee members. Rather, the immediate and specific intellectual, social, and political climates surrounding the documents' production and initial dissemination significantly mediated the content and style of the final texts. Smitherman's article thus serves as a timely reminder of the danger in assuming that the final documents speak unequivocally the intentions and concerns of those involved in drafting it. Nevertheless, recognition of the situatedness of all knowledge production should not keep us from positing situated readings of possible receptions of these documents within specific material contexts. For instance, how is either document likely to be read and used in intellectual and social climates where essentialist assumptions of language and functional approaches to literacy instruction predominate? How would we read and use either document if we are interested in helping students to enact deliberative uses of standardized rules?

With these questions in mind, I argue that although the resolution launches a solid fight for the legitimacy of all forms of English and students' right to use them, it doesn't go far enough against the logic of linguistic imperialism. That is, it allows for interpretations and usages that are likely to perpetuate rather than confront essentialist and functional assumptions to language learning. Instead of assimilation, the resolution promotes accommodation: It argues that "nontraditional" students should be allowed to acquire a new tool—a common language—while retaining rather than displacing their "home" languages. Although it replaces the logic of linguistic subtraction with a logic of linguistic addition, the "new" logic leaves intact the foundation of linguistic imperialism: the superpower status of a fossilized "common" language (Horner, "'Students' Right'").

I have three major contentions with the 1974 resolution. First, using such categories as public vs. private, standard vs. dialectal, and common vs. home, the resolution not only reduces the living process of language into discrete and self-evident tools but also ranks them according to the interests of the status quo. The "common" language is made dominant by the logic of simple arithmetic—the number of institutions requiring it and thus the number of people needing it. This logic of simple arithmetic covers up the foundation of linguistic imperialism, which is a logic of power: the power of the few to dictate how all perceive and work the world. Two, the dichotomy of "deep meaning" vs. "surface structure" turns "common" language into a neutral tool: a mere surface—formal—structure for wording preexisting "deep meaning" rather than a material force mediating how we produce meaning and thus work the world (for a more detailed analysis, see Lu, "Importing 'Science'"). Third, the resolution relies on linguistic theories sustained by essentialist notions of language and functionalist approaches to literacy; it uses these theories to present standardized English as a neutral, "common" language. As a result, the resolution inadvertently makes students whose home languages are not standardized English the only ones needing more than one language tool in their tool kit. In making these three moves, the 1974 resolution is more likely to be used to endorse research and pedagogy that centers on the question of what common language all students need and to render irrelevant research and pedagogy that examines how students might go about doing that language—that is, how they might struggle with the conflict between the established rules of that language and other languages meaningful to their daily existence when making decisions over how to work with and on these rules.

Fifteen years after the 1974 resolution, "Students' Right to Their Own Language," another committee was charged by the CCCC to draft a National Language Policy in response to English-only legislation in states such as California. The 1989 policy differs from the 1974 resolution by treating "the teaching of languages other than English" as good for all students. However, read with the two questions I have in mind, the superpower status of "literate competence in English" is not only retained but significantly expanded. "English," defined in part as "literate competence," remains "the language of wider communication." The "teaching of languages other than English" is now presented as good because it can ensure that "proficiency in one's mother tongue will not be lost" to certain groups of students and because it can enable "native speakers of English" to "rediscover the language of their heritage or learn a second language" ("National Language Policy" 369). By naming English to be the only "language of wider communication," it goes global, rendering other languages "narrower" and secondary and belonging to a former time period of "heritage" and the "mother." By reifying diverse discursive practices into discrete "languages" with relevance in seemingly discrete temporal and spatial zones, the 1989 Language Policy complies with the logic of linguistic imperialism by occluding attention to issues of power, conflict, and struggle at the heart of any move to institute a common English over Othered "tongues" (see Horner, "'Students' Right'"; Horner and Trimbur). Again, this type of position statement on students' language needs is more likely to be used to defend research and teaching that promote functional rather than deliberative uses of standardized rules.

As Smitherman puts it, the Language Policy of 1989 "stresses the need . . . for . . . all Americans to be bi- or multi-lingual in order to be prepared for citizenship in a global, multicultural society" (369). This suggests that the essentialist notions of language and functionalist approaches to literacy instruction had found new impetus in the 1980s in spite of, or as a result of, the academy's new, official charge to "prepare" students for "citizenship in a global, multicultural society." To argue for deliberative uses of standardized rules in the teaching and learning of writing, we need to take a more active role in debate over the meaning of *citizenship* in the so-called global economy, especially concerning how the academy might best go about helping students respond to the demands created by the "epochal shifts from Fordist to post-Fordist production, national to globalized societies, manufacturing to knowledge economies, the Cold War to the New World Order" (Trimbur, "Agency" 285).

Composition in the Regime of Flexible Accumulation

As James A. Berlin puts it, post-Fordism is a "regime of flexible accumulation" made possible through "the rapid means of communication and transportation encouraged by the technological compression of time and space" ("English Studies" 218). Control over information flow has become a vital weapon in global competition. Accordingly, the academy is pressured to produce workers who "combine greater flexibility and cooperation with greater intelligence and communicative ability" ("English Studies" 219).

The logic of linguistic addition embedded in policy statements such as the 1974 "Students' Right to Their Own Language" resolution or the 1989 National Policy Statement might lead us to focus attention solely on identifying the language or language skills all students supposedly need to thrive in the regime of flexible accumulation. To combat this logic, we should also deliberate over how we might do language—tinker with the language tools and skills we supposedly need in a new world ordered by the regulation and circulation of information. For instance, why is this new order only interested in flooding the world with certain types of information but not others? Why are some coding systems but not others valued? What kinds of flexibility, mobility, and connectivity for producing and distributing information are standardized by this new world order? What are the material consequences of conscripting our word work to its standard definitions of flexibility, mobility, and connectivity? For teachers and students interested in building a more sustainable world for all, how might one work on its standardized rules for producing and distributing information? Why?

For instance, it has become a truism that students need access to and experience in navigating the information superhighway. In classrooms that encourage deliberative uses of standardized rules, teachers and students could examine the ways in which corporate discourse polices how we do information when reading, writing, and learning. We might begin with a rhetorical analysis of one of the double-page advertisements in the campaign for *Microsoft Encarta,* such as the one rendered in the voice of children:

> We click the mouse and we hear Martin Luther King Jr. or Fidel Castro speak. (Castro is sort of hard to understand.) We can see the Berlin Wall being torn down or the propagation of a nerve impulse. We can rock out to Belgian guitarist Django Reinhardt or Classical Patt Waing of Burma. Alas (a word we learned from our *Microsoft Bookshelf* reference library), if we told you every single great thing *Encarta* does, we'd be up all night and there'd be no time for Dad's bedtime stories about Sartre and the existentialists. (qtd. in Cook 317)

According to the advertisement, this is how we should do language in the age of information: We need to be more childlike, striving for the kind of indiscriminate curiosity that children supposedly have. We should be more flexible and mobile in our consumption of information, traveling with a random click of the mouse across disciplines—history, politics, biology, philosophy, or music—as well as nations, cultures, and historical periods.

It is a mobility ensured by a willingness to move on while not quite fully understanding what we are seeing or hearing. It is a mobility more concerned with coverage than with probing the relations across seemingly discrete bits of information or taking responsibility for how we link and sequence them. Most of all, it is a mobility that would not require us to ever leave the security and comfort of our home or even couch. That is, we—the technology-rich—have the right and need to be more flexible and mobile in our access to the world, but we have no need to become more self-reflexive about the partiality of the information we produce, nor do we need to become more able to transform our discursive and material locations.

When analyzing how corporate discourse encourages us to consume information, we might also pose questions that can help us experiment with alternative ways of doing information. How has digitized information been fashioned? Which viewpoints are expounded or delegitimized by individual pieces of information? In strictly reproducing such information when accessing and circulating it, are we enhancing or impeding our effort to build the kind of sustainable world we envision? How should we do—or undo—that information when using it so that our word work would indeed build the kind of world we envision? Using these questions, students might compose counter expositions to the Microsoft advertisement by taking into account the effect digitization has on our sense of what counts as knowledge and by considering not only the "every single great thing *Encarta* does" *for* and *to* its ideal consumers but also the kinds of homes most likely to be housing such consumers and the material location of such homes on the geopolitical map of the U.S. and the world.[2] Or, they might examine the kinds of English most likely to be endorsed in technology-rich homes. For instance, what discursive logic is guiding the use of the conjunction—the word *or*—in the English spoken by the childlike consumers in the Microsoft advertisement? Why are the words of Martin Luther King Jr. perceived as conjunctural to those of Fidel Castro, according to which dichotomies of self and other?

Writing assignments in these classrooms can ask students to try out different connectives across the bits of information featured in the advertisement to expound different points about what "great thing *Encarta*" can and cannot do. For instance, students might explore whether the commercial's projected consumer finds Castro "sort of hard to understand" because of language differences or conflicts in ideology. How might we question that consumer's implicit confidence in his or her ability to fully understand Martin Luther King Jr.? What in King's word work is likely to be glossed over, even violated by the version of English sanctioned in technology-rich dwellings? In order to build the kind of world each of us envisions, what argument can be made that the residents of technology-rich dwellings need to pay more attention to particular aspects of King's word work that are likely to be glossed over by the English we use? Or, students might consider the new perspectives likely to emerge when one dislodges the conjuncture established by the Microsoft advertisement between the image of "the Berlin Wall being torn down" and "the propagation of the nerve impulse" and instead, put the image of the fall of the Berlin Wall next to the sound of Martin Luther King Jr. speaking. Having explored these questions, students might then design Web pages or linkages that acknowledge not only our right and need to access digitized information but also our right and need to deliberate over how we do information, including our need to pose alternative routes for navigating the information superhighway. And they might experiment with ways of disseminating their composition digitally and otherwise.

Learning to make deliberative uses of digitized information is one way that composition studies might "demonstrate its relevance and effectiveness" as our nation tries to make sense of and take action in response to the attacks on New York City's World Trade Center towers on September 11, 2001 (as Gilyard suggests in this volume). For anyone who might receive email messages such as "The Binch" and the "Special Report: Terrorism in the US" among others over the span of about one minute (as Gilyard relates), the particular connectives one works out and posts across these bits of information would be critical for the future of this world. Instead of spontaneously clicking the forward button as one reads through the messages in the order they appear on the screen and to the first group of persons coming to one's mind, one might ponder over such questions as which of these messages ought to be forwarded to a particular person or group, in which sequence, with what comments, images, sounds, attached to each piece, if one hopes to post routes for navigating the Internet that might help to build a world more sustainable for all, peace-loving Muslims as well as non-Muslims. How we click the forward button is one of the moments where the meanings of buzz words such as *patriotism, freedom, justice,* etc. get fought out. Deliberative uses of such technology and digitized information are the ethical responsibility of all email users.

This line of deliberation should be cogent for classrooms populated by students accrediting themselves for the most well-compensated sectors of the regime of flexible accumulation: I have in mind new professions such as systems engineering, organizational management, or biotechnology as well as advertising and public relations (Berlin, "English Studies" 219; Cook 314). Instead of focusing attention merely on identifying the information and skills that can increase one's chance to compete in these well-compensated sectors, faculty and students might explore the extent to which cybernetic (feedback-controlled) systems theories in telephone technology, computer design, weapons deployment, or database construction and maintenance reduce "the world into a problem of coding" (Haraway 161). Or, faculty and students might consider the ways in which molecular genetics, ecology, sociobiological evolutionary theory, or immunobiology translates the organism into problems of genetic coding and read-out. Students might also consider the different consequences individual systems of coding might bring to different peoples worldwide. Whose viewpoints, voices, and ways of life are ignored by the coding we design and distribute? How and why should these peoples have more say in the production and distribution of such coding (Haraway 163; Giroux, "Cultural Studies"; Berlin, "English Studies")?

Classrooms across the general curriculum might also examine the linkage between technology and literacy. To what extent has that link exacerbated current educational and social inequality in the U.S. along axes of class, gender, and race (Selfe, "Technology"; Giroux, "Cultural Studies"; Berlin, "English Studies"; Ohmann)? How have employment patterns changed in the regime of flexible accumulation? For instance, what types of wages, benefits, and working conditions are provided for people working as "clerical, secretarial, and routine and lesser-skilled manual workers" and the even less secure part-timers, temporaries, and public trainees (Berlin, "English Studies" 218)? Do all students have equal access to those universities, programs, or disciplines accredited to confer degrees that are most likely to open doors to the best-compensated professions? How? Why (Ohmann 683)? We might also consider the material consequences of flexible accumulation on those living in technology-poor countries.

In short, approaching students' language needs and rights in terms of how they do language might help faculty and students avoid the trap of either ignoring or surrendering to current pressures to turn the academy into a mere training ground for corporate berths. As many cultural critics have argued, corporate America calls for "workers who are at once creative and aggressive in identifying and solving problems and submissive and unquestioningly cooperative in carrying out the orders of superiors" (Berlin, "English Studies" 221; *see also* Blitz and Hurlbert). Foregrounding our need and right to deliberate over how we do language can help us turn the orders of corporate America on their head: to train workers who are creative and aggressive in identifying not only those problems and solutions we have been ordered by global capital to produce and circulate but also those problems and solutions we have been ordered to render peripheral, irrelevant, or even erroneous. Then students might gain access not only to the language tools they have been ordered to acquire by the regime of flexible accumulation but also to ways of working on those tools and skills in the interest of building a more sustainable world for all.

Let me end with a quick invocation. As Smitherman reminds us, one cannot erase "with the stroke of a pen" long-held attitudes and deeply entrenched biases transmitted through the generations. Those working consciously and unconsciously to perpetuate essentialist notions of language and functionalist approaches to literacy are "products of the school (and the college, though in fewer numbers) because everybody goes through school" (370). School is a major player in shaping language attitudes. So is, I'd like to add, home—patriarchal or alternative, public or private. The stories of language we tell in college classrooms across the curriculum matter because all college classrooms are involved, to different extents, in producing not only the nation's future K-through-12–level teachers but also the adult part of homes. Composition studies needs to find more creative ways of sharing with faculty and students across the curriculum the many counter stories we have to tell about our students' rights and needs to deliberate over how they do language so that we have a better chance of dislodging the academy's current commitments to diversity, interdisciplinarity, and active learning from the tyranny of linguistic imperialism.

Notes

1. The kinds of word work I have in mind here are compatible with the kind of "cross-boundary discourses" Jacquelyn Jones Royster calls for ("When"), the tactics of "rhetorical listening" Krista Ratcliffe proposes ("Rhetorical Listening"), the movement "besides ourselves" for which Susan C. Jarratt argues ("Besides"), the "rhetorical sovereignty" Scott Lyons depicts American Indians as striving for ("Rhetorical Sovereignty"), the "deliberative discourse" outlined by Dennis A. Lynch and his colleagues ("Agonistic"), and the "critical affirmation" I have posed ("Redefining").

2. See Nedra Reynolds on the need to treat reading and writing as "made possible by forms of dwelling as well as forms of travel" (564).

18 Working with Difference: Critical Race Studies and the Teaching of Composition

GARY A. OLSON

> Race is an inevitable feature of the classroom; it is the ineluctable product
> of the racialization of American society.
> —Michael Eric Dyson, "Race and the Public Intellectual"

In April of 1992, Los Angeles was rocked by devastating riots after three police officers were acquitted of "assault under color of authority" for the brutal beating of Rodney King. The riots were responsible for fifty deaths, for nearly a billion dollars in property damage, and for focusing the national public attention on issues of race relations and cultural difference. It was in an attempt to quell these riots, to cool the heat of racial passions, that King himself addressed the nation and uttered the haunting question that will forever signify liberal anxiety: "Can't we all just get along?" In six short words, King had in effect managed to express an entire political philosophy that had begun as far back as seventeenth-century England, a philosophy impelled by bourgeois dread of conflict; white, middle-class fear of otherness (how ironic that these six words were uttered by a working-class black man); liberal insistence on papering over all cultural difference by insisting that "deep down" all humans are "the same," that our differences are only on the surface ("skin-deep," as they say) and thus are of little consequence.

This liberal ideology of homogenization has been a part of American political philosophy since the inception of the United States as an independent nation, and it is perhaps represented most aptly in the metaphor of the melting pot. This image of homogenization, of the blending of all difference into one single mass, is so burned into the consciousness of all citizens that it hardly seems conceivable to question whether a melting pot really is a desirable approach to constructing a multicultural society, whether erasing cultural difference benefits all citizens or just those in dominant positions, whether what melts away is really all the ethnic and racial traits that mark certain people as *not* white, *not* Western European, *not* Christian, and so on. So ingrained in the national imaginary is this understanding of what a true democracy is, that to many it hardly seems worthwhile to train a critical lens on it. Yet, difference, especially racial difference, has become a key factor of analysis in many contemporary critical discourses, and it is becoming an ever-increasing concern for anyone involved in higher education because the demographics of the student population are shifting dramatically: With each passing year the population becomes more racially, ethnically, and nationally diverse.

As the general population of the U.S. is becoming more diverse, record numbers of minorities and international students are enrolling in college. For example, from 1980 to 1999 the number of African Americans enrolled in college in the U.S. rose by half, the number of Native Americans almost doubled, the number of international students almost doubled, the number of Hispanics almost tripled, and the number of Asian Americans more than tripled. In contrast, the number of whites enrolled in college barely changed (*Chronicle* 20). These trends are expected to intensify in the next few decades. Clearly, in the years to come the student population in U.S. colleges will be substantially different from what it has been throughout the history of higher education in this country: predominately white and middle class. Even a cursory glance at composition scholarship, however, indicates that writing instructors and writing program directors are not well equipped to cope, both pedagogically and administratively, with the influx of students of difference.

Certainly, several scholars in composition have examined issues of race, and increasingly more compositionists are recognizing the importance of race scholarship. Thomas Fox, Keith Gilyard, Gail Y. Okawa, and Jacqueline Jones Royster, among others, have written about composition instruction and people of color, and these have been valuable contributions.[1] Nevertheless, the field has witnessed no sustained examination of race, racism, and the effects of both on composition instruction and effective writing program administration. Of course, it is true that many compositionists have attempted to address multiculturalism in general, often by appealing to Mary Louise Pratt's concept of the contact zone, but, as I have argued elsewhere, although compositionists have appropriated the contact zone metaphor to interrogate how teachers exercise power and authority, especially in the multicultural classroom, some have tended to deploy it in such a way as to defend a kind of liberal pluralism, thereby subverting attempts to come to terms with the truly colonizing effects of the pedagogical scenario. In this paper, I will suggest that to be prepared for the level of diversity that we can expect in the student population in the years to come, compositionists should become familiar with scholarship in critical race theory; doing so will help us extend and broaden the critique of race already begun by scholars such as those I just mentioned.[2]

The Origins of Critical Race Theory

Critical race theory is an intellectual movement dedicated to interrogating how dominant society constructs and represents both race and racism. It pays particular attention to how power and domination are always already inherent in racial relations and to how society's governing institutions, especially the law, enforce a regime of domination and subordination on all people vis-à-vis their race.[3] Although critical race theorists write from a variety of perspectives, employ a number of critical methodologies, and address a substantial array of interrelated (and sometimes unrelated) issues, they are united in a common project: to examine how and why U.S. society is organized according to a system of white privilege and minority subordination and to make interventions in our social practices— especially the law—in an attempt to change society's perceptions, understanding, and representations of race.

Although several crosscurrents contributed to the creation of critical race theory, the two most important are the civil rights movement and the critical legal studies movement. Although critical race theory emerged from these two movements, it is in effect a reaction against them. Critical legal studies is an oppositional discourse within legal studies devoted to examining the operations of the law and legal discourse from an ideologically leftist and activist perspective. It draws on various critical discourses (feminist, Marxist, and poststructuralist theory, in particular) to construct a critique of the legal establishment's standard operating procedures and the assumptions underlying those procedures. A central tenet of critical legal studies is that the law is not and cannot be neutral or disinterested, despite the prevailing mythology that justice is (and should be) blind. Critical legal studies scholars challenge this and many of the foundational beliefs that undergird the legal system in the United States. Since the 1970s, these oppositional scholars have amassed an impressive body of scholarship and have thereby established critical legal studies as one of the most important forms of critical theory in contemporary thought. Although some critical legal studies scholars did address race as a key factor in their analyses, little attempt was made to fully interrogate the dynamics of racial power. That is, although critical legal studies constituted a full-fledged challenge to the legal system's complicity in perpetuating regimes of domination and subordination, it failed, in the eyes of some, to provide an adequate account of how race is a central component of those very systems. As such, in the area of race, it was by default complicitous with the very legal system it had sought to contest. Dissatisfied with the failure of critical legal studies to recognize the centrality of race in its critiques, a number of members broke with the group in 1989 and formed critical race theory.[4]

These same secessionists were also dissatisfied with the mainstream civil rights movement. Specifically, mainstream society, with the blessing of the civil rights movement's leadership, subscribed to a notion of racism as mostly an individual act, not a systemic social condition. Racism was (and is) defined primarily as the actions of individual agents: people who hurl derogatory epithets, burn crosses on lawns, refuse to rent apartments to minorities, or insist on hiring only whites. Because racism was conceived in the popular imaginary only as the vicious acts of ignorant or irrational people, it seemed to follow that the main error here was to believe that race was significant, that someone's racial background mattered. Consequently, issues of racial difference were conveniently swept under the carpet on the premise that race consciousness was the problem in the first place. The effect of equating racism with race consciousness, of conceiving of racism as the transgressions of the few rather than as the way that social relations are organized in this society, was to place out of bounds any substantive analysis of the everyday practices and assumptions of ordinary citizens as well as the normal operations of society's institutions, including the family, the law, and education. The founders of critical race theory insisted that race very much matters, that far from being the genesis of racism, race consciousness is an important analytical tool that allows us to examine social and legal relations in contemporary society—and, perhaps, to alter those relations for the better.

By the 1980s, the opposite of race consciousness, *color blindness,* had become firmly entrenched as a principle in legal thought. Most legal scholars believed that the law and other social institutions could and should recognize and then eliminate all instances of race consciousness (and the biases thought to arise from it) from social, legal, and political policy. The legal establishment's approach to the interrelationships of race, racism, and law arose from a single ideological perspective: Race consciousness is to be avoided at all costs. To critical race theorists, however, ignoring racial difference is a way to maintain and even perpetuate the status quo with all of its deeply institutionalized injustices to racial minorities; that is, dismissing the importance of race is a way to guarantee that institutionalized and systematic racism continues and even prospers. They argued that the only way to eradicate racism is precisely to become *more* race conscious, to analyze and then highlight how race is often a submerged issue in the law, in policy making, in pedagogy, and in everyday practices.

One reason why the legal establishment adopted the perspective that race consciousness should be avoided at all costs is that traditional legal scholarship assumed that the law is distinct from politics, that the law operates in a precinct above or outside of the political. This traditional notion of the law assumed that the law is always neutral, unbiased, apolitical, and disinterested—an attribute symbolized by the statue of blind Justice judiciously weighing the facts in her scales. This faith in the inherent rationality of the law and of legal agents caused many people to assume that over time racism would gradually be extirpated as the law in its boundless wisdom methodically expunged such vestiges of irrationality from society. By the time that critical race theory was formed, critical legal studies scholars had already launched a massive assault on such thinking, pointing out that the notion of law as disinterested is yet another instance of Enlightenment rationalism writ large in the institution of law. All institutions and their agents are always already operating from within ideological perspectives and according to specific interests; indeed, it is impossible to operate otherwise. What these scholars did *not* do, however, was address the question of race and race consciousness adequately. Although the general critique of the law's fundamental interestedness was a necessary first step in exposing the law's complicity in regimes of domination and subordination, it did not go far enough in the eyes of those who founded the critical race theory movement.

In short, critical race theory arose primarily from an attempt both to revive, reenergize, and redirect a body of languishing civil rights scholarship and to extend the critique begun by critical legal studies scholars so that it more fully examined the dynamics of race and how institutions operate to maintain racial inequity. Thus, critical race theory was simultaneously a critical intervention in the discourse on race and an intervention in critical discourse itself. Although critical race theory began as a movement of legal scholars, it quickly spread throughout the academy, especially into the field of education.

Interrogating Race and Racism

> In part, what makes race a confounding problem and what causes many people to not know what race is, is the view that the problems of race are the problems of the racial minority. They are not. The problems of race belong to all of us, no matter where our ancestors come from, no matter what the color of our skin.
> —*State v. Buggs*

A principal belief of critical race studies is that the law is not simply reflective of racial inequity; it is constitutive of that inequity. The legal system establishes the rules and procedures that allow racism to flourish. Even when it enacts laws ostensibly designed to induce racial harmony or protect minorities from discrimination, it often operates to reinforce hegemonic control over the very people it pretends to liberate and protect. In the same way that feminists have argued that in a patriarchy, the primary institutions, especially the law, will inevitably operate in such a way as to further patriarchy even when it seems to endeavor to ensure gender equality, critical race theorists argue that so, too, in a racist society will the main institutions operate to further hegemonic control over racial minorities, even when these institutions pretend to accomplish the opposite. Thus, racial inequity in the law is not produced simply by a few prejudiced judges and lawmakers; it is shaped by and shapes the law itself. Critical race theory seeks to analyze how institutions such as the law operate to stifle race consciousness and to further racist agendas.

A key theme in critical race theory scholarship is how race is to be defined. Many prominent critical theorists over the last few decades have argued compellingly that race is a social construct more than a biological reality, that although certain racial attributes such as skin color do exist, those attributes go no further than these relatively surface-level signs of difference. This anti-essentialist critique of race emerged in part from the postmodern critique of identity and maintains that race is a convenient category or label that dominant groups employ to further economic and political agendas. This critique points to the fact that at any given time in history, certain groups may or may not be coded as raced. At one time in the United States, for example, Jews, Italians, and the Irish were considered to be nonwhite minorities; as these groups worked their way into the social structure (and as the labor skills they had to offer became more specialized and therefore more valued), they were accepted as white, while their Eastern European cousins were coded as nonwhite. Race, then, is an unstable category, and it is clear that even if human beings were originally divided into separate races, interbreeding over several millennia ensures that by this point in time, there is no such thing as a person reliably and unequivocally representative of a particular race. Thus, this critique insists that race simply does not exist; it is not a valid, "natural," or even useful category. Ironically, this postmodern critique of racial identity seemed to suggest that the newly created critical race theory was irrelevant: If race does not exist, if it is a socially constructed category, then it seems pointless to create an entire area of inquiry on that very concept. While most critical race theorists do believe that race is socially constructed, they point out that it nonetheless carries with it very real, material, substantial consequences. On the basis of race—socially constructed as it may be—people are denied jobs and housing, disproportionately arrested and imprisoned, and discriminated against in education and in just about every important sector of society. That is, being raced in U.S. society has very material consequences. Consequently, critical race scholarship attempts to balance a cognizance that race is more a political than a biological category with an analysis of how this category is deployed in order to maintain and further a system of domination and subordination based on race.

Central to critical race thought (and antithetical to the melting pot notion of difference) is the understanding that cultural differences cannot legitimately be isolated and considered separately from one another. That is, few people possess a single, immediately distinguishable, monolithic identity. You might be Asian *and* female *and* lesbian *and* a single mother *and* working class. Or you might be African American *and* female *and* upper-middle class, and so on. People are differently inflected by cultural difference and inhabit multiple and overlapping cultural identities. Membership in one form of cultural identity—Latina, say—reveals very little beyond this surface-level characteristic; it does not reveal what other racial and ethnic backgrounds a person may inhabit, how social class has combined with that background, what political allegiances arise from that person's background and experiences, and so on. Thus, while race consciousness is at the center of critical race theory analysis, so, too, is the understanding that considering one form of cultural difference independent of the other forms of difference that intersect with it is to perform a kind of analytical violence. A productive understanding of race and cultural difference is nuanced, sensitive to the complex interplay of multiple forms of difference.

One reason why so many people in this country tend to simplify issues of race and other forms of difference is that we seem to have fallen into a mode in which African Americans are by default held up as the prototypical or exemplary racial minority while members of other racial groups are ignored or subsumed under this umbrella category. In other words, we tend to think race literally in black-and-white terms, assuming that African Americans somehow stand in for or represent all nonwhite others. This dualistic conceptual framework is evident in legal and political discourse, in social policy, and in the classroom. Critical race theory seeks to think race not in this traditional black-and-white framework but in a framework that accounts for the multiplicity of intersecting racial and other cultural differences. At the same time, it assumes that minorities are differently raced, that dominant society "races" oppressed groups in different ways—in ways that tend to further dominant society's economic and material use of those groups. For example, we are not likely to hear Asians being typed as lazy and indolent, or hear African Americans being called foreigners and asked to produce green cards, or find Hispanics being classified as inscrutable bookworms who may very well be spies to boot. Part of the difficulty here is that the one word *race* is inadequate for describing the monumentally complex reality that it purports to characterize. In articulating a more sophisticated understanding of race and racism, critical race theory hopes to rectify some of these problems.

Underlying much of the perceived racism in this country is an elaborate system of white privilege.[5] Given how society is structured, those of us who are white, by virtue of being white, reap a disproportionate share of advantages and benefits—in the same way that those of us who are male, by virtue of being male, reap a disproportionate share of advantages and benefits. White privilege represents an intricate structure of unearned benefits that someone enjoys simply by being born into the dominant order. What's more, these advantages and benefits are typically invisible to those who experience them and are thus easily taken for granted. For example, unless unusual factors come into play, most whites can expect to go shopping without being scrutinized by store detectives, can expect to rent or buy a house in any part of town that they can afford, can drive down a suburban street without being stopped "on suspicion," and can generally go through daily life without their race being an impediment or even an issue.[6] The same cannot be said of most racial minorities. In other words, racism is a much more subtle and invidious phenomenon than the occasional person who utters hate speech; it is deeply ingrained in the fabric of society and thus touches each of us. In an article entitled "The Other Reader," Joe Harris argues that in cultural studies classes it is tempting and all too easy to assume that it is some *other* reader of a cultural text who may be "duped" by that text but not ourselves, that we are somehow above or immune from such traps; in the same way, we tend to believe that racism is something that infects and affects some *other* person, never ourselves.[7] Critical race theory brings to the foreground the workings of racism in the daily lives of all citizens, and it illustrates that we are all complicitous in a system of domination and subordination, advantage and disadvantage, structured according to racial categories.

One attempt to address the intricacies of white privilege and questions of race consciousness is the emerging area of critical whiteness studies—an area that in part grew out of critical race theory. This new area of investigation seeks to understand how we construct and represent whiteness. In the same way that critical race theory interrogates how nonwhite "races" are constructed, represented, and then assigned particular advantages or, usually, disadvantages as a result of those representations, critical whiteness studies is interrogating how whiteness is part of a similar process. As far back as the 1970s, some scholars called for critical intellectuals interested in social justice to begin to study whiteness as a race. Although it may have taken much longer than many of us would have liked, the study of whiteness is finally becoming an important and valuable area of inquiry.

Race Consciousness and Composition

At the very least, a familiarity with critical race studies better prepares us to devise pedagogies and writing programs that are sensitive to the complex issues of race and race consciousness.[8] It provides insight into how dominant society constructs and represents both race and racism and into how power and domination are always already inherent in racial relations. It makes us aware that if we equate racism with race consciousness, if we assume that racism means simply the transgressions of the few rather than the way that social relations are organized in this society, we preclude substantive analysis of the everyday practices and assumptions of ordinary citizens. We would understand instead that race very much matters, that race consciousness is an important analytical tool that allows us to examine our own pedagogies, writing programs, and institutions—and, perhaps, to alter them for the better. We would understand that our institutions are not simply reflective of racial inequity but are constitutive of that inequity and, thus, that we must structure our pedagogies and writing programs with great care. Importantly, we would understand that while race is primarily a social construction, it nonetheless carries with it very real, material, substantial consequences— consequences such as the denial of desirable jobs and housing and widespread discrimination in education and other important sectors of society. That is, we would be keenly aware that being raced in U.S. society has significant and tangible repercussions in people's lives.

Furthermore, we would know that cultural differences cannot legitimately be isolated and considered separately from one another, that few people possess a single, immediately distinguishable identity, that considering one form of cultural difference independent of the other forms of difference that intersect with it is to perform a kind of categorical or analytical violence. We instead would develop a more productive understanding of race and cultural difference, one that is nuanced and sensitive to the complex interplay of multiple forms of difference. In addition, we would be careful not to hold up one race as the prototypical or exemplary racial minority while ignoring members of other racial groups or subsuming them under one umbrella category. At the same time, we would assume that minorities are differently raced, that dominant society races oppressed groups in different ways—in ways that tend to further dominant society's economic and material use of these groups. We would, thus, strive to articulate a more sophisticated understanding of race and racism. What's more, we would be cognizant of and sensitive to the elaborate system of white privilege in which those of us who are white reap a disproportionate share of advantages and benefits, a structure of unearned benefits that some people enjoy simply by being born into the dominant order. In short, we would understand that racism is a much more subtle and pernicious phenomenon than the occasional person who utters hate speech; it is deeply ingrained in the social fabric and thus touches each of us. Racism operates in the daily lives of all citizens, and we are all therefore complicitous in a system of domination and subordination, advantage and disadvantage, structured according to racial categories. In fact, those of us who are white might even be tempted to begin to examine how whiteness is constructed and represented and how it functions within a system of racial supremacy.

As teachers of composition and administrators of writing programs, such knowledge will help us respond productively to the issues that are certain to become increasingly more prominent in our classrooms and programs as our student populations become more diverse. Such knowledge will help prevent us from making serious mistakes in our pedagogical approaches. For example, consider a confrontation that occurred in a peer-editing session that Andrea Greenbaum describes in a recent *Composition Forum* article. In that session, Brian, a white student, was editing a paper written by Johnnie, an African American classmate. When Brian pointed out that Johnnie was inconsistent in how he spelled certain words in his rendering of colloquial dialogue, Johnnie became irate and accused Brian of blatant racism. Johnnie insisted that Brian had accused him of being unable to spell and that he was doing so precisely because Johnnie was African American. Although Brian attempted to console Johnnie by declaring that he was only pointing out a matter of inconsistency, Johnnie remained indignant, and the other African American students in class united in solidarity with Johnnie. At that point, according to Greenbaum,

> Instantly, the class divided along racial lines, with the African American students erupting in shouts to Brian that he was racist and that his comment was inappropriate. Not surprisingly, the white students sided with Brian, arguing that his question was a legitimate one and that his job as editor and facilitator was to bring up all matters related to the text. (2)

Greenbaum realized that she had lost control of her class, and she felt trapped, a white woman instructor caught between collective black anger and equally collective and growing white anger. Rather than addressing the issues head-on and turning the situation into a pedagogical opportunity, Greenbaum dismissed class and, sadly, never discussed the situation further with her students. Johnnie never returned to class after that incident.

Clearly, this narrative is an example of how volatile race relations can become in the composition classroom, how racial anger can percolate to the surface and extinguish any possibility of learning—writing or anything else. Simply put, it is an example of how *not* to deal with race in the composition classroom. The instructor could have capitalized on this episode, intervening productively to lead students into discussions about the power of language, the capacity of language to injure people, the nature of colloquial dialogue, and questions of racial stereotyping and racial sensitivity. Rather than turn away from conflict, rather than echo Rodney King's plea that we just get along, the instructor had an exceptional opportunity to transform this confrontation into a powerful learning experience for the entire class—an experience that had the potential not only to enable the students to learn something about race but also to enable the classmates to work more productively with one another throughout the rest of the semester, thereby increasing the likelihood that they would learn more about the intricacies of language and composition. In Greenbaum's class, these rich opportunities dissolved, and the class was by all accounts a disaster. Johnnie left the class in humiliation, the white students were allowed to feel righteous, and the African American students remained disgruntled and resistant throughout the semester, accusing the instructor—and with good reason, as she herself points out—of being complicit with Brian's racism. In this class, *everybody* lost out, students and instructor. The mishandled dynamics of the class not only prevented any increased awareness of race, they virtually assured that the students learned very little about writing that semester.

Fortunately, Greenbaum was able in retrospect to draw some lessons from this scenario, so perhaps not all was lost. Her reading of works in postcolonial theory and critical race theory enabled her to revisit her disastrous class from a new perspective. She was able to step out of her previous perspective and to view the events from Johnnie's point of view; and, most importantly, she learned not to run from conflict but to embrace it, to turn it into a learning experience for all concerned. If the statistics about the changing demographics of the student population that I rehearsed in the beginning of this chapter suggest anything, it is that it is incumbent upon all of us to learn as much as possible about the dynamics of race. As teachers, we need to equip ourselves with the knowledge and sensitivity that will prevent us from making the same mistakes that Greenbaum did. As administrators, we can prevent similar difficulties by introducing readings and discussions of critical race theory into our teaching practica and training sessions for new teaching assistants and adjunct instructors. And of course, those of us who teach composition from a cultural studies perspective can always directly introduce readings in critical race theory for reading and class discussion. At the end of this chapter is a list of selected readings appropriate for both composition instructors and writing students.

Critical race theory, then, provides a conceptual framework from which we can prepare ourselves to be responsive to the increasingly more diverse student population. It equips us with a knowledge of the otherwise submerged or invisible operations of race and other forms of difference. With that knowledge, we can devise pedagogies and structure writing programs that speak to the needs of all, not just part, of our constituents. With that knowledge, we can sensitively and effectively deal with administrative and interpersonal conflicts in the "contact zone." With that knowledge we can enrich scholarship in rhetoric and composition, focusing the lens of critical race theory on how discourse itself helps to reinscribe regimes of domination and subordination, especially vis-à-vis race.

Notes

I would like to thank Allison Brimmer, Colleen Connolly, Toni Francis, Merry Perry, Deepa Sitaraman, and Lynn Worsham for commenting on drafts of this paper.

1. For other excellent works on race by compositionists, see Shirley Wilson Logan, Catherine Prendergast, Krista Ratcliffe, Thomas R. West, and Lynn Worsham.

2. I am purposely assuming a primarily white audience for this paper because the demographics of the field are such that the great preponderance of writing instructors are white, although the number of people of color in the field seems to be increasing of late. In addition, I assume that most people of color are already acutely aware of critical race theory and the issues it addresses.

3. Where I say *law* in this paper, one could just as easily and appropriately read *education* or *pedagogy*.

4. Most critical race theorists date the formal origin of the group to its first conference in 1989. Friction had grown between many critical legal studies scholars and those members who were doing race analysis, and, as a consequence, the new group was formed; however, it is true that the members who broke off to form the new group had been engaged in critical race scholarship since the late 1970s. Founding members included Derrick Bell, Kimberlé Crenshaw, Richard Delgado, Neil Gotanda, Angela Harris, Charles Lawrence, Mari Matsuda, Stephanie Phillips, Patricia Williams, and others.

5. Marilyn Frye argues that we should stop speaking of "racism" and should instead start speaking of "white supremacy" because this term more accurately identifies the root of the problem.

6. Over the years, many compositionists have used Peggy McIntosh's famous article on white privilege as a reading and discussion prompt. Although McIntosh is not part of the critical race theory movement, her attempt to raise consciousness about how white privilege is part and parcel of the structure of racism that characterizes this society is illustrative of the kinds of analysis done by critical race theorists in an attempt to raise race consciousness.

7. Thomas West makes this very point in "The Racist Other."

8. Of course, critical race theory may also have more direct benefits. Those of us who center writing classes on important cultural issues such as sexism and

racism will find that there are quite a few critical race theory texts that would serve as excellent materials for reading and class discussion.

Selected Readings in Critical Race Theory

Armour, Jody David. *Negrophobia and Reasonable Racism: The Hidden Costs of Being Black in America.* New York: New York UP, 1997.

Bell, Derrick A., Jr. "Brown v. Board of Education and the Interest-Convergence Dilemma." *Harvard Law Review* 93 (1980): 518–33.

———. *Faces at the Bottom of the Well: The Permanence of Racism.* New York: Basic, 1993.

———. *Race, Racism, and American Law.* 4th ed. New York: Aspen, 2000.

———. "Racial Realism." *Connecticut Law Review* 24 (1992): 363–79.

———. "Serving Two Masters: Integration Ideals and Client Interests in School Desegregation Litigation." *Yale Law Journal* 85 (1976): 470–516.

Cameron, Christopher David Ruiz. "How the García Cousins Lost Their Accents: Understanding the Language of Title VII Decisions Approving English-Only Rules as the Product of Racial Dualism, Latino Invisibility, and Legal Indeterminacy." *California Law Review* 85 (1997): 1347–93.

Carbado, Devon. *Black Men on Race, Gender, and Sexuality: A Critical Reader.* New York: New York UP, 1999.

Chang, Robert S. *Disoriented: Asian Americans, Law, and the Nation-State.* New York: New York UP, 1999.

Crenshaw, Kimberly, et al. *Critical Race Theory: The Key Writings That Formed the Movement.* New York: New, 1996.

Delgado, Richard. "Campus Antiracism Rules: Constitutional Narratives in Collision." *Northwestern University Law Review* (1991): 343–87.

———. "Rodrigo's Fourteenth Chronicle: American Apocalypse." *Harvard Civil Rights–Civil Liberties Law Review* (1997): 275–99.

Delgado, Richard, and Jean Stefancic. *Critical Race Theory: An Introduction.* New York: New York UP, 2001.

———, eds. *Critical Race Theory: The Cutting Edge.* 2nd ed. Philadelphia: Temple UP, 2000.

Flagg, Barbara J. *Was Blind, but Now I See: White Race Consciousness and the Law.* New York: New York UP, 1997.

Guinier, Lani. "Groups, Representation, and Race-Conscious Districting: A Case of the Emperor's Clothes." *Texas Law Review* 71 (1993): 1589–642.

———. *Lift Every Voice: Turning a Civil Rights Setback into a New Vision of Social Justice.* New York: Simon, 1998.

———. "No Two Seats: The Elusive Quest for Political Equality." *Virginia Law Review* 77 (1991): 1413–514.

———. "The Triumph of Tokenism: The Voting Rights Act and the Theory of Black Electoral Success." *Michigan Law Review* 89 (1991): 1077–154.

———. *The Tyranny of the Majority: Fundamental Fairness in Representative Democracy.* New York: Free, 1994.

Harris, Paul. *Black Rage Confronts the Law.* New York: New York UP, 1999.

López, Gerald P. "Undocumented Mexican Migration: In Search of a Just Immigration Law and Policy." *University of California Los Angeles Law Review* 28 (1981): 615–714.

López, Ian F. Haney. *White by Law: The Legal Construction of Race.* New York: New York UP, 1998.

Matsuda, Mari J., et al. *Words That Wound: Critical Race Theory, Assaultive Speech, and the First Amendment.* Boulder, CO: Westview, 1993.

Rodríguez, Clara E. *Changing Race: Latinos, the Census, and the History of Ethnicity in the United States.* New York: New York UP, 2000.

Russell, Katheryn K. *The Color of Crime: Racial Hoaxes, White Fear, Black Protectionism, Police Harassment, and Other Macroaggressions.* New York: New York UP, 1997.

Russell, Margaret M. "Law and Racial Reelism: Black Women as Celluloid 'Legal' Heroines." *Feminism, Media, and the Law.* Ed. Martha A. Fineman and Martha T. McCluskey. London: Oxford UP, 1997. 136–45.

———. "Race and the Dominant Gaze: Narratives of Law and Inequality in Popular Film." *Legal Studies Forum* 15 (1991): 243–54.

Williams, Patricia J. *Alchemy of Race and Rights: Diary of a Law Professor.* Cambridge: Harvard UP, 1991.

Wing, Adrien Katherine, ed. *Critical Race Feminism: A Reader.* New York: New York UP, 1997.

———, ed. *Global Critical Race Feminism: An International Reader.* New York: New York UP, 2000.

19 From Classroom to Program

RESPONSE BY JOSEPH HARRIS

What worried me about the conference of writing program administrators at Miami University was how little talk there was about administering writing programs. I heard much that interested me about teaching after September 11, about ways of defining composition as a field of study, about how taking on an administrative position can redirect the trajectory of a career, and especially about how we might rethink the work we do with students in writing courses—but I heard little about how the efforts of individual teachers might be imagined and supported as part of the collective work of a program. Summing up the history and prospects of composition for the special millennium issue of *PMLA*, David Bartholomae writes that "the problem of staffing will dominate the next decade" ("Composition" 1954), suggesting that the structures of programs—who teaches, with what training, and for what pay—will continue to decisively shape what goes on in the writing classrooms within them. These are precisely the sorts of institutional issues that many WPAs are well positioned to influence, but we cannot do so simply by advocating particular approaches to teaching. We need instead to learn how to think about programs as well as classrooms, about the workforce as well as the curriculum of composition.

In responding to the essays here by Gary A. Olson and Min-Zhan Lu, then, I find myself trying to imagine what consequences their views might hold for me not only as an individual teacher or intellectual but also as someone charged with directing and representing the work of a program faculty. So, for instance, when Olson argues that critical race theory can help us "understand that our institutions are not simply reflective of racial inequity but are constitutive of that inequity and, thus, that we must structure our pedagogies and writing programs with great care," I would like to know more about what such care might involve. If it merely means urging mostly white, middle-class teachers to change how they discuss race with mostly white, middle-class students, then the impact of critical race theory on work in composition will be slight. What if we instead drew on such theory to ask why so many composition programs still routinely sort students into categories—"basic," "mainstream," "honors," "exempt"—that correspond insidiously with divisions of race, ethnicity, and social class? What if we worked less at changing what teachers and students talk about and more on changing who is in the room? How might we create programs that speak to the needs and interests of minority and working-class students or that recruit faculty of color to join our work? I don't have any ready answers to such questions—although, ironically, I am confident enough in my ability to lead an informed classroom discussion about race in America. But that's my point. The most pressing task facing us now is not retheorizing the writing classroom but reforming the institutions in which we work.

So, while I agree with Lu that we need to help students learn how to analyze corporate discourse and to resist "pressures to turn the academy into a mere training ground for corporate berths," I also wonder about the power of a form of critique that rarely circulates outside the classroom. In *Work Time*, Evan Watkins points to the disconnect between the subversive value that English professors like to assign to the work they do in their courses and the ways in which a good grade earned in English often functions outside those courses simply as proof for future employers that a student is verbally adept. The ability to analyze corporate discourse, for instance, will surely be a prized asset for any student planning to enter the corporate world. And while critiquing Microsoft ads may awaken some students to the workings of power in language, such a task is also likely to function as simply one more assignment to be completed for others. I don't think this is a problem that can be solved at the level of the individual classroom. However, I do think that writing *programs* might throw some static into the hegemonic flow of grades, meanings, and values by making certain kinds of subaltern intellectual work more visible—by sponsoring student journals, Web sites, and essay contests, for instance; or by listing writing courses by instructor, title, and description (rather than simply by section) in college catalogs; or by creating forums for college faculty to discuss their work as teachers with one another; or by publishing goals and standards for composition courses that do more than simply echo tired calls for clarity and correctness.

I have long been committed to working with beginning undergraduates, and my hunch is that Olson, Lu, and I teach similar sorts of writing courses. Certainly, I admire the kinds of work with students that they describe in their essays. However, to achieve the political goals that Olson and Lu argue for, I think we need to speak and act not just as teachers (and not just to one another) but as public advocates of reform in our programs, departments, colleges, and universities. This was a theme that arose often in response to the talks given by Olson and Lu at Miami. Elizabeth Vander Lei asked how, given finite resources, we might try to equip teachers to attempt new and critical sorts of work in writing classrooms, and Charles Schuster particularized this question by suggesting that as program directors we need to realize that we are often in the position of asking young and inexperienced instructors to attempt a difficult and volatile form of teaching. Peter Mortensen asked whether and how institutional critique might lead to institutional reform, and Alice Gilliam similarly wondered how we might make critical race theory more than just a subject of classroom talk and writing. Donte Cornish continued this line of thought by asking how we can try to build writing programs whose faculty more fully reflect the racial and class diversity of the students we teach. These are urgent questions for those of us charged with directing the intellectual and institutional work of composition. I hope they will soon be taken up in books like this.

Part 7   What Political and Social Issues Have Shaped Composition Studies in the Past and Will Shape This Field in the Future?

20 Composition and the Critical Moment

KEITH GILYARD

Not long ago, with a fairly quick sweep of the bookshelves in my office, I scooped up such books as Barry Kanpol's *Critical Pedagogy*, Ira Shor and Caroline Pari's *Critical Literacy in Action*, and Cathy Fleisher and David Schaafsma's *Literacy and Democracy*, which includes an essay, "Three Codifications of Critical Literacy," by Thomas Philion. Caught in this movement was a handful of journals with articles such as Min-Zhan Lu's "Redefining the Literate Self: The Politics of Critical Affirmation," Lu and Bruce Horner's "The Problematic of Experience: Redefining Critical Work in Ethnography and Pedagogy," Robert P. Yagelski's "The Ambivalence of Reflection: Critical Pedagogies, Identity, and the Writing Teacher," and a review essay by Gary A. Olson titled "Critical Pedagogy and Composition Scholarship," in which he reviews several works including Judith Goleman's *Working Theory: Critical Composition Studies for Students and Teachers*. Goleman's book was also reviewed in a different journal by Thomas E. Recchio in an essay titled "Some Versions of Critical Pedagogy." In short order, I also happened upon Gesa E. Kirsch's review essay, "Feminist Critical Pedagogy and Composition," in which Carmen Luke and Jennifer Gore's *Feminisms and Critical Pedagogy* is among the books discussed. Included in my haul was Amy Goodburn's "Processing the 'Critical' in Literacy Research: Issues of Authority, Ownership, and Representation."

I sensed I could quickly generate, right in my office, a fairly current Top-40 list of composition-studies hits with the word *critical* in their titles. I also figured I could simultaneously get to work on a critical-pedagogy hall of fame by pulling oldies but goodies from my shelves like Paulo Freire's *Education for Critical Consciousness* and including works that are not titled as critical but are integrally connected to the aforementioned scholarship. I am thinking of essays like Kate Ronald and Hephzibah Roskelly's "Untested Feasibility: Imagining the Pragmatic Possibility of Paulo Freire" and various entries by Henry A. Giroux, the most notable for my current purposes being *Corporate Culture and the Attack on Higher*

Education and Public Schooling. So, such discourse encoded immediately around me is what I was calling the *critical moment,* a moment that certainly began before the first Composition in the Twenty-First Century Conference in 1993 but has gained much greater discursive force, as I am indicating, since then. Moreover, the voluminous outpouring of critical writings in and of themselves seems to constitute a significant variable impacting composition studies. Olson and Yagelski suggest that critical has gone mainstream. It is almost as if we could all chant, on three, textual production inscribed by asymmetrical power relations.

I did not have a specific crisis in mind as I attempted to assess this moment although critical pedagogy addresses itself generally to long-standing social inequity and other vagaries of life under late capitalism. However, a specific crisis was made manifest on September 11, 2001 as we moved past the beginnings of the commercial and the mathematical millennia to the onset of the political one. Composition studies could not help but address this development in significant ways. Whatever else was at stake with composition teaching, whatever a practitioner or theorist had wished to advocate about students as rational subjects, cognitive objects, pawns, postmodern wonders, or radically democratic agents in training and regardless of expressions about identity formations relative to such conceptions, all pedagogy was jolted to its very foundations—or antifoundations if you prefer. How the numerous essays related to the World Trade Center and Pentagon bombings written by students under the auspices of composition studies are produced and consumed—again, sheer volume signals a considerable social force—will have a major impact on directions taken by the American citizenry. This is not to suggest that no other events of great political magnitude loom on the horizon. Surely, such events always will, although one hopes the consequences are not so horrible. Nonetheless, if a major strand in student texts of exploring issues of internationalism persists, as I suspect it will, and if concomitant concerns about domestic security and the proper measure of civil liberties also remain popular writing topics, as I also imagine will be the case, and if teachers and scholars have parallel responses, as I am surmising, then we will look back upon the bombings as the events that ushered in this particular era of composition studies. Thus, the dynamics surrounding that watershed event ought to be examined as carefully as we can manage, which means in part to frame them historically and theoretically as we continue to search for the best lessons to be learned. What I aim to do in this chapter, therefore, is to link pedagogical concerns grounded in the September 11 occurrences and their aftermath to the broader critical configuration inside which they function.

At the 1993 conference, James A. Berlin sketched a still-relevant explanation of some of the large social forces that were affecting and would affect higher education in general and composition studies in particular. Specifically, he described the shift from a Fordist to a post-Fordist economy, that is, the movement from classic assembly-line production to what David Harvey, echoed by Lu in this volume, termed the regime of flexible accumulation. Under the former arrangement, set-up costs were relatively high, which meant that long cycles of consumption for particular products were encouraged—and markets had to be protected—so that manufacturers could reach the phase in their production processes where their unit costs had decreased dramatically enough to ensure the desired profits. Unskilled manual labor was in great demand, and the managerial component was an extremely bureaucratic sector where creativity by subordinates was little encouraged.

In contrast, the new economy is marked by international competition, global dispersal of manufacturing operations and markets, and an emphasis on diverse and rapidly shifting production. Fewer manual laborers are required, a development accompanied by the rise of a managerial elite who are flexible, nimble, and collaborative and who communicate well in writing, especially through electronic media. According to Berlin, there will be intense competition for these jobs, which will be precious few. In his view, the oft-noted observation that the current generation of college graduates is pessimistic about their financial futures will continue to have resonance. Given some projections, we may now be living in a nation where one-third of the college graduates are unemployed or underemployed (Greenwald). The upshot for educators, among whose number are many compositionists, is that they will be helping to prepare students to pursue jobs in an economy where desirable jobs are becoming increasingly fewer. Part of the good news for writing teachers, information that may ring ironic in some quarters, is that a market emphasis on excellent written communication and collaborative problem-solving lines up well with a pedagogy that stresses the same. This may enable writing instructors to make a case for their continuing relevance, a point not to be overlooked given the creeping corporate tendencies in higher education. However, alignment of curricular goals and market ideals, although a more-than-trivial occurrence, should not function as the total justification for the work of writing teachers; certainly no critical pedagogue would be satisfied with such rationale. The fact remains that a very small number of students, however we teach them, will operate at the highest levels of the post-Fordist economy, so composition instruction, in order to remain widely meaningful, has to stay linked to a mission other than corporate expediency. It is this broader mission that critical pedagogues, and Berlin in particular, have in mind when they call for critical literacy. They advocate that students attain a thorough understanding of the political economy and its attendant discourses in order to achieve an informed evaluation of the social order and to perform an analysis of the best way for them to impact or change the system should they see fit to try, and of course all critical pedagogues want them to try (Berlin, "English Studies" 222–25). Critical composition instructors, the assumption goes, will serve as models of the critically literate citizen with the concomitant commitment to reducing social and economic inequality.

Although Berlin is explicit in his description of the phenomena the critically literate will confront, he is less sharp in defining what critical literacy actually is and suggesting concrete actions. Shor's more recent work is instructive on this score:

> Critical literacy thus challenges the status quo in an effort to discover alternative paths for social and self-development. This kind of literacy—words rethinking worlds, self dissenting in society—connects the political and the personal, the public and the private, the global and the local, the economic and the pedagogical, for reinventing our lives and for promoting justice in place of inequity. (1)

Obviously aware of common charges about theoretical obscurity and vagueness leveled against critical literacy theorists, Shor refuses simply to beg the question of social inequality. Rather, he embellishes his argument with data about alarming child-poverty rates, the digital divide, and ethnic, class, and gender discrimination as well as related wage-parity issues (4–7). In Shor's conception, these issues ought to form the basis of writing curriculums. Indeed, all curricular implementation ought to be judged in light of how it contributes to a critical literacy project.

In *Corporate Culture,* Giroux amplifies the articulations of Berlin and Shor, which he helped to shape, and provides a view of how the tensions suggested play out in an academy under siege by those primarily interested in market values. Giroux defines corporate culture to be an "ensemble of ideological and institutional forces that functions politically and pedagogically to both govern organizational life through senior managerial control and to produce compliant workers, spectorial consumers, and passive citizens" (9). He sees colleges and universities as a major arena inside which a diametrical conflict between conceptions of citizenship is being enacted. On the one hand, citizenship is promoted as privatized, and one's primary social purpose is to amass material wealth. On the other hand, citizenship is viewed as operating in the interest of the greater public good. Of course, there will always be a debate about what the public good is, but by pointing out that more than one-quarter of the nation's children live in poverty, by referencing the attacks on affirmative action, by calling attention to the reduction of government investments in urban development, and by highlighting the increases in funding for corrections along with the corresponding decrease in expenditures for public higher education, Giroux makes a compelling case that in the interest of the many a stronger civil sector needs to be developed as a check on corporate power (11). In this analysis, higher education must be reclaimed or held as a public good, which requires a fight on campuses against corporate encroachment, a movement that itself is marked by downsizing, sponsorship deals with business interests, attempts to abolish tenure, and efforts to undermine or eliminate academic programs whose existences cannot be justified in terms of strict corporate logic (as can composition to some extent). In Giroux's view, as colleges and universities operate in terms of corporate competitiveness, there will be less access to higher education for ethnic minorities and the poor, and access for most students in any case will mean exposure to a pedagogy that preps most students for de-skilled work in the service sector (12–28). Giroux concludes by championing "citizen rights over consumer rights" (43) and calls for an alliance to protect schools as vehicles for promoting radical democracy.

Like Berlin, Giroux is attentive to the corporate call for hires with excellent writing and problem-solving skills. He is aware that such skills help to complete the profile of the managerial elite. In contrast to Berlin, however, (and I don't mean to overstate the distinction), he expresses no value in preparing students for the marketplace unless instruction remains firmly connected to questions of "ethics, equity, and justice" (18).

These latter questions are precisely what concern Lu as she, in painstaking fashion, adds greater clarity and precision to discussions of critical literacy and suggests a way for practitioners to model and thus operationalize it. Understanding literacy as a trope and borrowing terminology from Cornel West, Lu posits a literacy of "critical affirmation." To her, the ideal literate self uses reading and writing

(1) To end oppression rather than to empower a particular form of the self, group, or culture; (2) To grapple with one's privileges as well as one's experience of exclusion; (3) To approach more respectfully and responsibly those histories and experiences which appear different from what one calls one's own; and (4) To affirm a yearning for individual agency shared by individuals across social divisions without losing sight of the different material circumstances which shape this shared yearning and the different circumstances against which each of us must struggle when enacting such a yearning. ("Redefining the Literate Self" 173)

Lu is quite specific about undermining certain hierarchies, which is also evident as she joins Horner to reflect on the converging possibilities offered by critical composition and critical ethnography, constructions they see as countering not only teacher-student hierarchies but those among researchers and teachers. Goodburn is also attuned to the critical possibilities of ethnographic research, as her ideal is to "involve researchers and participants in a highly participatory framework for constructing knowledge, an inquiry that seeks to question, disrupt, or intervene in the conditions under study for some socially transformative end" ("Processing the 'Critical'" 121–22).

Yagelski deepens the practitioner considerations relative to critical pedagogy as he considers the role of teachers with respect to identity conflicts. Probing his own ambivalence as a so-called critical instructor, Yagelski feels that his own angst epitomizes the collective psyche of the critical practitioner group in composition. He reasons that even Freire, whose ideas he celebrates, "is more conflicted and complex than he seems to let on" ("Ambivalence of Reflection" 42). Despite talk of collaboration and co-intentionality, Yagelski observes, Freire did not totally shy away from the role of teacher as deliverer. In the end, Yagelski, aided in his formulations by the healthy skepticism and engagement with critical pedagogy evinced by Richard E. Miller in "The Arts of Complicity," urges us to embrace the authority—as there is no way around it anyway—that comes with being a teacher.

I have intended to show by this brief intellectual mapping that coming into 2001, there was an extensive and clear articulation of critical literacy and critical pedagogy inside composition studies' theoretical, practitioner, and research wings. It was not a monolithic impulse to be sure. There were conceptual shadings and self-conscious resistance, as Philion notes, to formulaic application. Nonetheless, a conglomerate of the critical seemed to be held together rather firmly by a shared commitment, as Kanpol insists, to undermining oppression, alienation, and subordination (137). As crews both literal and metaphoric try to untangle the physical and psychic rubble of a catastrophe, a long-term project to be sure, the critical coalition may face its most severe test in terms of demonstrating its relevance and effectiveness, for critical literacy matters as much these days as it ever will. Enlightened production and consumption of texts—in the broad poststructuralist sense—represent the nation's best chance to make sense of the events of September 11 and chart the best long-range course or, in other words, aim for the best national and international presence and best set of alliances—both intranational and international—in a world seemingly smaller, murkier, and more interdependent than many Americans had sensed it to be. Naturally, I am postulating that much of the preparation needed to sustain enlightened literacy will take place in composition classrooms, where, as indicated earlier, I suspect that foreign-policy discussions will be a major feature of our instructional contact zones, perhaps even surpassing conversation about race, gender, and class—or even talk about border crossings, that ever-popular, postmodern topic.

Indeed, the task for the critical coalition remains formidable and crucial as even a cursory sifting through the textual activity of the weeks immediately following September 11 suggests. I offer two brief examples, emails I received over the span of about a minute, as illustration.

The first message was titled "The Binch" and was parody of the Grinch tale. Authorship was attributed to a Rob Suggs. It begins:

> Every U down in Uville liked U.S. a lot,
> But the Binch, who lived Far East of Uville, did not.
> The Binch hated U.S.! the whole U.S. way!
> Now don't ask me why, for nobody can say,
> It could be his turban was screwed on too tight.
> Or the sun from the desert had beaten too bright
> But I think the most likely reason of all
> May have been that his heart was two sizes too small.

Over the course of eight additional stanzas, it is revealed that the Binch, only one letter away from having an expletive for a name, is irrational, jealous, and attempts to destroy the orderly way of life in Uville and wreck the spirit of the people by stealing U airplanes and crashing them into the Uville Twin Towers, an ultimately ineffective mission because U-Pride and U-Hope prevail. In the final stanza, the author drops Uville for America and our nation, and he asserts that the United States will survive because it is more than tall towers, wealth, and political powers, more than its enemies could ever guess.

The second posting was attributed to Seumas Milne of the British newspaper *The Guardian.* It was titled "Special Report: Terrorism in the U.S." and began:

> Nearly two days after the horrific suicide attacks on civilian workers in New York and Washington, it has become painfully clear that most Americans simply don't get it. From the president to passersby on the street, the message seems to be the same: this is an inexplicable assault on freedom and democracy, which must be answered with overwhelming force—just as soon as someone can construct a credible account of who was actually responsible. Shock, rage and grief there has been aplenty. But any glimmer of recognition of why people might have been driven to carry out such atrocities, sacrificing their own lives in the process—or why the United States is hated with such bitterness, not only in Arab and Muslim countries, but across the developing world—seems almost entirely absent. Perhaps it is too much to hope that, as rescue workers struggle to pull firefighters from the rubble, any but a small minority might make the

connection between what has been visited upon them and what their government has visited upon large parts of the world. But make the connection they must, if such tragedies are not to be repeated, potentially with even more devastating consequences.

The article goes on to lambaste American political leaders and British Prime Minister Tony Blair, rehearse arguments about the United States's displays of economic, diplomatic, and military power around the globe, including the backing of Israel's occupation of the West Bank and even the alliance with Osama bin Laden to depose the communist leader Mohammad Najibullah in Afghanistan.

Obviously, there's a big explanatory gap between "nobody can say . . . may have been that his heart was two sizes too small" and "connection between what has been visited upon them and what their government has visited upon large parts of the world." My purpose is not to criticize harshly these extremes but to outline the wide-ranging nature of the work to be done because as compositionists you will be sure to receive, if you have not already, student papers echoing positions similar to those articulated by Suggs and Milne. Undoubtedly, you will, in addition, receive voluminous musings on various conceptual points in-between. Although I am not at all against the morale boost attempted by Suggs, my outlook happens to be much closer to Milne's than to that of Suggs, as far as explanations go. I like to think that this would not matter that much in a classroom because I characteristically assume that all formulations are provisional and fallible and therefore would be putting pressure on them all, a statement I hope is believable and a point I wish to demonstrate by spending more time criticizing the text I find more persuasive, though I suppose I am open to the charge of being merely dismissive of a point of view I find uncaptivating.

Although Suggs's poem would not be much of a rejoinder to Milne's article, as I imagine many students could readily see, I would also urge them to critique the editorial. They should consult other sources (as should we all) in order to evaluate more fully Milne's spin on historical events. What even counts as a thorough critique? Who gets constructed as the typical American? Furthermore, if Milne's analysis is absolutely correct, what recommendations does it offer for creative direction? Many Americans, more than Milne seems to accept, understand the basic concept of "what goes around, comes around," which implies that what comes around goes around as well. I have heard much analysis in this vein, but the essential question is the question of when and how the go-around–come-around–go-around cycle gets broken. As I have been maintaining, some of the germane and emerging discourse is going to take place in composition classrooms. There is no way around that, and no eluding that social force, and all instructors

certainly have a responsibility to mediate discussion. Those who consider themselves critical teachers will want actively to shape such discourse, attempting to
model a process of full participation in civic affairs. This activity, by the way, is
not restricted to discussions of September 11 but should form the basis for discussions of a wide range of social issues. Tentative yet rigorous examination and
dialogic engagement are key forms of discourse despite the specific political concepts being addressed.

Of course, not all instructors desire to teach in the manner that I or the theorists and practitioners I have mentioned advocate. Some faculty directly oppose
a leftist sort of critical literacy and choose to focus upon the imparting of technical expertise. Others are sympathetic, particularly in the shadow of recent events,
to the politics of self-described critical pedagogues but profess to feel the student
and institutional pulls to teach where the commas go. I suggest mildly to both
groups that style will not be practiced upon thin air but in texts, and that all texts
are inherently political as are all teaching postures. No real contradiction exists
between facilitating technical expertise and helping students develop more critical sensibilities. The latter activity may be the greatest boost to the former. I also
suggest to all teachers, following Kanpol, that critical pedagogy in its most-rel-
evant form is not a uniform or static body of precepts. As Kanpol argues:

> To be a force, critical pedagogy must be incorporated into traditional and/or
> conservative and progressive mainstream school settings as part of our daily
> teaching and living. It can be part of any subject material. Critical pedagogy
> has some legitimacy as well—just like other forms of knowledge. It is not sim-
> ply a critical pedagogy framework that a school must adopt. Critical pedagogy
> is more about human beings digging into their guts (psychology), asking and
> answering questions about their past, students' past, the relationship of this
> to the content, and how this knowledge can undercut social relations that are
> oppressive. Critical pedagogy can occur at all places and at all times. (175)

Kanpol circumscribes a broad area inside which many teaching ideas can interact. He certainly privileges a radical political critique, but such viewpoint does
not exhaust the possibilities of critical pedagogy.

I suggest finally that embracing dialogic exchange and interrogating language
are parts of a long tradition, a critical tradition, in the liberal arts, although these
activities have not always been the dominant features of classrooms. I am reminded of my first sustained dialogic encounter with an instructor, which occurred in a graduate school course on educational foundations. Up until that time,
most papers I submitted for courses were returned with comments that indicated,

more or less, whether I had been a good or bad boy. Occasional questions had been posed, but never had it been required that I actually respond to them. In contrast, my education professor, the distinguished Henry Perkinson, insisted that we respond to his comments in writing. Then he would write responses to our responses, which might initiate yet another round of exchanges. We disagreed at one point on the antecedents of some concept. I forget the concept but not how fruitful and friendly was the dispute. It went something like this: I wrote that we could trace the idea to the early-twentieth century; the professor said the nineteenth, given what it was a reaction against; I said if we were going to talk about reactions against, then we can take it back to the eighteenth. I think we ended up taking it all the way back to the Middle Ages. I'm sure we went overboard, but I remember the value inside the process, the emphases on dialogue and the unsettling of absolute positions. On a far more recent occasion, post–September 11, I overheard a college student in a university cafeteria express puzzlement about the attacks by pointing out that "they didn't take over anything, so what's the point?" I won't attempt to analyze fully here a lengthy and complex conversation, and I'm sure that student eventually will achieve a broader outlook. I merely want to posit at this juncture that part of what may have been impeding understanding of "the point," if the statement really encapsulated a moment of sincere wonderment, was a deeply held metaphor that equated successful military strikes with geographical conquest, an understandable construct given that the history of the United States is largely one of territorial expansion by military means. Perhaps the unraveling of the mystery of "the point" will involve discussion of the limitation of the land-control metaphor, which constrains both social explanation and individual response. To reiterate, a concern with language scrutiny, as well as ongoing consideration of the participant structure of classrooms, seem to be intellectual moves that all teachers should be making. The moves represent a critical but not proselytizing engagement.

Regardless of one's ease or discomfort with the critical in composition studies, it will remain a force with which to be reckoned. And it should be welcomed. Mass bewilderment is not going to position the nation where it needs to be in the long run nor will psychic insularity nor the rhetoric of most current political leaders. If students follow the critical example or even help to establish it, this augurs well for our collective future. If in the pursuit of global justice, students and teachers push participatory democracy to a greater measure of probity, I could think of no better outcome for composition studies at any time.

21 The Uses of Literacy in a Globalized, Post–September 11 World

HARRIET MALINOWITZ

> For years, Walter Cronkite said on television every night: That's the way it
> is. The role of humanism is to say: No, that's not the way it is.
> —Edward Said, speaking at Long Island University,
> Brooklyn Campus, March 12, 2001

> *Question:* What do you consider the most reliable source of news covering
> the WTC and the alleged conspirators?
> *Answer:* The best thing to do is read widely and always skeptically.
> Remember everyone, including me, has their opinions and their goals and
> you have to think through them for yourself.
> —Noam Chomsky interview in the MSNBC chatroom, October 2, 2001

Near the end of Judith Rossner's bestselling 1983 novel *August,* a young woman terminating her psychoanalysis is apprehensive about moving from New York to Washington, D.C. The nation's capital, as she envisions it, is cold and averse to emotions, "a man's world, an external, WASPy kind of place where problems can be solved because they're only on the surface anyway" (499–500). Her analyst's response is that, on the contrary, many of the world's gravest problems are insoluble precisely *because* of the complicated, though unprobed, unconscious feelings of politicians and their constituents.

The analyst's gesture in the direction of what might broadly be called social psychology will certainly resonate with theorists and practitioners of what might broadly be called critical literacy. Liberatory pedagogy, cultural studies, multicul-turalism, and other socially based teaching practices took root in composition in the last decades of the twentieth century because reading, writing, rhetoric, lan-guage, and discourse came to be seen as constitutive, rather than merely descrip-tive, of events in the world. The distinction between the study of literary and non-literary texts—even, for that matter, between linguistically based and imagistic texts and between tangible textual artifacts (books, paintings, films) and cultural texts (sports, political movements, societal discourses of race or AIDS, religious sermons, nuggets of popular wisdom, depictions of geographical regions)—began to shrivel in importance, as far as English departments were concerned, as it became recognized that widely disparate texts could make similar sorts of demands on one's ability to make meaning. As Michael Bérubé has put it, interpretive study

> helps you notice textual detail, read for subplots, place texts in generic or historical contexts, or make something coherent out of seemingly random features of a text. It leads you, in a phrase, to get more out of what you read; and in recent decades . . . the discipline of English has begun to make the promise, implicitly and explicitly, that if you can learn to "get more out of" your reading of Jane Austen, you will also learn to get more out of your reading of other texts, discourses, and rhetorics, be they magazine articles, conversations, Supreme Court decisions, rhetorics of empire, or books by Stanley Fish. (*Employment* 147–48)

Contemporary teachers and students of cultural studies view this belief that the world can—and should—be read as foundational to the building of critical literacy. Thus, they are deeply indebted to, among other key figures, Richard Hoggart, founder of the Centre for Contemporary Cultural Studies in England and author of the pathbreaking 1957 book *The Uses of Literacy*. In *Uses,* Hoggart examined the effects of the mass media of his day on the thinking of the British working class. His findings left him none too sanguine:

> The ability to read the decent weeklies is not a *sine qua non* of the good life. It seems unlikely at any time . . . that a majority in any class will have strongly intellectual pursuits. There are other ways of being in the truth. The strongest objection to the more trivial popular entertainments is not that they prevent their readers from becoming highbrow, but that they make it harder for people without an intellectual bent to become wise in their own way. (262)

Composition in the twenty-first century, more than in the twentieth and *far* more than in the nineteenth, is a realm devoted to the edification of students across the class spectrum who seek higher education not to develop strongly intellectual pursuits, but rather, strongly marketable ones. The new global economy provides the dominant framework in which knowledge—including the world views and personal goals of students—comes to be formed. But even though core English studies in the contemporary corporatized university, encased within a market-driven world, are enduring ever-dimmer prospects for luring students into the life of the mind, we may still hope to lure students' minds into a more critical analysis of their lives—to help them to become wise in their own way.

Doing so, however, requires an understanding of what the mass media and other forces have made of them and how it has done so. Such an understanding will draw both on the analyst in *August*'s assertion that the political is psychological and on Hoggart's demonstration that the literary is sociological. (And, in both cases, vice versa.) It will draw, too, on the Foucauldian idea that the constitution of reality is rhetorical. I would further add the harsh assessment—and I believe that Hoggart, if he were alive now, might agree that this represents an unfortunate extension of his own observations half a century ago—that the media (as well as government and, indeed, many other arms of our culture) today have interests in and finely honed methods of promoting what I have come to call *stupidification* of their audiences. Exploring the ways that stupidification has come to be not only a mass cultural practice but also a mass cultural value is an essential prerequisite to comprehending why critical analysis is something so many of our students—and so many people in our society generally—are reluctant and ill-equipped to take on.

The late literary scholar Bill Readings notably tied globalization to the contemporary university in his 1996 book, *The University in Ruins*. Readings analyzes the role of the academy in an era when the sovereignty of the nation-state has withered away in the face of transnational corporate power. Readings contends that in such an age, the function of the university is accordingly transformed. Historically, "the Kantian concept of reason" (as embodied in the humanities) and, later, "the Humboldtian idea of culture" (as embodied in the German research university) provided the frameworks within which the university bolstered national cultures and identities (14). However, the left's notion, drawn from Louis Althusser, of the university as an ideological cultural apparatus of the nation-state is now obsolete, as the university has dissociated itself from the ideology of the nation—becoming instead, as Readings puts it, an "apparatus of management" (47), wrapped in "the techno-bureaucratic notion of excellence" (14). The individual that the university interpolates is no longer the citizen-subject but a consumer.

This shift has implications for the notion of multiculturalism—an ideology that has been a staple of composition's diet for many years now, yet that has undergone something of a transformation. It is no longer a subversive, or even especially controversial, word; it represents the economic interests (albeit in a new, twisted sense) of transnational corporations and of cities such as New York, Los

Angeles, Tokyo, London, Frankfurt, and Hong Kong, whose cultures reflect their role as centers of international business and finance (Sassen).

These centers subsume both an international professional and managerial class and a class of extremely poorly paid, mostly immigrant workers who service the vast new infrastructure that accommodates the business community. The former group's emergence was heralded by corporate diversity-training workshops in the 1990s, premised on the idea of "Workplace 2000"—the time when the increased presence of women and minorities was expected to radically alter the culture of the workplace—and that portrayed multiculturalism as a reality that the wise and serious careerist must cheerfully prepare for. Meanwhile, members of the other group—janitors, hotel chambermaids, messengers, nannies, delivery people, street vendors, taxi drivers, house cleaners, food and restaurant workers—often working part-time and/or off-the-books, without benefits, nonunionized or poorly represented by unions—provide for the essential maintenance of the busy, cosmopolitan lifestyles of the first group.

Over the years, in the higher educational institutions of diverse status in which I've taught in New York, members of both these classes of multicultural people have been my students. Some have come to reap the glories of capitalism, whereas others have come attempting to escape the ravages of capitalism. As the student antisweatshop and larger antiglobalization movement have made widely known, many in the latter group have come precisely to escape the near-slave-wage manufacturing jobs U.S. companies have exported to their countries of origin—at the expense of living-wage union jobs here and traditional livelihoods there.

Having read hundreds of their personal narratives over the years, I've realized that despite the hype we hear on TV, it's a rare immigrant who will cite, as a reason for coming here, liberty. Yet, the United States is tireless in its promotion of itself as beneficent superpower, beacon of enduring ideals, guardian of the freest freedom, the justest justice. So unpunctured is its self-congratulation on its goodness (flip from network to network and see if you can find a news story that says otherwise) that most citizens could only conclude, when we were attacked on September 11, 2001, that others had gone mad with democracy-envy; no other explanation for our newfound status as object of hatred seemed plausible. And it's true that, for those lunging from CNN to Fox News to CBS to NPR to AOL and reading the dailies, there *were* almost no available bases for alternative theories, even if one earnestly sought to construct one. However, those Americans who started to read the foreign and independent press on the Internet in the months following September 11 (National Public Radio reported that the British *Guardian,* for example, had experienced a massive jump in its American online readership that fall) became aware, many for the first time, that while the famous melting pot continues to absorb the huddled masses yearning to breathe free, it is, less obviously to many who live here, also a major cause of the masses' respiratory problems.

Sustaining pride in our country's self-professed values (freedom, democracy, opportunity) in the face of trade practices and foreign policies bespeaking a less savory set of values (materialism, exploitation, support of dictatorships) often requires what George Orwell famously called *doublethink*. Doublethink, the rhetorical foundation of Orwell's dystopic society in the novel *1984*, was "a vast system of mental cheating" (191) via which the government maintained absolute control of truth:

> To know and not to know, to be conscious of complete truthfulness while telling carefully constructed lies, to hold simultaneously two opinions which cancelled out, knowing them to be contradictory and believing in both of them, to use logic against logic, to repudiate morality while laying claim to it, to believe that democracy was impossible and that the Party was the guardian of democracy, to forget, whatever it was necessary to forget, then to draw it back into memory again at the moment when it was needed, and then promptly forget it again, and above all, to apply the same process to the process itself—that was the ultimate subtlety: consciously to induce unconsciousness, and then, once again, to become unconscious of the act of hypnosis you had just performed. Even to understand the word *doublethink* involved the use of doublethink. (31)

Consciously to induce unconsciousness: doublethink is a key ingredient of the phenomenon I call stupidification. To not-know what one knows, to be confident that what one does not know does not exist—indeed, to find the nonexistence of what one doesn't know ratified on every news channel, in every government utterance, in the enaction of the law, in the school curriculum—within this epistemological framework, virtually anything is possible. When symbols are revered or despised as meaningful fields in themselves, severed from the circumstances they purport to represent, they can engender sentiments, motivate actions, and justify policies and beliefs that might seem if actually subjected to close empirical inspection to be at great odds with the conditions that gave rise to them.

Noam Chomsky has argued that unlike totalitarian societies, which use violence to maintain control, democracies achieve many of the same ends through rhetoric. The "genius of democratic systems of thought control," he says, lies in societies' ability to keep certain ideas "outside the spectrum of thinkable thought" ("Manufacture" 131). I would modify Chomsky slightly to argue that, in some ways, democratic and totalitarian methods of propaganda and thought-reduction are not altogether different from one another. Just as Orwell explained that, for instance, the meaning of the *Declaration of Independence* could not be translated into the government-constructed language of *1984* called *Newspeak* (which relied on the elimination of words to shrink the conceptual repertoire)—except perhaps to render it in the single word *crimethink* (278)—the notion that the United States has been guilty of barbarism, repression, slavery, and mass impoverishment and has thus earned the righteous vengeance of others is virtually unutterable in contemporary mass public discourse—except when rendered simply as *anti-American* or *unpatriotic.* (Conversely, on the left, visions of how the United States would ideally operate in the world are often shrunken to the words *justice* or *peace,* which are held to stand for all that is good and escape substantive definition. There is also that marvelous tautology, seemingly invented by guilty liberals for such occasions as when one is paying an undocumented nanny exploitative wages without social security, or succumbing to the pleasures of a boycotted product, or including in one's stock portfolio a company that damages the environment but pays a handsome dividend: "Ya gotta do what ya gotta do.")

A typical example of our society's unquestioning acceptance of doublethink occurred when New York was engulfed by a tidal wave of patriotism following the September 11 attacks. Whipped into an instant marketing frenzy and emboldened by the president's announcement that shopping could help to save America, wholesalers in the city provided symbols for the consumption of a fervent citizenry:

> They ran to their computers to design rhinestone twin tower brooches and "We Will Never Forget" pins and zipped them off to their manufacturers in Asia. These manufacturers were able to retool their metal presses and churn out disaster memorabilia in as little as four days. (Holloway D1)

Flags, "God Bless America" and "I Can't Believe I Got Out" T-shirts, and other paraphernalia proclaiming loyalty and homage to our country also appeared on the streets of New York. Made not by U.S. workers but rather by workers in Korea and China (whose wages remain conveniently unknown to the bearers of these souvenirs), many of these items sold at markups of 300 to 500 hundred percent (Holloway). Lest one imagine that such kitsch was only for the ignorant masses, up at Bloomingdale's, miniature Waterford crystal flags sold for $99. An ad explained their meaning: "Honoring our past. Saluting our future. Reminding us now more than ever of freedom, tolerance and bravery" ("The Stuff of Patriotism" 7).

If Americans are unconscious of their unbalanced relationship to the rest of the world and thus hindered in their ability to critically evaluate it, it may be because education, literature, science, media, and ideas have, like virtually everything else, been brought under the aegis of corporate culture. A few cases in point:

- "Product placement"—a longtime practice in movies and television, in which a company pays for, say, the star to drive a Ford or sip a Diet Coke or shop at Barnes and Noble—has entered the realm of literature to the applause of publishers. The well-known British writer Fay Weldon was paid a commission from Bulgari, the Italian jewelry company, to write *The Bulgari Connection*, a 2001 novel that showcased the company's products amidst a charged plot. A trend may well be afoot: Weldon's agent spoke enthusiastically of future plans for liquor, cigarette, and clothing brands to appear in "chick lit" books for young women (Kirkpatrick A1, A12).

- Conservative think tanks such as the Heritage Foundation (which is financed by corporate donors and which helped shape the Reaganomics policies of the 1980s [Susan George]) exist not to generate objective, high-quality scholarship but to produce catchy rationales for right-wing programs—"an alternative that would influence Congress directly, something closer to a lobby." Heritage's "annual budget of about $30 million allows it to flood politicians and editorialists with ready-made policies and easy-to-digest talking points" (Greenberg 26). These appealingly packaged policies can then be tested on focus groups, whose responses will in turn go on to create the terms of political oratory. (George Bush the First's famous campaign phrases—"kinder, gentler America" and "a thousand points of light"—were launched after they proved to be major hits in focus groups, despite the fact that not a single focus group knew what "a thousand points of light" meant [Edwards 28]).

- A study surveying 789 articles on biology and genetics published in 1992 in fourteen leading journals found that "thirty-four percent of the articles examined had a financial interest in the described research" (Miyoshi 25–26). In none of these cases were the conflicts of interest disclosed to readers (Press and Washburn 45).

- Fossil-fuel companies fund studies of global warming, corporate sponsors reserve the right to edit the academic research they fund, and, according to an article in *Atlantic Monthly,* "Freeport McMoRan, a mining company embroiled in allegations of environmental misconduct in Indonesia, has created a chair in environmental studies at Tulane" (Press and Washburn 41, 45).

- It's good, as Chomsky suggests in the epigram that prefaces this article, to read widely before you form an opinion. But if you tried to formulate ideas by perusing the information available at, say, CNN, Court TV, Comedy Central, *Time, Life, People,* America Online, Netscape, books published by Warner or Little, Brown, and a long roster of other venues, you probably wouldn't be too mired in intellectual conflict—seeing as how they all represent the world according to AOL–Time Warner, the owner of the $36.2 billion revenue-producing conglomerate ("Big Ten" 27–28). It's what they call *synergy:* the media giants' practice of simultaneously owning television networks, newspapers, magazines, film companies, book companies, radio stations, music labels, and internet services, "with the same firms gaining ownership of content and the means to distribute it" (McChesney 11).

To judge by these examples, critical literacy is a hard thing to achieve these days, as most available news and information sources provide and confirm the authenticity of the same news and information; in addition, their fare is oriented toward the interests of corporations (because both the news sources and sponsors are, of course, corporations). The old scoff, "Don't believe everything you read in the paper" must be broadened to include scientific journals, expert opinions on momentous medical research, supposedly inspired creative work—and virtually everything else one encounters, from school textbooks to the floors of the New York subways, which have, as of this writing, begun to feature advertisements.

It is precisely because critical literacy *is* so hard to achieve—because there are so many obstacles placed between an active mind and the world one would want, or at least need, to understand—that the other epigram I have included here, the one by Edward Said, is so pedagogically important. The humanities, marginalized at the dawn of the twenty-first century because of their perceived irrelevance in a corporatized world, are among the last sites available where the guileless believers might hear *anyone* say, "No, that's *not* the way it is."

The academy is not as extrinsic a force to the "real world" as one might think. On the contrary, we are occasionally singled out as the only real threat to an otherwise harmonious world order. In November, 2001, a report called "How Our Universities are Failing America and What Can Be Done About It" was published by the American Council of Trustees and Alumni, a conservative think tank (Martin and Neal). Its intended recipients included three thousand college and university trustees (Eakin). Proclaiming itself the first project of the "Defense of Civilization Fund," promoted by ACTA affiliate Lynne Cheney, the report indicts academe for "demurring" from the "nearly unanimous" and "wholehearted" support that the nation gave President George Bush in "calling evil by its rightful name" and for his planned military intervention in Afghanistan in the weeks following the September 11 attacks. It proceeds to cite 116 examples of purportedly egregious comments uttered by faculty, administrators, and students at teach-ins and other public forums. As the authors decline to supply responses or analyses explaining precisely what *is* misguided about the remarks, the egregiousness of those comments is presumably self-evident. The report thus reads like a tabloidesque expression of shock and scandal rather than an argument refuting, or in any way negotiating with, the statements on parade (Martin and Neal).

Perhaps this is not to be considered a shortcoming of the report, which some might laud as a model of vacuously effective persuasion—a genre enjoying ever-broader circles of acceptance. (New York University communications professor Todd Gitlin called the report "a record-breaking event in the annals of shoddy scholarship" [Eakin]). Its medium seems to be its message: the real villains are not those who think badly of U.S. foreign policy but simply those who think. It would seem that the ultimate transgression of the quoted speakers lies not in the content of their views but in their daring to question putatively sacred, and thus incontestable, ideas at all. "How Our Universities Are Failing America" insinuates that people who read books and get degrees are inherently suspect; that reflection is evil, while homespun, received wisdom (in particular, unquestioned patriotism) is good; and that it's the uneducated who get to have the last laugh—now that intellectuals are exposed as stupider than their compatriots, with Harvard students proven to be the stupidest of all. (This last point is made implicitly by including the results of a poll: Ninety-two percent of the American public thought America should take military action even if casualties occurred while only 28 percent of Harvard students thought so. There's no question about who got it "right.")

Knowledge is once again the pernicious fruit that God doesn't want us to eat: The reporters are aghast that universities added courses, including courses in Islam and Asian cultures, in the wake of the terrorist attacks. (This despite the fact that immediately after September 11, the government frantically sought to recruit people with expertise in precisely these areas to hone the U.S.'s flagging intelligence capabilities—and couldn't find enough of them.) The report's logic could make the most postmodern compositionist long for a return to the teaching of rhetorical modes: definition, cause and effect, comparison and contrast, classification, and analysis are all beyond the purview of its invective. Instead, we get a few examples—also uninterrogated—of the enlightened "public response" (which stands in counterpoint to the benighted "campus responses") such as this by then-New York mayor Rudolph Giuliani:

> You're either with civilization or with terrorists. On one side is democracy, the rule of law, and respect for human life; on the other is tyranny, arbitrary executions, and mass murder. We're right and they're wrong. It's as simple as that.

Whereas we idiots in academe might question the truth of rigid binaries, ask for evidence to support the assertions, consider the unstable nature of words like *right* and *wrong* and *civilization* and *terrorists,* and suggest a closer reading of this and other public rhetoric that emerged at the time, Giuliani's statement forecloses on any sort of analysis at all: "It's as simple as that."

Given this affirmation of the simple, it's almost silly that some fairly mild, warm-hearted peacenik clichés—"Break the cycle of violence," "An eye for an eye leaves the world blind," "We should build bridges and relationships, not simply bombs and walls," "Our grief is not a cry for war"—generate alarm that the speakers are with terrorists. More disturbing, though, is that statements proposing inquiry and analysis are held to speak damningly for themselves, so that critical thinking itself appears to be the enemy:

- "Ignorance breeds hate." Speaker from the Islamic Academy of Las Vegas.

- "We need to hear more than one perspective on how we can make the world a safer place. We need to understand the reasons behind the terrifying hatred directed against the United States and find ways to act that will not foment more hatred for generations to come." Professor emerita of women's studies, University of Oregon.

- "The question we should explore is not who we should bomb or where we should bomb, but why we were targeted. When we have the answer to why, then we will have the ability to prevent terrorist attacks tomorrow." Speaker at "Understanding the Attack on America: An Alternate View," University of North Carolina–Chapel Hill. (Martin and Neal)

Are we as a nation, then, in favor of ignorance? Is it best to base our opinions on only one perspective, seek no explanations for problems, and eschew all understanding that would help us to prevent these problems from recurring in the future? What does it mean that a "yes" to these questions is considered the smart response by the former head of the National Endowment for the Humanities?

In the weeks following the September 11 attacks, the nation heard repeatedly that *we* were *good* (while *they* were *evil*), *civilized* (while *they* were *barbaric*), *innocent* (while *they* were malevolent *devils*), *democratic patriots* (while *they* were *Islamic fundamentalists*), *crusaders* for *infinite justice* (while *they* were *fanatics* waging a *holy war*), stoically accepting of necessary *collateral damage* (while *they* *murdered innocent civilians*), and in support, as always, of *freedom fighters* (who are committed to exterminating *terrorists*). The world, we learned, was divided into two camps, those with us and those against us—those *with* to be sheltered under the iconic banner of *America,* those *against* to be lined up against the wall beside the equally iconic *bin Laden. We* were experiencing, as Bush put it, "the first war of the twenty-first century"; *their* wars—in Israel-Palestine, Colombia, Chechnya, and Kosovo—apparently never occurred or perhaps occurred on a non-Christian calendar and therefore had nothing to do with *us.*

As Columbia University professor Mahmood Mamdani pointed out, we also had the birth of the much-touted distinction between "good Muslims" and "bad

Muslims" (as opposed to, say, "between good and bad persons" or "between criminals and civic citizens") (Mamdani). On the other side of the same coin, Yale professor Immanuel Wallerstein objected to the notion that American values or traditions, endlessly invoked, were monolithic entities:[1]

> The America that welcomes immigrants and the America that rejects them are both American traditions. . . . The America of equality and of inequality are both American traditions. There is no essence there. There is no there there. (Wallerstein)

In addition to the profusion of binaries that became household words, semantic-ideological equations were also manufactured. Media critic Laura Flanders cited a few: "The United States='America'", "America='The Civilized World'", "Democracy=Bipartisanship", "an attack on the World Trade Towers or the Pentagon=an attack on the American 'way of life'" (Flanders). *Terrorist* took its place with *Communist* and *witch* in American lexical history, though actually defining *terrorism* was studiously avoided. (For good reason. Even the U.S. Department of Defense and the FBI's definitions diverge, while the United Nations' version—"all war crimes will be considered acts of terrorism"—would certainly not do [LeVine]).

Jeff Baxter, a military-technology expert addressing war-industry figures in business and politics at the Potomac Institute for Policy Studies, declared that this new war was "an information war . . . a war fought with ideas," one that required "perception engineering"—psychological warfare, propaganda campaigns, and the like (Corn). Sure enough, as the bombs started to drop, the Pentagon hired the Rendon Group, a public relations firm, so that, in Defense Secretary Donald Rumsfeld's words, people would not be "confused as to what this is about." (Those people were not only in the U.S. but in seventy-nine target countries.) The Rendon Group has previously handled the public-relations needs of trade organizations and "post-privatization management" (Solomon)—most important in an era of globalization when more and more governments are relinquishing control of their own infrastructures to privately owned companies.

Perceptions were engineered not just with words, but also with images. Old West–style "WANTED" posters with bin Laden's picture dotted the landscape— conflating, in the public imagination, Hollywood's cowboy movies with its war movies, which for many decades have been partly financed by the Pentagon at taxpayer expense. The Pentagon lends material and personnel support—from battleships to troops—to what, in its determination, are positive film portrayals of the U.S. in warfare and extracts in return the prerogative to rewrite scripts according to its own interests. Burnishing its image in this way boosts recruitment, allotments of Congressional funds, and public approval of its various incursions; therefore, it retains on its staff a Defense Department Hollywood liaison (*Military in the Movies*).

This juggernaut of false dichotomies, putative equivalencies, spurious use of terms, focus-group–tested sales pitches, and hokey images went virtually unchallenged except in the independent media (mostly on the Internet) and—as the Cheney mob will attest—in some parts of the academy. The us-good, them-evil binary and most of what followed sustained itself via a popular blizzard of Orwellian language, logic, and lunacy. As Jacob Levich wrote in an article called "Happy New Year: It's 1984":

> In George Orwell's dreary classic, the totalitarian state of Oceania is perpetually at war with either Eurasia or Eastasia. Although the enemy changes periodically, the war is permanent; its true purpose is to control dissent and sustain dictatorship by nurturing popular fear and hatred. The permanent war undergirds every aspect of Big Brother's authoritarian program, excusing censorship, propaganda, secret police, and privation.

He goes on to enumerate some of the infamous mantras of Oceania that also proved remarkably palatable in the U.S. crisis:

> WAR IS PEACE. A reckless war that will likely bring about a deadly cycle of retaliation is being sold to us as the means to guarantee our safety. . . . FREEDOM IS SLAVERY. . . . Americans are about to lose many of their most cherished liberties in a frenzy of paranoid legislation. . . . IGNORANCE IS STRENGTH. America's "new war" against terrorism will be fought with unprecedented secrecy, including heavy press restrictions not seen for years, the Pentagon has advised.

American students frequently read *1984* in their high school English classes and are amazed that anyone could be induced to accept such patently absurd maxims, to agree that two plus two equals five. We ask such questions, too, of the Holocaust: How could the people have actually let it happen? Why did they let Adolph Hitler come to power? Hitler achieved power through the deployment of transcendent ideals that masses of people took at face value: patriotism, national unity, the need to spur the economy, to stave off Communism, and to redress the humiliations visited upon Germans by the Versailles Treaty.

Furthermore, he did it entirely through legal means. He had tremendous popular support, with all sorts of strange bedfellows—industrialists and trade unionists, fascists and socialists, Catholics and enemies of the Catholics—succumbing to his persuasive powers; and almost 90 percent of the 95 percent of the German people who voted voted "yes" on the plebiscite approving his final consolidation of power as Fuhrer and Reich Chancellor (Bullock 171). He also made good use of propaganda, scapegoating, fictions of plotted coups, shameless duplicity, and inspired rhetoric that reassured the people that they could once again become the true Germans of yesteryear.

It wasn't until he was in power that he rapidly changed the laws. Among a stunning array of maneuvers, he asserted that the Communists were plotting terrorist activities, and he thus justified issuing a decree suspending civil liberties "for the protection of the People and the State" (Bullock 144–45). Perhaps most strikingly, he managed to convince those whom he would soon ban and kill to pass the Enabling Bill, which gave him powers to act without the approval of the Reichstag, to override provisions of the Constitution, and to single-handedly enact foreign treaties. In a speech before the vote, he invoked the spirit of national unity and promised he would only resort to using the new law when it was "essential for carrying out vitally necessary measures" (Bullock 147). He concluded, "It is for you, gentlemen of the Reichstag, to decide between war and peace" (Bullock 148).

Some of this may have an eerily familiar ring. You may, in that case, also be interested to know that Joseph Goebbels, the Nazi director of propaganda, wrote in his diary in 1933, "The struggle is a light one now, since we are able to employ all the means of the State. Radio and Press are at our disposal. We shall achieve a masterpiece of propaganda" (Bullock 142).

After September 11, 2001, many people said that Americans had lost their innocence due to finally experiencing destruction on their own soil. I think, on the contrary, that losing our innocence is precisely what we still most need to do. It is especially hard to do this in a climate in which asking questions, reading skeptically, and analyzing closely—three essential components of intellectual work—can lead to charges of anti-Americanism or justifying terrorism. Writers such as Arundhati Roy, Susan Sontag, Ward Churchill, and Seumas Milne ("They Can't See") were vilified and dismissed in just this way when, in the immediate aftermath of September 11, they addressed Americans' ignorance about U.S. actions that have tormented and enraged the world.

I am not, finally, saying that the mission for compositionists in the twenty-first century is for all to become radical-leftist critiquers of globalization and American foreign policy. (Though I do agree with Keith Gilyard's hypothesis, in his essay in this volume, about the ascendance of foreign policy discussions in the "instructional contact zones" of composition classes: There is "no eluding that social force," and hence it's vital that as teachers we creatively seize the "critical moment.") I am saying, though, that, just as the analyst in *August* said (quite rightly) that the world's problems are underwritten by unexplored and therefore dangerously powerful feelings, they are also underwritten by unexplored and therefore dangerously powerful ideas. Politics is not just the province of the social sciences; if anything, I hope that I have demonstrated the extent to which politics—very dependent upon the formation of mass opinion—is shaped by language and rhetoric and in some ways can *best* be studied through those lenses.

Globalization is a vast phenomenon injuring the majority of people it touches. The purported clash of Islam and the West is certain to produce a lot more suffering for millions of the world's people, including Americans. Yet, I've discovered that even a great many people with PhDs in English know little or nothing about the actual workings of the World Trade Organization or the history of the immensely powerful international organizations—Keynesian in conception and now thoroughly neoliberal in theory and deed—that came out of the 1944 Bretton Woods Conference or about contemporary trade treaties or about the specifics of U.S. foreign policy—that include, besides more than 130 military interventions between 1890 and 2001 (Grossman), many other actions that could be deemed terrorist. (Or perhaps not. The point is that one has to know about them and define terrorism before one is in a position to make such a determination).

As Cheney's report ironically makes clear, we are among the very few people available to let students know that critical thinking is *not* a sin or a crime and that they *do* have the power and the resources to interpret and describe this world thickly[2] through reading and writing. In order to help them activate this power, we have to do our own homework. This may include using independent media in our teaching and our research (there's plenty to be found on the Internet—enabling one to genuinely, as Chomsky suggests, read both "widely" and "skeptically"); listening to the many good questions asked at press conferences that go unanswered (and noticing when the questions go unreported, too, as if they had never been posed); reading all the metaphoric fine print we can (e.g., actual transcripts of reported speeches, the texts of Congressional bills and executive orders, articles that may contradict their headlines, television images that may tell a different story than the commentator does); consulting the Web sites and related links of organizations representing unpopular, suppressed, or unfamiliar views; engaging with programs and groups on campus that may also espouse such views; and learning, following Orwell's example, to "guess the truth by the way the other side [tells] lies" (James 76). It will be worth it. Because critical literacy is on the critical list.

Notes

I am deeply indebted to Kerryn Higgs for her brilliant Internet, research, and editorial skills, and her good grace when I spilled wine on her laptop in the middle of it all. I am also grateful to Long Island University for providing research released time for the writing of this article.

1. Wallerstein's argument interestingly paralleled Edward Said's simultaneous rebuttal ("Clash of Ignorance") of Samuel Huntington's alleged implication, in *The Clash of Civilizations,* that Islam was a monolithic entity. When I read Huntington myself, I felt that Said had been a bit hard on him—an example of why it's a good idea to maintain some skepticism about even your most-admired writers' accounts.

2. See historian Jeffrey N. Wasserstrom on bringing Clifford Geertz's method of interpreting Balinese cock fights to the discussion about September 11. See also political psychologist Marc Howard Ross for an interesting discussion of using narrative analysis for greater cross-cultural understanding. Both are excellent examples of the role of critical reading and writing in political contexts.

22 Teaching after September 11

RESPONSE BY RICHARD E. MILLER

Where were you when the planes hit the towers?

This is a question that will be asked for years to come. And it was a question that was very much in the air when we met at Miami University to discuss the future of composition in the twenty-first century, just one month after the attacks on the World Trade Center and the Pentagon. There is no right or even good answer to this question. What activity would have been appropriate? What should one have been doing when news of the terrorist attacks arrived? But this is partly the point of the question. We ask it so that we can share our sense of disruption. Our confusion. To reassure ourselves that none of us, whatever our education, our life experiences, or our political leanings, quite knew what to do or think in that moment when it seemed the world was going to go up in flames.

Can you believe it? we say. I was washing the dishes. Listening to the radio. Preparing for class. Worrying about next year. Walking through Manhattan, counting the falling bodies. This is what I was doing when the apocalypse appeared to be at hand.

And you, what were you doing?

Traveling to Oxford, Ohio from northern New Jersey, the plane banking over New York's altered skyline, flying just three weeks after I'd vowed never to do so again, I can't get this *New Yorker* cartoon out of my head. There's an image of a man waiting at a ticket counter. In response to the question, "Where would you like to go?" he says, simply, "September 10th."

I, too, want to go backward, but I'm learning all over again that there's no going back. There is only what lies ahead.

At the end of the conference, Keith Gilyard and Harriet Malinowitz discussed their own responses to September 11. Gilyard turned to his bookshelf and found a rich set of resources for the critical pedagogue; Malinowitz turned to the Internet for fast-breaking news on the Taliban and the consequences of globalization. They found, I would say, a record of ideas, teaching practices, and intellectual stances that had currency and that exercised some power before September 11; like the *New Yorker*'s nostalgic traveler, they found the relics of a suddenly bygone era.

What will it mean, though, to teach after September 11? Although the image of the critical pedagogue is sure to retain its enduring appeal, as will the image of the revolutionary teacher spreading alternate understandings of current events, I believe that the important work in writing program administration, and in the humanities more generally, lies elsewhere. For writing programs and the teachers who work in them to assume a meaningful role in preparing students to respond to the challenges posed by the twenty-first century, we must all ask ourselves the following questions:

- How have we contributed to producing a citizenry that is so woefully ill-informed about world religions? Global politics? International trade and finance?

- What role have we played in training the future's military advisors? Political analysts? Legislators? Public policy makers? And if the answer is "none," then why is that?

- What have we done to prepare students to live in a less-than-ideal world, a world of seemingly intractable, seemingly insoluble problems?

- And, finally, what work have we done at the local level with other departments and disciplines to ensure that our students receive an education that provides sustained instruction in thinking about the problems and the opportunities that globalization has made and will continue to make possible?

In asking these questions, I mean to focus attention squarely on those areas where writing teachers and writing program administrators already exercise considerable control: the curriculum, its goals, and the teaching practices that bring the curriculum to life. We can look at the world after September 11 and conclude that we got here because powerful interests have colluded to thwart the weak; or we can recognize that the humanities, in general, and writing programs, in particular, have contributed to producing future leaders and laborers who are ill-prepared to think and act on a political stage where alliances are fluid and ideals and commitments get negotiated and renegotiated in the moment.

Will writing programs be here a hundred years from now? And, if so, what will they do? As we figure out what it means to teach after September 11, we will also be figuring out the answers to these questions. My own position on this may appear paradoxical, but I'd like to suggest that the intellectual growth and development of the field of composition have been limited by an overestimation of the power of the written word. For those who believe the pen is mightier than the sword, the most important activity to engage in is the act of writing; and, at the professional level, in our field, it is writing that critiques something else—a position, an approach, and, at times, even an individual—that is the most important writing of all. The limited value of such work, which was never very easily concealed from the general public, is now obvious to us all. What difference would it make to produce a critique of media representations of the collapse of the twin towers? Of the roles that fashion and gender have played in reporting the war in Afghanistan? Of the emergence of women's rights as a concern in the Bush administration? As long as we elect to write in ways that produce arguments that never circulate beyond the confines of our field, as long as we devote our energies to assessing the past without thought of future action, then our political, cultural, and intellectual irrelevance is self-willed.

We can, however, imagine other ways to teach after September 11, as well as other content areas, and other goals for our teaching. There is valuable work that could go on in our classrooms besides training students to analyze and critique, work that would involve teaching students how to propose viable solutions to the insoluble problems of the twenty-first century: the conflict between religious and corporate efforts at globalization; the environmental consequences of modernization; the jobless future; democracy's fate in the age of technology, for example. Solving the insoluble is the paradox that lies at the heart of any significant social act: what must be done, can't be done, yet we must go forward. What can be done to alter the relations between Israel and Palestine? Between India and Pakistan? Between the United States and the Arab world? Can the global impact of civilization be reduced, or is environmental devastation inevitable? Is it possible to argue for universal human rights while respecting cultural differences and the right to self-determination? These are some of the questions that define our present and that will shape our collective future. If we do not provide our students with a curriculum that asks them to propose solutions to problems of this kind and to then assess the viability of their proposals, if we do not prepare them to play an active role in making a more hospitable future, who will?

After the conference, I returned to my university and attended a breakfast meeting on academic leadership. The vice-president of the university used his introductory remarks to reflect on the impact that September 11 had had on the community: A number of alumni had perished in the towers; students had lost their parents; ROTC members had been called up for active duty; and there was a steady stream of new requirements regarding foreign students. The vice-president described, as well, the economic consequences of the attack, the looming budget-ary crisis that would follow the drop in the stock market, the loss of jobs, the decline in tax revenues. It was a grim picture but not one that was totally devoid of opportunity, he insisted. As difficult as it was to think about what areas would prosper after the attacks, the vice-president noted, there was sure to be increased government funding in the sciences for work on biological warfare and defense and in the social sciences for work that involved the study of the roots of terror-ism, improved surveillance techniques, and foreign languages. While speculating in this way might seem ghoulish, it is the vice-president's job to consider shifting trends in the funding of higher education and to respond accordingly. The vice-president cannot, in other words, simply analyze and critique what others have done; he must propose and then act. This is what it means to be a social agent in the world, as opposed to a social critic on the sidelines of world events.

What most struck me about the vice-president's remarks was the fact that the humanities were not even mentioned as an area that might contribute to the fu-ture health and vitality of the university. The new version of the humanities I've sketched out here, though, could play such a role by assisting students in learn-ing how to formulate and test solutions to insoluble problems. In the humani-ties, so defined, the goal is to show students the human dimension of *all* knowl-edge and to train them how to read, write, think, create, and imagine in a world where all solutions are provisional and subject to change without notice.

What kind of world did you commit yourself to building after September 11?

Writing teachers have few tools to work with in embarking on such a task: a handful of reading and writing assignments, a grading system, some face time with the students over the course of the semester. These tools have tended to be used to construct worlds either where nothing can be done because the problems are so immense or where everything is subject to change, as long as the writer has a strong-enough argument and solid-enough command of the conventions of prose. The tools have been used, in other words, to foment despair or a kind of social dementia. In the real world, though, where terrible things happen all the time, neither of these approaches can support sustained efforts to improve the human condition. For that to happen, one must learn how to think through the failures, rejections, setbacks, and revisions that accompany any serious project of reform. One must learn, in other words, that critical optimism, the habit of mind I've described here, is an intellectual achievement and that it is best acquired by work-ing on the unfolding world-in-the-making that the world always is and always has been.

Conclusion: Everything Has Changed; Nothing Has Changed

SHANE BORROWMAN AND EDWARD M. WHITE

Composition in the Twenty-First Century: Crisis and Change—the volume that pre-ceded this one—was first published in 1996, was released in paperback in 1997, sold out, and went into a second printing in 2001. These dates are important only in a bibliographical entry or on a curriculum vitae, for the book—like most any book—exists outside of time. The debates it addresses still rage: controversies over the abolition of composition, the breadth and depth of this field of study, the ethi-cal means of assessment, the best methodologies for research, the most appro-priate ways to administer writing programs and writing centers, and, above all, the most effective ways to teach undergraduate and graduate students. There is, however, a radical difference between that volume and this one: Few contribu-tors to the earlier volume mention the world outside of composition as they con-sider either crisis or change. A hint of what is to come does appear in Lynn Z. Bloom's concluding essay: We "approach the new century far from complacent about the past, uncomfortable with the present, uneasy about the future" (273), but she also argues that, despite occasional unease, the world of composition is "a world of hope, a world without end" (277).

Composition Studies in the New Millennium: Rereading the Past, Rewriting the Future exists in a very different place than its predecessor, in a world where hope seemed suddenly hard to come by, a world that felt as if it had just experi-enced its end. The conference at which the chapters in this book were presented as talks ran from October 5 through October 7, 2001—less than a month after that second infamous day. September 11, 2001, anchors this collection in a spe-cific moment in time, a moment tied to moving images, powerful emotions, per-sonal trauma, national and international tragedy, and war. Many chapters in this collection reflect these connections.

256

The editors found themselves unable to extricate the book from its narrative, from the conference that followed this national tragedy so closely. September 11 was, as Robert J. Connors might have said, our lion in the road: We could get around it by working hard and stepping carefully but could not ignore it. We tried. With an eye to the book's future beyond September 11, we encouraged contributors revising their oral presentations into book chapters to expand the implications of their texts beyond the immediate: "As 2001 fades further into the past, and readers new to the professional conversation come into contact with the book, references to the events of September 11 and narratives on the physical activity of attending the Writing Program Administrators conference will work less and less well." So the contributors did revise. They reworded, they cut, and they tried to move the experience of attending a conference in October from the shadow of September. Yet, the crises and changes in 2001 were not the same as those of 1993, and this book, based as it is on the 2001 conference, has remained firmly, obstinately, anchored in its own time and resistant to all efforts to cut it loose.

The question for readers reflecting on the book as a whole is whether the terrorist attack in 2001 that cast such a large shadow over the conference was one local event, already receding in time as business as usual reasserted its claims, or whether it set out a new reality for the twenty-first century. Our answer as the book goes to press is that both statements are true. Reality has changed, as terrorism becomes the new and ghostly enemy, ever present in our lives, our research, and our classrooms. Furthermore, reality has changed for other reasons as well: the advances in technology described so powerfully in part 5, the research developments set out in part 1, and, indeed, the continued development of composition studies detailed in every essay in this volume. Yet, reality has not changed, because the gulf between composition specialists and the practitioners in their classrooms is as large as ever. Classroom teachers do not seem to be doing much that is different from what they did when the first volume was published or, really, much that is different from when the Braddock team in 1963 described knowledge of composition in the memorable metaphor of chemistry emerging from alchemy.

So, everything has changed but nothing has changed. What does this paradox suggest for the rewriting of the future that our subtitle proclaims with such hubris? Time has passed since the first volume in this series, and the questions asked within composition and rhetoric have changed. One of the original questions in *Crisis and Change* was What is composition and why do we teach it? which asks for a definition and a rationale: What are we doing and why are we doing it? Now, in this volume, the question is What do/should we teach when we teach composition? No definition is called for here; instead, the issue is What are we doing and ought we to be doing it? Similarly, Who should teach composition and what should they know? has become Where will composition be taught and who will teach it? Both questions are concerned with pedagogy and knowledge, yet the original question gets at matters of staffing and disciplinarity while the new question strikes closer to the roots, asking, ultimately, where composition belongs in the modern-university structure. Such shifts in wording represent the changes in thinking in composition studies, the maturation of a discipline built upon questioning its own subject's validity. As Ellen Cushman suggests in her response to Art Young and Mark Reynolds in part 3, composition is being reborn as writing and is moving well beyond its traditional home and boundaries in English departments. The sheer energy of this new-old discipline, well represented in this volume, is bursting the old boundaries and seeking new ways to fit into—and out of—the university.

On two of the questions asked in *Crisis and Change,* this current volume is silent, although both questions represent ongoing issues for every contributor to the book, every participant at the conference, every member of the field of composition: Who will assess composition in the twenty-first century and how will they assess it? and What issues will writing program administrators confront in the twenty-first century? Rather than representing a dismissal of these issues, that these two questions are not directly asked suggests their pervasiveness, their absolute importance to the field of composition. This is particularly true of assessment, for the national obsession with assessing students at all levels of education has gained momentum exponentially since 1996 and is unlikely to stall in the near future. Assessment, like the work of writing program administrators, is such a fundamental component of our work that direct questions about its place in the new century would be redundant.

Ultimately, contributors to this volume answered a new question, best articulated by Richard E. Miller in his response to Keith Gilyard and Harriet Malinowitz: "Where were you when the planes hit the towers?" For readers, teachers, and students of composition and rhetoric, this question may become "Where will composition go, now that the planes have hit the towers? And where should it go?" These new questions, rooted in the specific moment of crisis and change, may indeed be those that demand a rereading of the past and rewriting of the future of composition studies.

Or perhaps not.

As we consider the future of composition and reexamine its past, we may have stumbled and been mauled by the lion that had already left scratches on the chapters in this volume. Recent history certainly suggests that this could be the case: Many postsecondary institutions were disrupted or entirely closed on September 11. Few saw similar disruptions on September 12 or later. The same can be seen in the professional conversation on the WPA-L, an active listserv based at Arizona State University to which hundreds of professionals in and out of composition contribute. After the initial spate of postings on terrorism and the events in New York, Virginia, and Pennsylvania and even amongst such posts, talk of ongoing job searches and MLA interviews, first-year and advanced composition, placement and plagiarism, and dozens of other topics reasserted their dominance. As individual members of the listserv dealt with local responses to the attacks and contemplated the national moves towards war, the professional conversation quickly turned to business as usual.

So, September 11 was a lion in the road for the authors and editors of this volume as they wrote their chapters, but we may be underestimating the powerful pull of normality. We argue that everything has changed for Americans and their understanding of terrorism—changed in the ways that the Vietnam War altered the relationship of citizens towards the military, changed in the ways that Watergate altered attitudes towards government. We argue that a fundamental shift has taken place in the way Americans think about the world. Yet, we also argue that nothing has changed. The Vietnam War and Watergate, like the impeachment of William Jefferson Clinton and the Florida problem in the 2000 presidential election, changed the way Americans think about various aspects of their culture without seriously changing the ways in which those activities continue to occur. Since 1975, the U.S. military has been involved in dozens of conflicts of escalating size and cost throughout the world. Since 2000, few states have moved towards reforming their technologies of voting. And composition has continued in its course since September 11, 2001, extending its scope no doubt, but not radically altering the trajectory or nature of that development.

We know that composition studies will not be the same in the twenty-first century as it was in the twentieth, although continuities will certainly exist. Class sizes will be contested fiercely between teachers and administrators, between administrators and public- and private-funding sources. Theoretically and pedagogically valid direct assessments of writing will continue to compete with statistically reliable indirect assessments. The list of continuing issues could itself continue—could, undoubtedly, fill a third volume on composition studies. Yet, the future of composition, we can assert with some confidence, is not what it used to be. Some of the changes in the twenty-first century, such as ever-newer technologies or the increasing corporatization of the university, seem inevitable from where we stand in 2003. Other changes, such as the movement of composition beyond the campus or outside the control of the conventional college English department, seem probable but uncertain. Even less sure is the civic undertaking that would move composition studies into political action and even confrontation, in the wake of terrorist acts and governmental reactions to (or exploitations of) these acts. No doubt readers of this book a half century from now will find naivete to smile at and predictions to wonder at—if, indeed, there are still books at hand and interested readers to pick up this volume. We cannot, of course, truly rewrite our future, but we can continuously reread our past to understand and improve our present. That may be as close as we can come to altering the future of our profession and our discipline.

Works Cited   Contributors   Index

Works Cited

ADE Ad Hoc Committee on Staffing. "Report of the ADE Ad Hoc Committee on Staffing." *ADE Bulletin* 122 (1999): 7–26.

Alberti, John. "Returning to Class: Creating Opportunities for Multicultural Reform at Majority Second-Tier Schools." *College English* 63 (2001): 561–84.

Allison, Libby, Lizbeth Bryant, and Maureen Hourigan, eds. *Grading in the Post-Process Classroom: From Theory to Practice.* Portsmouth, NH: Heinemann, 1997.

American Accent Training. 2001 <http://www.americanaccent.com/intonation.html>.

American Heritage Dictionary. 4th ed. Boston: Houghton, 2000. 714.

Anderson, Paul. Email to Gesa E. Kirsch. 19 March 2002.

———. "Simple Gifts: Ethical Issues in the Conduct of Person-Based Composition Research." *CCC* 49 (1998): 63–89.

Anson, Chris M. "Teaching Writing in a Culture of Technology." *College English* 61 (1999): 261–80.

Anzaldúa, Gloria. *Borderlands/La Frontera: The New Mestiza.* San Francisco: Aunt Lute, 1987.

Arndt, Bettina. *Private Lives.* New York: Penguin, 1986.

Atwell, Nancie. *In the Middle: Writing, Reading, and Learning with Adolescents.* Portsmouth, NH: Heinemann, 1987.

Bakhtin, Mikhail. "Discourse in Life and Discourse in Art (Concerning Sociological Poetics)." *Freudianism: A Marxist Critique.* By V. N. Volosinov. Trans. I. R. Titunik. Ed. Neal H. Bruss. New York: Academic, 1976. 93–116.

———. [V. H. Volosinov?]. *Marxism and the Philosophy of Language.* Cambridge, MA: Harvard UP, 1986.

Bartholomae, David. "Composition: 1900–2000." *Publications of the MLA* 115 (2000): 1950–54.

———. "Inventing the University." *When a Writer Can't Write: Studies in Writer's Block and Other Composing-Process Problems.* Ed. Mike Rose. New York: Guilford, 1985. 134–65.

———. "What Is Composition and (If You Know What That Is) Why Do We Teach It?" Bloom, Daiker, and White 11–28.

———. "Writing with Teachers: A Conversation with Peter Elbow." *CCC* 46 (1995): 62–71.

Bartholomae, David, and Anthony Petrosky, eds. *Ways of Reading.* New York: St. Martin's, 1987.

Barton, David, and Mary Hamilton. *Local Literacies: Reading and Writing in One Community.* London: Routledge, 1988.

Barton, Ellen. "More Methodological Matters: Against Negative Argumentation." *CCC* 51 (2000): 399–416.

Baudrillard, Jean. "Plastic Surgery for the Other." Trans. François Debrix. Ed. Baudrillard and Marc Guillaume. *Figures de l'alterite.* Paris: Descartes, 1994. 8 April 1997 <http://www.uta.edu/english/apt/collab/texts/plastic.html>.

Bazerman, Charles. *The Languages of Edison's Light.* Cambridge, Mass: MIT P, 1999.

Benjamin, Walter. "The Work of Art in the Age of Mechanical Reproduction." *Illuminations.* Trans. Harry Zohn. Ed. Hannah Arendt. New York: Harcourt, 1968. 217–51.

Berkenkotter, Carol, and Thomas N. Huckin. *Genre Knowledge in Disciplinary Communication: Cognition/Culture/Power.* Hillsdale, NJ: Erlbaum, 1995.

Berkow, Peter, prod. *English Composition: Writing for an Audience.* Videocassette. The Annenberg Center for Public Broadcasting Project. PBS, 2001.

Berlin, James A. "Contemporary Composition: The Major Pedagogical Theories." *College English* 44 (1982): 765–77.

———. "English Studies, Work, and Politics in the New Economy." Bloom, Daiker, and White 215–25.

Bernstein, Susan Naomi, Ann E. Green, and Cecilia Ready. "Off the Radar Screen: Gender, Adjuncting, and Teaching Institutions." *CCC* 53 (2001): 149–52.

Bérubé, Michael. Address. NCTE Convention. Chicago Hilton, Chicago. 21 Nov. 1996.

———. *The Employment of English.* New York: New York UP, 1998.

Bewick, Thomas. *History of British Birds.* Newcastle: Beilby, 1797–1804.

"The Big Ten." *Nation* 7–14 Jan. 2002: 27–30.

Bishop, Wendy. *Teaching Lives: Essays and Stories.* Logan: Utah State UP, 1997.

Bizzell, Patricia. "Composing Processes: An Overview." *The Teaching of Writing.* Ed. Anthony Petrosky and David Bartholomae. Chicago: U of Chicago P, 1986. 49–70.

Blair, Kristine, and Pamela Takayoshi, eds. *Feminist Cyberscapes: Mapping Gendered Academic Spaces.* Stamford, CT: Ablex, 1999.

Bleich, David. "What Can Be Done about Grading?" Allison, Bryant, and Hourigan 15–35.

Blitz, Michael, and C. Mark Hurlbert. "Cults of Culture." *Cultural Studies in the English Classroom.* Ed. James A. Berlin and Michael J. Vivion. Portsmouth, NH: Boynton, 1992.

Bloom, Harold. *The Western Canon: The Books and School of the Ages.* New York: Harcourt, 1994.

Bloom, Lynn Z. "Composition Studies as a Middle-Class Enterprise." *Composition Studies as a Creative Art: Teaching, Writing, Scholarship, Administration.* Logan: Utah State UP, 1998. 33–53.

———. "Conclusion: Mapping Composition's New Geography." Bloom, Daiker, and White 273–80.

———. "Teaching My Class." *Composition Studies as a Creative Art: Teaching, Writing, Scholarship, Administration.* Logan: Utah State UP, 1998. 25–32.

Bloom, Lynn Z., Donald A. Daiker, and Edward M. White. *Composition in the Twenty-First Century: Crisis and Change.* Carbondale: Southern Illinois UP, 1996.

Boehm, Beth A. "Fear and Loathing in English 101: What Happens When English Faculty Members Reenter the First-Year Composition Classroom?" *ADE Bulletin* 128 (2001): 48–52.

Bolter, Jay David, and Richard Grusin. *Remediation: Understanding New Media.* Cambridge, MA: MIT P, 1999.

Booth, Stephen. *Precious Nonsense: The Gettysburg Address, Ben Jonson's Epitaphs on His Children, and Twelfth Night.* Berkeley: U California P, 1998.

Braddock, Richard, Richard Lloyd-Jones, and Lowell Schoer. *Research in Written Composition.* Urbana, IL: NCTE, 1963.

Bradshaw, Andy. "NWP Evaluation Continues to Show Positive Results." *The Voice: A Newsletter of the National Writing Project* 6.4 (2001): 1+.

Brand, Alice Glarden, and Richard L. Graves, eds. *Presence of Mind: Writing and the Domain Beyond the Cognitive.* Portsmouth, NH: Heinemann, 1997.

Brandt, Deborah. "Accumulating Literacy: Writing and Learning to Write in the Twentieth Century." *College English* 57 (1995): 649–68.

———. *Literacy in American Lives.* New York: Cambridge UP, 2001.

———. "Sponsors of Literacy." *CCC* 49 (1998): 165–85.

Brandt, Deborah, Ellen Cushman, Anne Ruggles Gere, Anne Herrington, Richard E. Miller, Victor Villanueva, Min-Zhan Lu, and Gesa E. Kirsch. "The Politics of the Personal: Storying Our Lives Against the Grain." *College English* 64 (2001): 41–62.

Bridges, William. *JobShift: How to Prosper in a Workplace Without Jobs.* Reading, MA: Addison-Wesley, 1994.

Britton, James, Tony Burgess, Nancy Martin, Alex McLeod, and Harold Rosen. *The Development of Writing Abilities (11–18).* London: Macmillan, 1975.

Brown, Stuart C., Rebecca Jackson, and Theresa Enos. "The Arrival of Rhetoric in the Twenty-First Century: The 1999 Survey of Doctoral Programs in Rhetoric." *Rhetoric Review* 28 (2000): 233–42.

Bruce, Bertram, and Maureen P. Hogan. "The Disappearance of Technology: Toward an Ecological Model of Literacy." *Handbook of Literacy and Technology: Transformations in a Post-Typographic World.* Ed. David Reinking, Michael C. McKenna, Linda L. Labbo, and Ronald D. Kieffer. Mahwah, NJ: Erlbaum, 1998. 269–81.

Brueggemann, Brenda Jo. *Lend Me Your Ear: Rhetorical Constructions of Deafness.* Washington, DC: Gallaudet, 1999.

Brumberger, Eva. "The Best of Times, The Worst of Times: One Version of the 'Humane' Lectureship." Schell and Stock. 91–106.

Brummett, Barry. *Rhetoric in Popular Culture.* New York: St. Martin's, 1994.

Bullock, Alan. *Hitler: A Study in Tyranny.* Abr. ed. New York: Harper, 1991.

Canagarajah, A. Suresh. *Resisting Linguistic Imperialism in English Teaching.* Oxford: Oxford UP, 1999.

Carroll, Jill. "Being Professional in an Unprofessional Climate." *Chronicle: Career Network* 5 Oct. 2001. 11 Oct. 2001 <http://chronicle.com/jobs2001/10/>.

Cassebaum, Anne. "Crossing Class Lines: A Diary." *Academe* (July–August 2001): 37–41.

Castells, Manuel. *End of the Millennium.* Vol. 3. *The Information Age: Economy, Society, and Culture.* Malden, MA: Blackwell, 1998.

———. *The Power of Identity.* Vol. 2. *The Information Age: Economy, Society, and Culture.* Malden, MA: Blackwell, 1997.

———. *The Rise of the Network Society.* Vol. 1. *The Information Age: Economy, Society, and Culture.* Malden, MA: Blackwell, 1996.

"CCCC Guidelines for the Ethical Treatment of Students and Student Writing in Composition Studies." *CCC* 52 (2001): 485–90. (*See also* <http://www.ncte.org/cccc/positions/ethics.shtml>.)

Chafe, Wallace. "Punctuation and the Prosody of Written Language." Technical Report 11. Berkeley: Center for the Study of Writing, 1987.

Charney, Davida. "Empiricism Is Not a Four-Letter Word." *CCC* 47 (1996): 567–93.

Chiseri-Strater, Elizabeth, and Bonnie Stone Sunstein. *FieldWorking: Reading and Writing Research.* Upper Saddle River, NJ: Prentice, 1997.

Chomsky, Noam. "Chatting With Chomsky." Interview. MSNBC chatroom. Will Femia, host. 2 Oct. 2001 <http://www.zmag.org/chatwithchom.htm>.

———. "The Manufacture of Consent." *The Chomsky Reader.* Ed. James Peck. New York: Pantheon, 1987: 121–36.

Chronicle of Higher Education. Almanac. 2001–2002. 48.1 Aug. 2001.

Churchill, Ward. "'Some People Push Back': On the Justice of Roosting Chickens." *Pockets of Resistance* 11. Supplement of *Dark Night Field Notes* Sept. 2001 <http://www.columbia.edu/~lnp3/ward_churchill.htm>.

Clifford, John, and Elizabeth Ervin. "The Ethics of Process." Kent 179–97.

"Coalition on the Academic Workforce Report." 22 Nov. 2000. American Historical Association. 1 Dec. 2000 <http://www.theaha.org/caw/cawreport.htm>.

Connors, Robert J. "The Abolition Debate in Composition: A Short History." Bloom, Daiker, and White 47–63.

———. *Composition-Rhetoric: Backgrounds, Theory, and Pedagogy.* Pittsburgh: U of Pittsburgh P, 1997.

Connors, Robert J., and Andrea Lunsford. *The St. Martin's Handbook.* New York: St. Martin's, 1989.

Cook, Jon. "The Techno-University and the Future of Knowledge: Thoughts after Lyotard." *The Practice of Cultural Analysis: Exposing Interdisciplinary Interpretation.* Ed. Mieke Bal. Stanford: Stanford UP, 1999. 303–24.

Cooper, Marilyn M. "The Ecology of Writing." *College English* 48 (1986): 364–75.

Cooper, Marilyn M., and Michael Holzman. *Writing as Social Action.* Portsmouth, NH: Heinemann, 1989.

Cope, Bill, and Mary Kalantzis, eds. *Multiliteracies: Literacy Learning and the Design of Social Futures.* London: Routledge, 2000.

Corbett, Edward P. J., Nancy Myers, and Gary Tate, eds. *The Writing Teacher's Source Book.* 4th ed. New York: Oxford UP, 2000.

Corn, David. "Unlikely Doves: Counter-terrorism Experts." *AlterNet.* 28 Sept. 2001. Oct. 2001 <http://www.alternet.org/print.html?StoryID=11601>.

Couture, Barbara. "Modeling and Emulating: Rethinking Agency in the Writing Process." Kent 30–48.

Crosby, Faye J. *Juggling: The Unexpected Advantages of Balancing Career and Home for Women and Their Families.* New York: Free, 1991.

Crowley, Sharon. "Around 1971: Current-Traditional Rhetoric and Process Models of Composing." Bloom, Daiker, and White 64–74.

———. *Composition in the University: Historical and Polemical Essays.* Pittsburgh: U of Pittsburgh P, 1998.

———. *The Methodical Memory: Invention in Current Traditional Rhetoric.* Carbondale: Southern Illinois UP, 1990.

———. "A Personal Essay on Freshman English." *Pre/Text* 20.3–4 (1999): 156–76.

Cushman, Ellen. "The Rhetorician as an Agent of Social Change." *CCC* (1996): 7–28.

———. *The Struggle and the Tools: Oral and Literate Strategies in an Inner City Community.* Albany: State U of New York P, 1998.

Cushman, Ellen, and Terese Guinsatao Monberg. "Re-Centering Authority: Social Reflexivity and Re-Positioning in Composition Research." Farris and Anson, *Under Construction* 166–80.

Daiker, Donald A. "Introduction: The New Geography of Composition." Bloom, Daiker, and White 1–7.

Danielewicz, Jane, and Wallace Chafe. "How 'Normal' Speaking Leads to 'Erroneous' Punctuating." *The Acquisition of Written Language: Response and Revision.* Ed. Sarah Freedman. Norwood, NJ: Ablex, 1985.

Daniell, Beth. "Narratives of Literacy: Connecting Composition to Culture." *CCC* 50 (1999): 393–410.

Dawkins, John. "Teaching Punctuation as a Rhetorical Tool." *CCC* 46 (1995): 533–48.

Deans, Thomas. *Writing Partnerships: Service-Learning in Composition.* Urbana, IL: NCTE, 2000.

DeGenero, William. "Social Utility and Needs-Based Education: Writing Instruction at the Early Junior College." *Teaching English in the Two-Year College* 28 (2000): 129–40.

Deibert, Ronald J. *Parchment, Printing, and Hypermedia: Communication in World Order Transformation.* New York: Columbia UP, 1997.

DeJoy, Nancy. "I Was a Process-Model Baby." Kent 163–78.

Delbanco, Andrew. "The Decline and Fall of Literature." *New York Review of Books* 4 Nov. 1999: 32–38.

Deletiner, Carole. "Beware the Researcher." Email response to Paul Anderson's "Simple Gifts: Ethical Issues in the Conduct of Person-Based Composition Research." *CCC Online* <http://www.ncte.org/ccc/7/sub/49_1anderson.html> 28 Jan. 1999. 1–4.

DeVoss, Dànielle, Dawn Hayden, Cynthia L. Selfe, and Richard J. Selfe Jr. "Distance Education: Political and Professional Agency for Adjunct and Part-Time Faculty, and GTAs." Schell and Stock 261–86.

Doucette, Don, and John E. Roueche. "Arguments with Which to Combat Elitism and Ignorance about Community Colleges." *Leadership Abstracts* 4.13 (1991).

Dyson, Michael Eric. "Race and the Public Intellectual: A Conversation with Michael Eric Dyson." Interview with Sidney I. Dobrin. *Race, Rhetoric, and the Postcolonial.* Ed. Gary A. Olson and Lynn Worsham. Albany: State U of New York P, 1999. 81–126.

Eakin, Emily. "On the Lookout for Patriotic Incorrectness." *New York Times* 24 Nov. 2001: A15+.

Ede, Lisa. *Situating Composition: Composition Studies and the Politics of Location.* Carbondale: Southern Illinois UP, forthcoming.

Edwards, Linda. "The Focusing of the President 1992." *Village Voice,* 23 June 1992: 25–29.

Elbow, Peter. "Breathing Life into the Text." *When Writing Teachers Teach Literature.* Ed. Art Young and Toby Fulwiler. New York: Heinemann, 1995. 193–205. Rpt. in *Everyone Can Write: Essays Toward a Hopeful Theory of Writing and Teaching Writing.* New York: Oxford UP, 2000. 360–71.

———. "Introduction. About Voice and Writing." *Landmark Essays on Voice and Writing.* Davis, CA: Hermagoras, 1994. xi–xlvii. Rpt. in *Everyone Can Write: Essays Toward a Hopeful Theory of Writing and Teaching Writing.* New York: Oxford UP, 2000. 184–222.

———. "The Shifting Relationships Between Speech and Writing," *CCC* 36 (1985): 283–303. Rpt. in *Everyone Can Write: Essays Toward a Hopeful Theory of Writing and Teaching Writing.* New York: Oxford UP, 2000. 149–67.

———. *What Is English?* New York: MLA, 1990.

———. *Writing Without Teachers.* New York: Oxford UP, 1973.

———. *Writing with Power: Techniques for Mastering the Writing Process.* New York: Oxford UP, 1981.

Emerson, Caryl. "The Outer Word and Inner Speech: Bakhtin, Vygotosky, and the Internalization of Language." *Critical Inquiry* 10 (1983): 21–40.

Emig, Janet. *The Composing Processes of Twelfth Graders.* Urbana, IL: NCTE, 1971.

Faigley, Lester. "Competing Theories of Process: A Critique and Proposal." *College English* 48 (1986): 527–42.

———. *Fragments of Rationality: Postmodernity and the Subject of Composition.* Pittsburgh: U of Pittsburgh P, 1992.

———. "Material Literacy and Visual Design." *Rhetorical Bodies: Toward a Material Rhetoric.* Ed. Jack Selzer and Sharon Crowley. Madison: U of Wisconsin P, 1999. 171–201.

Farber, Jerry. "Learning How to Teach: A Progress Report." Corbett, Myers, and Tate 273–78.

Farris, Christine, and Chris M. Anson. "Introduction: Complicating Composition." Farris and Anson, *Under Construction* 1–7.

———, eds. *Under Construction: Working at the Intersections of Composition Theory, Research, and Practice.* Logan, UT: Utah State UP, 1998.

Fasnacht, Nancy. "Why I Like Being a Contract Faculty Member." *Chronicle of Higher Education.* 6 July 2001. 10 July 2001 <http://chronicle.com/2001/07/2001070602c.htm>.

Flanders, Laura. "Welcome to the Warnacular." ZNet Commentary. 19 Sept. 2001. <http://www.zmag.org>.

Fleisher, Cathy, and David Schaafsma, eds. *Literacy and Democracy: Teacher Research and Composition Studies in Pursuit of Habitable Spaces.* Urbana, IL: NCTE, 1998.

Flower, Linda. "Cognition, Context, and Theory Building." *CCC* 40 (1989): 282–311.

———. *The Construction of Negotiated Meaning: A Social Cognitive Theory of Writing.* Carbondale: Southern Illinois UP, 1994.

———. "Literate Action." Bloom, Daiker, and White 249–60.

———. *Problem-Solving Strategies for Writing.* Fort Worth: Harcourt, 1981.

Flower, Linda, and John R. Hayes. "A Cognitive Process Theory of Writing." *CCC* 32 (1981): 365–87.

———. "Images, Plans, and Prose: The Representation of Meaning in Writing." *Written Communication* 1 (1984): 120–60.

Foehr, Regina Paxton, and Susan A. Schiller, eds. *The Spiritual Side of Writing: Releasing the Learner's Whole Potential.* Portsmouth, NH: Heinemann, 1997.

Fontaine, Sheryl I., and Susan M. Hunter, eds. *Foregrounding Ethical Awareness in Composition and English Studies.* Portsmouth, NH: Heinemann, 1998.

Foucault, Michel. *Discipline and Punish: The Birth of the Prison.* Trans. Alan Sheridan. New York: Pantheon, 1977.

———. "Space, Knowledge and Power." *The Foucault Reader.* Ed. Paul Rabinow. New York: Pantheon, 1984. 239–56.

Fox, Thomas. "Repositioning the Profession: Teaching Writing to African American Students." *JAC* 12 (1992): 291–303.

Franklin, Phyllis. "October 2000 Employment Trends." *MLA Newsletter* 33.1 (2001) 4–7.

Freedman, Sarah Warshaur. "Moving Writing Research in the Twenty-First Century." Bloom, Daiker, and White 183–93.

Freire, Paulo. *Education for Critical Consciousness.* New York: Seabury, 1973.

Frey, Olivia. "Beyond Literary Darwinism: Women's Voices and Critical Discourse." *College English* 52 (1990): 507–26.

Frost, Robert. Preface. "A Way Out." *Selected Prose of Robert Frost.* Ed. Hyde Cox and Edward Connerey Lathem. New York: Holt, 1966.

Frye, Marilyn. "On Being White: Thinking Toward a Feminist Understanding of Race and Race Supremacy." *The Politics of Reality: Essays in Feminist Theory.* Freedom: Crossing, 1983. 110–27.

Fulwiler, Toby, ed. *The Journal Book.* Portsmouth, NH: Boynton, 1987.

"The Future Just Happened." *BBC Online.* 29 July 2001. 27 Aug. 2001 <http://news.bbc.co.uk/hi/english/static/in_depth/programmes/2001/future/tv_series_1.stm>.

Gavaskar, Vandana S. "'I Don't Identify with the Text': Exploring the Boundaries of Personal/Cultural in a Postcolonial Pedagogy." *JAC* 18 (1998): 137–52.

Gee, John. *Social Linguistics and Literacies: Ideology in Discourses.* Brighton, Gt. Brit.: Falmer, 1990.

Gendlin, Eugene T. *Experiencing and the Creation of Meaning.* New York: Free, 1962.

———. *Focusing.* New York: Bantam, 1978.

George, Diana. "From Analysis to Design: Visual Communication in the Teaching of Writing." *CCC* 54 (2002) 11–39.

George, Diana, and Diane Shoos. "Dropping Bread Crumbs in the Intertextual Forest: Critical Literacy in a Postmodern Age or: We Should Have Brought a Compass." *Passions, Pedagogies, and Twenty-First Century Technologies.* Ed. Gail E. Hawisher and Cynthia L. Selfe. Logan: Utah State UP, 1999. 115–26.

George, Diana, and John Trimbur. "The 'Communication Battle,' or, Whatever Happened to the 4th C?" *CCC* 50 (1999): 682–98.

George, Susan. "A Short History of Neo-liberalism: Twenty Years of Elite Economics and Emerging Opportunities for Structural Change." Conference on Economic Sovereignty in a Globalising World. Bangkok. 24–26 March 1999 <http://www.millennium-round.org/>.

Gere, Anne Ruggles. *Intimate Practices: Literacy and Cultural Work in U.S. Women's Clubs, 1880–1920.* Urbana, IL: U of Illinois P, 1997.

Gilyard, Keith, ed. *Race, Rhetoric, and Composition.* Portsmouth, NH: Boynton, 1999.

Giroux, Henry A. *Corporate Culture and the Attack on Higher Education and Public Schooling.* Bloomington, IN: Phi Delta Kappa Educ. Foundation, 1999.

———. "Cultural Studies and the Culture of Politics." *JAC* 20 (2000): 505–40.

Glenn, Cheryl. "The Last Good Job in America." *Forum* 4 (2000): A12–A15. Insert in *CCC* 52 (2000).

Godfather Part II. Screenplay by Mario Puzo and Francis Ford Coppola. Dir. Francis Ford Coppola. Paramount, 1974.

Goleman, Judith. *Working Theory: Critical Composition Studies for Students and Teachers.* Westport: Bergin, 1995.

Gombrich, E. H. *Art and Illusion: A Study in the Psychology of Pictorial Representation.* Princeton: Princeton UP, 1960.

Goodburn, Amy. "Processing the 'Critical' in Literacy Research: Issues of Authority, Ownership, and Representation." *English Education* 30 (1998): 121–45.

Gould, Jane S. *Juggling: A Memoir of Work, Family, and Feminism.* New York: Feminist, 1997.

Graff, H. J. *The Legacy of Literacy: Continuities and Contradictions in Western Culture and Society.* Bloomington, IN: Indiana UP, 1987.

Greenbaum, Andrea. "What'cha Think? I Can't Spell?" *Composition Forum* 9 (1998): 1–9.

Greenberg, David. "Right Thinking." Review of *The Power of Ideas: The Heritage Foundation at 25 Years.* By Lee Edwards. *New York Times Book Review* 10 May 1998: 26.

Greenwald, John. "Bellboys with B.A.s." *Time* 22 Nov. 1993: 36–37.

Grimshaw, Anna, and Keith Hart. "Anthropology and the Crisis of the Intellectuals." *Critical Anthropology* 14 (1994): 227–61.

Grossman, Zoltan. "From Wounded Knee to Afghanistan: A Century of U.S. Military Interventions." Rev. 8 Oct. 2001. Oct. 2001 <http://www.zmag.org/list2.htm>.

Hairston, Maxine. "The Winds of Change: Thomas Kuhn and the Revolution in the Teaching of Writing." *CCC* 33 (1982): 76–88.

Haraway, Donna J. *Simians, Cyborgs, and Women: The Representation of Nature.* New York: Routledge, 1991.

Harris, Joseph. "Meet the New Boss, Same as the Old Boss: Class Consciousness in Composition." *CCC* 52 (2000): 43–68.

———. "The Other Reader." *Composition Theory for the Postmodern Classroom.* Ed. Gary A. Olson and Sidney I. Dobrin. Albany: State U of New York P, 1994. 225–35.

——— *A Teaching Subject: Composition since 1966.* Upper Saddle River, NJ: Prentice, 1997.

Harvey, David. *The Conditions of Postmodernity.* Oxford: Blackwell, 1989.

Hawisher, Gail E., and Cynthia L. Selfe, eds. *Passions, Pedagogies, and Twenty-First-Century Technologies.* Logan: Utah State UP, 1999.

Heath, Shirley Brice. "Work, Class, and Categories: Dilemmas of Identity." Bloom, Daiker, and White 226–42.

Herrington, Anne, and Charles Moran. "What Happens When Machines Read Our Students' Writing?" *College English* 63 (2001): 480–99.

Herzberg, Bruce. "Community Service and Critical Teaching." *CCC* 45 (1994): 307–19.

Hesse, Doug. "Saving a Place for Essayist Literacy." Hawisher and Selfe 34–48.

Hillocks, George. *Research on Written Composition: New Directions for Teaching.* Urbana, IL: NCTE, 1986.

Hochman, Will. "Re: FT Compositionists@Southern Ct State U." Email to Art Young. 4 Sept. 2001.

Hoggart, Richard. *The Uses of Literacy.* 1957. New Brunswick: Transaction, 1998.

Holloway, Lynette. "Seeing the Green Amid the Red, White, and Blue." *New York Times* 8 Dec. 2001: D1.

Horner, Bruce. "Mapping Errors and Expectations for Basic Writing: From the 'Frontier Field' to 'Border Country.'" Horner and Lu 117–36.

———. "'Students' Right,' English Only, and Re-imagining the Politics of Language." *College English* 63 (2001): 741–58.

———. *Terms of Work for Composition: A Materialist Critique.* Albany: State U of New York P, 2000.

———. "Traditions and Professionalization: Reconceiving Work in Composition." *CCC* 51 (2000), 366–98.

Horner, Bruce, and Min-Zhan Lu. "Expectations, Interpretations, and Contributions of Basic Writing." *Journal of Basic Writing* 19.1 (2000): 23–32.

———. *Representing the "Other": Basic Writers and the Teaching of Basic Writing.* Urbana, IL: NCTE, 1999.

Horner, Bruce, and John Trimbur. "English Only and U.S. College Composition." *CCC* 53 (2002): 594–630.

Hoy, Pat. *Instinct for Survival.* Athens: U of Georgia P, 1992.

Hunt, Russ. "Speech Genres, Writing Genres, School Genres, and Computer Genres." *Learning and Teaching Genre.* Ed. Aviva Freedman and Peter Medway. Portsmouth, NH: Heinemann, 1992. 243–62. (*See also* <http://www.StThomasU.ca/*hunt/selpubs.htm>).

Huntington, Samuel. *The Clash of Civilizations.* New York: Simon, 1996.

Interactive English. 10 CD-ROM. 12 notebooks with readings. Mountain View: Academic, 1997–1999.

James, Clive. "The Truthteller." *New Yorker* 18 Jan. 1999: 72–78.

Jarratt, Susan C. "Besides Ourselves: Rhetoric and Representation in Postcolonial Feminist Writing." *JAC* 18 (1998): 57–75.

Johnson, Steven. *Interface Culture: How New Technology Transforms the Way We Create and Communicate.* New York: Harper, 1997.

Johnson-Eilola, Johndan. "Reading and Writing in Hypertext: Vertigo and Euphoria." *Literacy and Computers: The Complications of Teaching and Learning with Technology.* New York: MLA, 1994. 195–219.

Journet, Debra. "Redefining the Mission of the English Department at the University of Louisville: Two Years Later." *ADE Bulletin* 128 (Spring 2001): 44–47.

———. "Rethinking General Education and Increasing the Number of Professorial Faculty Members; or, When Opportunity Knocks." *ADE Bulletin* 122 (Spring 1999): 27–30.

Kanpol, Barry. *Critical Pedagogy: An Introduction.* Westport: Bergin, 1994.

Kaufer, David S., and Brian S. Butler. *Rhetoric and the Arts of Design.* Mahwah, NJ: Erlbaum, 1996.

Kaufer, David S., and Patricia Dunmire. "Integrating Cultural Reflection and Production in College Writing Curricula." *Reconceiving Writing, Rethinking Writing Instruction.* Ed. Joseph Petraglia. Mahwah, NJ: Erlbaum, 1995. 217–38.

Kent, Thomas. Introduction. Kent 1–6.

———, ed. *Post-Process Theory: Beyond the Writing-Process Paradigm.* Carbondale: Southern Illinois UP, 1999.

Kirkpatrick, David D. "Now, Many Words from Our Sponsor." *New York Times* 3 Sept. 2001: A1, A12.

Kirsch, Gesa E. *Ethical Dilemmas in Feminist Research: The Politics of Location, Interpretation, and Publication.* Albany: State U of New York P, 1999.

———. "Feminist Critical Pedagogy and Composition." *College English* 57 (1995): 723–29.

Klein, William Dixon. "The Political and Economic Impacts of Writing Across the Curriculum in Chemistry at the University of Missouri–St. Louis." Diss. Michigan Technological U, 1999. *DAI* 60 (1999): 0730.

Knight, Charles. *The Old Printer and the Modern Press.* London: Murray, 1854.

Knodt, Ellen Andrews. "If at First You Don't Succeed: Effective Strategies for Teaching Composition in the Two-Year College." *Two-Year College English: Essays for a New Century.* Ed. Mark Reynolds. Urbana, IL: NCTE, 1994. 120–33.

Kress, Gunther. "'English' at the Crossroads: Rethinking Curricula of Communication in the Context of the Turn to the Visual." Hawisher and Selfe 66–88.

Kress, Gunther, and Theo Van Leeuwen. *Multimodal Discourse: The Modes and Media of Contemporary Communication.* London: Arnold, 2001.

Kuhn, Thomas S. *The Structure of Scientific Revolutions.* 2nd ed. Chicago: U of Chicago P, 1970.

Kytle, Ray. *Prewriting: Strategies for Exploration and Discovery.* New York: Random, 1972.

———. "Slaves, Serfs, or Colleagues—Who Shall Teach College Composition?" *CCC* 22 (1971): 339–41.

Lalicker, Bill. "Re: University of Colorado at Boulder." Online posting. 26 Sept. 2001. Writing Program Administrators Discussion List. 29 Sept. 2001 <http://lists.asu.edu/archives/wpa-l.html>.

Larson, Gary. *The Prehistory of the Far Side: A 10th Anniversary Exhibit.* Kansas City, KS: Andrews, 1980.

Levich, Jacob. "Happy New Year: It's 1984." Common Dreams News Center. 22 Sept. 2001. <http://www.commondreams.org/views01/0922-07.htm>.

LeVine, Mark. "10 Things to Know about Terrorism." AlterNet, 4 Oct. 2001. <http://www.alternet.org/print.html?StoryID=11647>.

Lewiecki-Wilson, Cynthia, and Jeff Sommers. "Professing at the Fault Lines: Composition at Open Admissions Institutions." *CCC* 50 (1999): 438–62.

Lewis, Michael. "Faking It." *New York Times* 15 July 2001, late ed., sec. 6: 32+. 24 Aug. 2001 <http://www.nytimes.com/2001/07/15/magazine/15INTERNET.html>.

———. "Jonathan Lebed's Extracurricular Activities." *New York Times* 25 Feb. 2001, late ed., sec. 6: 26+. 24 Aug. 2001 <http://www.nytimes.com/2001/02/25/magazine/25STOCK-TRADER.html>.

———. *Liar's Poker: Rising Through the Wreckage on Wall Street.* New York: Norton, 1989.

———. *The Next New Thing: A Silicon Valley Story.* New York: Norton, 2000.

———. *Next: The Future Just Happened.* New York: Norton, 2001.

Lindemann, Erika. "Guidelines for Employing Lecturers." Online posting. 27 June 2001. Writing Program Administrators Discussion List. 30 June 2001 <http://lists.asu.edu/archives/wpa-l.html>.

———. "Re: request." Email to Art Young. 12 Sept. 2001.

Little Feat. *Under the Radar.* New York: CMC Intl. Records, 1998.

Logan, Shirley Wilson. "'When and Where I Enter': Race, Gender, and Composition Studies." *Feminism and Composition Studies: In Other Words.* Ed. Susan C. Jarratt and Lynn Worsham. New York: MLA, 1998. 45–57.

Lu, Min-Zhan. "Importing 'Science': Neutralizing Basic Writing." Horner and Lu, *Representing* 56–104.

———. "Professing Multiculturalism: The Politics of Style in the Contact Zone." Horner and Lu, *Representing* 166–90.

———. "Redefining the Literate Self: The Politics of Critical Affirmation." *CCC* 51 (1999): 172–94.

Lu, Min-Zhan, and Bruce Horner. "The Problematic of Experience: Redefining Critical Work in Ethnography and Pedagogy." *College English* 60 (1998): 257–77.

Luke, Carmen, and Jennifer Gore, eds. *Feminisms and Critical Pedagogy.* New York: Routledge, 1992.

Lunsford, Andrea. "Towards a Mestiza Rhetoric: Gloria Anzaldúa on Composition and Postcoloniality." *JAC* 18 (1998): 1–27.

Lupton, Ellen, and J. Abbott Miller. *Design, Writing, Research: Writing on Graphic Design.* New York: Kiosk, 1996.

Lynch, Dennis A., Diana George, and Marilyn M. Cooper. "Agonistic Inquiry and Confrontational Cooperation." *CCC* 48 (1997): 61–85.

Lyons, Scott. "Rhetorical Sovereignty: What Do American Indians Want from Writing?" *CCC* 51 (2000): 447–68.

MacDonald, Susan Peck. "Voices of Research: Methodological Choices of a Disciplinary Community." Farris and Anson, *Under Construction* 111–23.

MacFarquhar, Larissa. "The Dean's List." *New Yorker* 11 June 2001: 62–72.

Mahiri, Jabari. *Shooting for Excellence: African American and Youth Culture in New Century Schools.* Urbana, IL: NCTE, 1998.

Malinowitz, Harriet. *Textual Orientations: Lesbian and Gay Students and the Making of Discourse Communities.* Portsmouth, NH: Heinemann, 1995.

Mamdani, Mahmood. "Good Muslim, Bad Muslim—An African Perspective." Social Science Research Council/After Sept. 11 Website. <http://www.ssrc.org/sept11/essays/Mamdani.htm>.

Martin, Jerry L., and Anne D. Neal. "How Our Universities Are Failing America and What Can Be Done about It." November, 2001. A Project of the Defense of Civilization Fund, The American Council of Trustees and Alumni. Washington, D.C. 11 Nov. 2001 <http://www.goacta.org/Reports/defciv.pdf>.

Matalene, Carolyn. "Experience as Evidence: Teaching Students to Write Honestly and Knowledgeably about Public Issues." Corbett, Myers, and Tate 180–90.

Mathieu, Paula. "'Not Your Mama's Bus Tour:' A Case for 'Radically Insufficient' Writing." *City Comp.* Ed. Bruce McComiskey and Cynthia Ryan. Albany: State U of New York P, 2003.

McChesney, Robert W. "The New Global Media." *Nation* 29 Nov. 1999: 11–15.

McCrimmon, James. *Writing With a Purpose.* Boston: Houghton, 1950.

McIntosh, Peggy. "White Privilege and Male Privilege: A Personal Account of Coming to See Correspondences Through Work in Women's Studies." 10 Nov. 2002 <http://www.wcwonline.org.title108.html>.

McLeod, Susan H. "Job Opportunity." Online posting. 19 Sept. 2001. Writing Program Administrators Discussion List. 19 Sept. 2001 <http://lists.asu.edu/archives/wpa-l.html>.

———. *Notes on the Heart: Affective Issues in the Writing Classroom.* Carbondale: Southern Illinois UP, 1999.

———. "Re: job opening." Email to Art Young. 20 Sept. 2001.

McLuhan, Marshall. *Understanding Media: The Extensions of Man.* New York: New American Lib., 1964.

McLuhan, Marshall, and Quentin Fiore. *The Medium Is the Massage.* New York: Bantam, 1967.

———. *War and Peace in the Global Village: An Inventory of Some of the Current Spastic Situations That Could Be Eliminated by More Feedforward.* New York: Bantam, 1968.

Messaris, Paul. *Visual "Literacy": Image, Mind, and Reality.* Boulder: Westfield, 1994.

Micciche, Laura. "More Than a Feeling: Disappointment and WPA Work." *College English* 64 (2002): 432–58.

The Military in the Movies. Dir. John J. Shanahan. Prod. Center for Defense Information, Washington, D.C., and the Media Education Foundation, Northampton, MA, 1997.

Miller, Richard E. "The Arts of Complicity: Pragmatism and the Culture of Schooling." *College English* 61 (1998): 10–28.

———. *As If Learning Mattered: Reforming Higher Education.* Ithaca: Cornell UP, 1998.

———. "'Let's Do the Numbers': Comp Droids and the Prophets of Doom." *Profession* 99 (1999): 96–105.

Miller, Susan. "How I Teach Writing: How to Teach Writing? To Teach Writing?" *Pedagogy* 1 (2001): 479–88.

———. *Textual Carnivals: The Politics of Composition.* Carbondale: Southern Illinois UP, 1990.

———. "Writing Theory: Theory Writing." *Methods and Methodology in Composition Research.* Ed. Gesa E. Kirsch and Patricia A. Sullivan. Carbondale: Southern Illinois UP, 1992. 62–83.

Miller, Thomas. *The Formation of College English.* Pittsburgh: Pittsburgh UP, 1997.

Milne, Seumas. "Special Report: Terrorism in the U.S." *Guardian* 13 Sept. 2001. 20 Sept. 2001 <http://www.guardian.co.uk/comment/story/0,3604,551036,00.html>.

———. "They Can't See Why They Are Hated." *Guardian* 13 Sept. 2001. Sept. 2001 <http://chss.montclair.edu/english/furr/pol/wtc/milne091301.html>.

Mitchell, W. J. T. *Picture Theory: Essays on Verbal and Visual Representation.* Chicago: U of Chicago P, 1994.

Miyoshi, Masao. "Ivory Tower in Escrow." *Boundary 2* 27.1 (Spring 2000): 7–50.

MLA Committee on Professional Employment. *Final Report of the MLA Committee on Professional Employment.* PMLA 113 (1999): 1154–87.

Moffett, James. *Student-Centered Language Arts Curriculum K–13.* 1968. Portsmouth, NH: Boynton-Cook, 1992.

———. *Teaching the Universe of Discourse.* Boston: Houghton, 1968.

Moghtader, Michael, Alanna Cotch, and Kristen Hague. "The First-Year Composition Requirement Revisited: A Survey." *CCC* 52 (2001): 455–61.

Morenberg, Max, Donald A. Daiker, and Andrew Kerek. "Sentence Combining at the College Level." *Research in the Teaching of English* 12 (1978): 245–56.

Morgan, Dan. "Ethical Issues Raised by Students' Personal Writing." Corbett, Myers, and Tate 87–93.

Morrison, Toni. *Lecture and Speech of Acceptance, upon the Award of the Nobel Prize for Literature, Delivered in Stockholm on the Seventh of December 1993.* New York: Knopf, 1994.

Mortensen, Peter, and Gesa E. Kirsch, eds. *Ethics and Representation in Qualitative Studies of Literacy.* Urbana, IL: NCTE, 1996.

Moss, Beverly. "Creating a Community: Literacy Events in African-American Churches." *Literacy Across Communities.* Ed. Beverly Moss. Cresskill, NJ: Hampton, 1994. 147–78.

Moxley, Joseph M. "If Not Now, When?" *Writing and Publishing for Academic Authors.* Ed. Moxley and Todd Taylor. 2nd ed. Lanham, MD: Rowman, 1997. 3–18.

Mullin, Joan. Email to Gesa E. Kirsch. 9 Oct. 2001.

Murphy, Michael. "New Faculty for a New University: Toward a Full-Time Teaching-Intensive Faculty Track in Composition. *CCC* 52 (2000): 14–42.

Murphy, Richard J., Jr. *The Calculus of Intimacy: A Teaching Life.* Columbus: Ohio State UP, 1993.

Murray, Donald. "Teach Writing as Process Not Product." *Rhetoric and Composition: A Sourcebook for Teachers.* Ed. Richard Graves. New Rochelle, NJ: Hayden, 1976. 179–82.

———. *A Writer Teaches Writing.* Boston: Houghton, 1968.

———. *Write to Learn.* New York: Holt, 1984.

Myers, Miles. *Changing Our Minds: Negotiating English and Literacy.* Urbana, IL: NCTE, 1996.

National Center for Educational Statistics. "1999 National Study of Postsecondary Faculty." 1 Nov. 2001 <http://nces.ed.gov/pubsearch/pubsinfo.asp?pubid=2001201>.

———. "Postsecondary Education." *Digest of Educational Statistics, 2000.* 21 Sept. 2001. <http:nces.ed.gov/pubs2001/digest/ch3.html>.

"National Language Policy." NCTE, 1989. <www.ncte.org/positions/national.shtml>.

Newkirk, Thomas. "Seduction and Betrayal in Qualitative Research." *Ethics and Representation in Qualitative Studies of Literacy.* Ed. Peter Mortensen and Gesa E. Kirsch. Urbana, IL: NCTE, 1996. 3–16.

New London Group. "A Pedagogy of Multiliteracies: Designing Social Futures." *Harvard Education Review* 66.1 (1996): 60–92.

Norgaard, Rolf. "University of Colorado at Boulder." Online posting. 26 Sept. 2001. Writing Program Administrators Discussion List. 29 Sept. 2001 <http://lists.asu.edu/archives/wpa-l.html>.

North, Stephen M. "The Death of Paradigm Hope, the End of Paradigm Guilt, and the Future of Research in Composition." Bloom, Daiker, and White 194–207.

———. *The Making of Knowledge in Composition: Portrait of an Emerging Field.* Portsmouth, NH: Boynton, 1987.

Odell, Lee, and Dixie Goswami. "Writing in a Non-Academic Setting." *Research in the Teaching of English* 16 (1982): 201–23.

O'Hare, Frank. *Sentence-Combining: Improving Student Writing Without Formal Grammar Instruction.* Urbana, IL: NCTE, 1973.

Ohmann, Richard. "Literacy, Technology, and Monopoly Capital." *College English* 47 (1985): 675–89.

Okawa, Gail Y. "Removing Masks: Confronting Graceful Evasion and Bad Habits in a Graduate English Class." *Race, Rhetoric, and Composition.* Ed. Keith Gilyard. Portsmouth, NH: Boynton, 1999. 124–43.

Oliver, Kenneth. "The One-Legged, Wingless Bird of Freshman English." *CCC* 1 (1950): 3–6.

Olson, Gary A. "Critical Pedagogy and Composition Scholarship." *CCC* 48 (1997): 297–303.

———. "The Death of Composition as an Intellectual Discipline." *Composition Studies* 28.2 (2000): 33–41.

———. "Encountering the Other: Postcolonial Theory and Composition Scholarship." *JAC* 18 (1998): 45–55.

———. "Toward a Post-Process Composition: Abandoning the Rhetoric of Assertion." Kent 7–15.

O'Reilley, Mary Rose. *The Peaceable Classroom.* Portsmouth, NH: Boynton, 1993.

Orr, David W. *Ecological Literacy: Education and the Transition to a Postmodern World.* New York: New York UP, 1992.

Orwell, George. *1984.* 1949. New York: Plume, 1981.

Oury, Scott. "What's Past Is Prologue: The 2001 COCAL Conference." *Forum* 5 (2001): A6–A8. Insert in *CCC* 53 (2001).

Panofsky, Erwin. *Perspective as Symbolic Form.* Trans. Christopher W. Wood. New York: Zone, 1991.

Perl, Sondra. "Understanding Composing." *CCC* 31 (1980): 363–69.

Petraglia, Joseph. "Is There Life after Process? The Role of Social Scientism in a Changing Discipline." Kent 49–64.

Philion, Thomas. "Three Codifications of Critical Literacy." *Literacy and Democracy: Teacher Research and Composition Studies in Pursuit of Habitable Spaces.* Ed. Cathy Fleisher and David Schaafsma. Urbana, IL: NCTE, 1998. 53–81.

Phillipe, Kent A. *National Profile of Community Colleges.* 3rd ed. Washington: Amer. Assoc. of Community Colleges, 2000.

Pinker, Steven. *The Language Instinct: How the Mind Creates Language.* 1994. New York: Harper, 2000.

Porter, James. *Rhetorical Ethics and Internetworked Writing.* Greenwich, CT: Ablex, 1998.

Porter, James, Patricia A. Sullivan, Jeffrey Grabill, Stuart Blythe, and Libby Miles. "Institutional Critique: A Rhetorical Methodology for Change." *CCC* 51 (2000): 610–42.

Pratt, Mary Louise. "Arts of the Contact Zone." *Profession '91* (1991): 33–40.

Preface. *Illustrated London News* 14 May 1842, 1.

Preface to volume 1. *Penny Magazine of the Society for the Diffusion of Useful Knowledge* 1 (1832): iii–iv.

Prendergast, Catherine. "Race: The Absent Presence in Composition Studies." *CCC* 50 (1999): 36–53.

Press, Eyal, and Jennifer Washburn. "The Kept University." *Atlantic Monthly* March 2000: 39–54.

Pullman, George. "Stepping Yet Again into the Same Current." Kent 16–29.

Ratcliffe, Krista. "Eavesdropping as Rhetorical Tactic: History, Whiteness, and Rhetoric." *JAC* 20 (2000): 87–119.

———. "Rhetorical Listening." *CCC* 51 (1999): 195–224.

Ray, Ruth. *Beyond Nostalgia: Aging and Life-Story Writing.* Charlottesville: U of Virginia P, 2000.

Readings, Bill. *The University in Ruins.* Cambridge, MA: Harvard UP, 1996.

Recchio, Thomas E. "Some Versions of Critical Pedagogy." *College English* 58 (1996): 845–52.

R.E.M. "Losing My Religion." *Out of Time.* Warner Bros., 1991.

Reynolds, Joshua. *Seven Discourses Delivered in the Royal Academy.* London: Cadell, 1778.

Reynolds, Mark. "The Intellectual Work of Two-Year College Teaching." *ADE Bulletin* 121 (Winter 1998): 37–40.

Reynolds, Nedra. "Who's Going to Cross this Border? Travel Metaphors, Material Conditions, and Contested Places." *JAC* 20 (2000): 541–64.

Rinaldi, Jacqueline. "Journeys Through Illness: Connecting Body and Spirit." *The Spiritual Side of Writing: Releasing the Learner's Whole Potential.* Portsmouth, NH: Heinemann, 1997. 118–28.

Robertson, Linda, Sharon Crowley, and Frank Lentricchia. "The Wyoming Conference Resolution Opposing Unfair Salaries and Working Conditions for Post-Secondary Teachers of Writing." *College English* 49 (1987): 274–80.

Roemer, Marjorie, Lucille M. Schultz, and Russel K. Durst. "Reframing the Great Debate on First-Year Writing." *CCC* 50 (1999): 377–92.

Ronald, Kate, and Hephzibah Roskelly. "Untested Feasibility: Imagining the Pragmatic Possibility of Paulo Freire." *College English* 63 (2001): 612–32.

Rose, Mike. *Lives on the Boundary.* New York: Free, 1989.

———. *Writer's Block: The Cognitive Dimension.* Carbondale: Southern Illinois UP, 1984.

Rosenblatt, Louise M. *Literature as Exploration.* 1938. 4th ed. New York: MLA, 1983.

Ross, Marc Howard. "The Political Psychology of Competing Narratives: September 11 and Beyond." Social Science Research Council. <http:www.ssrc.org/sept11/essays/ross_text_only.htm>.

Rossner, Judith. *August.* New York: Warner, 1984.

Roy, Arundhati. "The Algebra of Infinite Justice." *Guardian.* London. 29 Sept. 2001. 30 Sept. 2001 <http://www.zmag.org/raycalam.htm>.

Royster, Jacqueline Jones. *Traces of a Stream: Literacy and Social Change among African American Women.* Pittsburgh: U of Pittsburgh P, 2000.

———. "When the First Voice You Hear Is Not Your Own." *CCC* 47 (1996): 29–40.

Royster, Jacqueline Jones, and Jean C. Williams. "History in the Spaces Left: African American Presence and Narratives of Composition Studies. *CCC* 50 (1999): 563–84.

Russell, David. "Activity Theory and Process Approaches: Writing (Power) in School and Society." Kent 80–95.

Said, Edward. "American Humanism." Paumonok Lecture. Long Island University, Brooklyn. 13 Mar. 2001.

———. "The Clash of Ignorance." *Nation* 22 Oct. 2001: 11–13.

Sassen, Saskia. *Globalization and Its Discontents.* New York: New, 1998.

Schell, Eileen E. *Gypsy Academics and Mother Teachers: Gender, Contingent Labor, and Writing Instruction.* Portsmouth, NH: Boynton/Cook, 1998.

———."What's the Bottom Line? Literacy and Quality Education in the Twenty-First Century." Schell and Stock 324–40.

Schell, Eileen E., and Patricia Lambert Stock. "Introduction: Working Contingent Faculty in[to] Higher Education." Schell and Stock 1–44.

————, eds. *Moving a Mountain: Transforming the Role of Contingent Faculty in Composition Studies and Higher Education.* Urbana, IL: NCTE, 2001.

Schuster, Charles I. "Seeking a Disciplinary Reformation." Bloom, Daiker, and White 146–49.

Selfe, Cynthia L. "Literacy, Technology, and the Academy: A Case Study." Watson Conference on Composition and Rhetoric, Louisville, KY. 11 Oct. 2000.

————. "Technology and Literacy: A Story about the Perils of Not Paying Attention." *CCC* 50 (1999): 411–36.

Shaughnessy, Mina P. *Errors and Expectations: A Guide for the Teacher of Basic Writing.* New York: Oxford UP, 1977.

Sheridan-Rabideau, Mary. "The Stuff That Myths Are Made Of: Myth Building as Social Action." *Written Communication* 18.4 (2001): 440–69.

Shor, Ira. "What Is Critical Literacy?" Shor and Pari 1–30.

Shor, Ira, and Caroline Pari, eds. *Critical Literacy in Action: Writing Words, Changing Worlds.* Portsmouth, NH: Boynton/Cook, 1999.

Sledd, James. "On Buying In and Selling Out: A Note for Bosses Old and New." *CCC* 53 (2001): 146–49.

————. "Why the Wyoming Resolution Had to Be Emasculated: A History and a Quixotism." *JAC* 11 (1991): 269–81.

Smallwood, Scott. "An Adjunct Calls for Less Whining and More Teaching." *Chronicle of Higher Education* 3 Aug. 2001: A12–A14.

Smith, Jeff. "Students' Goals, Gatekeeping, and Some Questions of Ethics." *College English* 59 (1997): 299–320.

Smith, Zadie. *White Teeth.* New York: Random, 2000.

Smitherman, Geneva. "CCCC's Role in the Struggle for Language Rights." *CCC* 50 (1999): 349–76.

Snyder, William, Jr. "Preciousness of Imperfection." *In Praise of Pedagogy: Poetry, Flash Fiction, and Essays on Composing.* Ed. Wendy Bishop and David Starkey. Portsmouth, ME: Calendar, 2000. 46.

Solomon, Norman. "War Needs Good Public Relations." ZNet Commentary. 26 Oct. 2001. 29 Oct. 2001 <http://www.zmag.org/sustainers/content/2001-10/26solomon.cfm>.

Sontag, Susan. from "The Talk of the Town." *New Yorker* 24 Sept. 2001. Oct. 2001 <http://www.newyorker.com/talk/content/?010924ta_talk_wc>.

Spellmeyer, Kurt. *The Arts of Living: Reinventing the Humanities for the Twenty-First Century.* Albany: State U of New York P, forthcoming 2003.

————. "Inventing the University Student." Bloom, Daiker, and White 34–44.

State v. Buggs. 581 NW 2d 329, 344. MN Super. Ct. 1998.

Sternglass, Marilyn. *Time to Know Them: A Longitudinal Study of Writing and Learning at the College Level.* Mahwah, NJ: Erlbaum, 1997.

Street, Brian V. *Social Literacies: Critical Approaches to Literacy in Development, Ethnography, and Education.* London: Longman, 1995.

Stuckey, J. Elspeth. *The Violence of Literacy.* Portsmouth, NH: Heinemann, 1991.

"The Stuff of Patriotism, and Cheap, Too." *New York Times* 14 Oct. 2001, week in review: 7.

Stygall, Gail. "At the Century's End: The Job Market in Rhetoric and Composition." *Rhetoric Review* 28 (2000): 375–89.

Suggs, Rob. "The Binch." <l-poconater@lists.psu.edu> 13 Sept. 2001. 20 Sept. 2001.

Swales, John. *Genre Analysis: English in Academic and Research Settings.* Cambridge, England: Cambridge UP, 1990.

Swearingen, C. Jan. "Prim Irony: Suzuki Method of Composition in the Twenty-First Century." Bloom, Daiker, and White 75–82.

Tavris, Carol. *The Mismeasure of Woman.* New York: Simon, 1992.

Taylor, Marcy, and Jennifer Holberg. "'Tales of Neglect and Sadism':" Disciplinarity and the Figuring of the Graduate Student in Composition." *CCC* 50 (1999): 607–25.

Taylor, Sarah Stewart. "Bogged Down in the Basics?" *Community College Week* 19 Mar. 2001: 6–8.

Thompson, Bruce E. R. "Emissaries from Beyond: The Authenticity of Adjuncts." *Chronicle of Higher Education* 27 July 2001: B16.

Thompson, Patrick W. "Were Lions to Speak, We Wouldn't Understand." *Journal of Mathematical Behavior* 3 (1982): 147–65.

Tinberg, Howard. "An Interview with Ira Shor—Part I." *Teaching English in the Two-Year College* 27 (1999): 51–60.

Tingle, Nicholas, and Judy Kirscht. "A Place to Stand: The Role of Unions in the Development of Writing Programs." Schell and Stock 218–31.

Trainor, Jennifer Seibel, and Amanda Godley. "After Wyoming: Labor Practices in Two University Writing Programs." *CCC* 50 (1998): 153–81.

Trimbur, John. "Agency and the Death of the Author: A Partial Defense of Modernism." *JAC* 20 (2000): 283–98.

———. "Articulation Theory and the Problem of Determination: A Reading of *Lives on the Boundary*." *Composition Theory for the Postmodern Classroom.* Ed. Gary A. Olson and Sidney I. Dobrin. Albany: State U of New York P, 1994. 236–53. Rpt. of "Articulation Theory and the Problem of Determination: A Reading of *Lives on the Boundary*." *JAC* 13.1 (1993): 33–50.

———. "Taking the Social Turn: Teaching Writing Post-Process." *CCC* 45 (1994): 108–18.

———. "Writing Instruction and the Politics of Professionalization." Bloom, Daiker, and White 133–45.

Trimmer, Joseph, ed. *Narration as Knowledge: Tales of the Teaching Life.* Portsmouth, NH: Heinemann, 1997.

Trower, Cathy. "Negotiating the Non–Tenure Track." *Chronicle of Higher Education* 6 July 2001. 10 July 2001 <http://chronicle.com/jobs/2001/07/2001070601c.htm>.

Villanueva, Victor, Jr. Afterword. "Bearing Repetition: Some Assumptions." Allison, Bryant, and Hourigan 176–79.

———. *Bootstraps: From an American Academic of Color.* Urbana, IL: NCTE, 1993.

Wallerstein, Immanuel. "America and the World: Twin Towers as Metaphor." Social Science Research Council/After Sept. 11 Website. Oct. 2001. <http://www.ssrc.org/sept.11/essays/wallerstein/htm.>.

Ward, Irene. Personal communication with Ellen Cushman. 22 Oct. 2001.

Ward, Irene, and William Carpenter, eds. *The Allyn and Bacon Sourcebook for Writing Program Administrators*. Boston: Allyn, 2002.

Wasserstrom, Jeffrey N. "Anti-Americanisms, Thick Description, and Collective Action," Social Science Research Council. <http://www.ssrc.org/sept11/essays/wasserstrom_text_only.htm>.

Watkins, Evan. *Work Time: English Departments and the Circulation of Cultural Value*. Stanford: Stanford UP, 1989.

Weaver, Beth. "The Portrayal of Gender in the WWF." University of Texas. Dec. 2000. 27 Aug. 2001 <http://www.cwrl.utexas.edu/~onderdonk/2000fall309/wwf/index.html>.

Weiser, Irvin. Notes. Unpublished. Composition Studies in the Twenty-First Century: Rereading the Past, Rewriting the Future conference. Miami University, Oxford, Ohio. 5–7 Oct. 2001.

West, Cornel. *Race Matters*. New York: Vintage, 1994.

West, Thomas R. "The Racist Other." *JAC* 17 (1997): 215–26.

———. *Signs of Struggle: The Rhetorical Politics of Cultural Difference*. New York: State U of New York P, 2002.

Whitney, Robert. "Why I Hate to Freewrite." *Nothing Begins with N: New Explorations of Freewriting*. Ed. Pat Belanoff, Peter Elbow, and Sheryl Fontaine. Carbondale: Southern Illinois UP, 1990. 214–30.

Williams, Lynna. "Scenes from the 'Teaching Moment' Lounge." *In Praise of Pedagogy: Poetry, Flash Fiction, and Essays on Composing*. Ed. Wendy Bishop and David Starkey. Portsmouth, ME: Calendar, 2000. 142–44.

Winslow, Rosemary. "Poetry, Community, and the Vision of Hospitality: Writing for Life in a Women's Shelter." *The Literacy Connection*. Ed. Ronald A. Sudol and Alice S. Horning. Cresskill, NJ: Hampton, 1999. 181–204.

Witte, Stephen P., and Lester Faigley. *Evaluating College Writing Programs*. Carbondale: Southern Illinois UP, 1983.

Wolf, Barbara, dir., prod. "Degrees of Shame: Part-Time Faculty: Migrant Workers of the Information Economy." Videocassette. Barbara Wolf Video Work, 1997.

Woolf, Virginia. *A Room of One's Own*. San Diego: Harcourt, 1929.

Worsham, Lynn. "After Words: A Choice of Words Remains." *Feminism and Composition Studies: In Other Words*. Ed. Susan C. Jarratt and Lynn Worsham. New York: MLA, 1998. 329–56.

WPA-L. "Re: Regional Cs." Writing Program Administration Listserv. 4–6 Sep. 2001. wpa-asu.edu. 30 Sep. 2001 (http://lists.asu.edu/archives/wpa-l.html).

Wysocki, Anne Frances, and Johndan Johnson-Eilola. "Blinded by the Letter: Why Are We Using Literacy as a Metaphor for Everything Else?" Hawisher and Selfe 349–68.

Yagelski, Robert P. "The Ambivalence of Reflection: Critical Pedagogies, Identity, and the Writing Teacher." *CCC* 51 (1999): 32–50.

Yancey, Kathleen Blake. *Reflection in the Writing Classroom*. Logan: Utah State UP, 1998.

Contributors

Wendy Bishop, Kellogg W. Hunt Professor of English, teaches writing at Florida State University. She is the author or editor of a number of books, including *Released into Language; Teaching Lives: Essays and Stories; Elements of Alternate Style; Ethnographic Writing Research; Thirteen Ways of Looking for a Poem; The Subject Is Writing; The Subject Is Reading; The Subject Is Research; The Subject Is Story;* and *Reading into Writing.* She lives in Tallahassee and Alligator Point, Florida.

Lynn Z. Bloom is Board of Trustees Distinguished Professor and Aetna Chair of Writing at the University of Connecticut and past president of WPA (1989 and 1990). Her publications include composition studies ("The Essay Canon," *Composition Studies as a Creative Art,* and *Composition in the Twenty-First Century,* of which she was a coeditor); biography *(Doctor Spock);* autobiography *(Forbidden Diary* and *Forbidden Family);* textbooks *(The Arlington Reader,* with L. Z. Smith; *The Essay Connection,* 7th ed.; *Inquiry,* with Edward M. White and Shane Borrowman; and *The St. Martin's Custom Reader,* with L. Z. Smith); and creative nonfiction ("Teaching College English as a Woman").

Shane Borrowman is the director of composition studies at Gonzaga University, where he teaches business writing; first-year composition and introductory literature courses; Vietnam War literature; and advanced studies in writing, pedagogy, fiction, and drama. His most recent work has appeared in *Alternative Rhetorics: Challenges to the Rhetorical Tradition* and *Writing with Elbow.* He is currently editing a collection of essays that focus on the teaching of writing in the wake of national trauma and researching the history of paper manufacturing and book-dealing in ancient Greece and the eastern Mediterranean.

Brenda Jo Brueggemann is an associate professor of English at Ohio State University, where she has directed the writing center and the first-year writing program (in different years). She is the author of *Lend Me Your Ear: Rhetorical Constructions of Deafness* (1999) and coeditor of *Disability Studies: Enabling the Humanities* (2002).

Ellen Cushman, an assistant professor of English at Michigan State University, researches community literacy *(The Struggle and the Tools,* 1998), service learning, and multimedia composing. Her essays have been published in *Language and*

Learning Across the Disciplines, College Composition and Communication, College English, and *Research in the Teaching of English.* She is coeditor, with Eugene Kintgen, Barry Kroll, and Mike Rose, of *Literacy: a Critical Sourcebook* (2001).

Donald A. Daiker is a professor of English at Miami University in Oxford, Ohio, where he teaches courses in composition, American literature, the short story, boundary crossing, and the teaching of writing. His books include *Sentence Combining: A Rhetorical Perspective* (1985), *The Writing Teacher as Researcher* (1990), and *New Directions in Portfolio Assessment* (1994). He has published on responding to writing, holistic evaluation, writing groups, and high school teaching as well as on Poe, Hawthorne, Melville, Hurston, and Hemingway.

Dànielle Nicole DeVoss is an assistant professor in the Department of American Thought and Language at Michigan State University. Her work has most recently appeared in the *Writing Center Journal, Taking Flight with OWLs, CyberPsychology and Behavior,* and *Moving a Mountain.* She teaches composition, technical writing, and Web-authoring courses, and her teaching and research interests include computer and technological literacies, feminist interpretations of and interventions in computer technologies, philosophy of technology and technoscience, computer technologies in writing centers, gender and identity play in online spaces, and online representation and embodiment.

Peter Elbow is a professor emeritus of English at the University of Massachusetts–Amherst. He directed the writing program there and at SUNY–Stony Brook and taught at MIT, Franconia College, and Evergreen State College. His recent book, *Everyone Can Write: Essays Toward a Hopeful Theory of Writing and Teaching Writing,* was awarded the James Britton Prize by the College English Association. The National Council of Teachers of English recently awarded him the James Squire Award "for his transforming influence and lasting intellectual contribution."

Lester Faigley holds the Robert Adger Law and Thomas H. Law Professorship in Humanities at the University of Texas at Austin. He was the founding director of both the Division of Rhetoric and Composition and the Concentration in Technology, Literacy, and Culture at Texas. He has also served as chair of the Conference on College Composition and Communication.

Christine Farris is an associate professor of English at Indiana University, where she has served as associate chair and director of composition. She is the author of *Subject to Change: New Composition Instructors' Theory and Practice* (1996) and a coeditor, with Chris Anson, of *Under Construction: Working at the Intersections of Composition Theory, Research, and Practice* (1998). She has also published on writing across the curriculum, composition as cultural studies, and the teaching of women's literature.

Keith Gilyard is a professor of English at Pennsylvania State University and a former chair of the Conference on College Composition and Communication.

He has served on the Conference on English Education Executive Committee, as chair of the National Council of Teachers of English Committee on Public Doublespeak, and as vice-president and president of the NCTE–CCCC Black Caucus. He has written numerous essays on language and education. His books include *Voices of the Self: A Study of Language Competence,* for which he received the American Book Award; *Let's Flip the Script; An African American Discourse on Language, Literature, and Learning;* and the edited collection *Race, Rhetoric, and Composition.*

Joseph Harris directs the Center for Teaching, Learning, and Writing at Duke University, where he also teaches courses in academic writing, critical reading, literature and social class, and teaching composition. He is the author of *A Teaching Subject: Composition since 1966* (1997). From 1994 to 1999, he edited *College Composition and Communication.*

Joseph Johansen began his college education in computer engineering at Ricks College in Idaho. He spent two years in the Wallone area of France, Belgium, and Luxembourg doing missionary work for the Church of Jesus Christ of Latter-day Saints. Upon returning to the United States, he continued his education at Lander University, where he received a BFA. He is currently completing his master's degree in professional communication at Clemson University.

Gesa E. Kirsch is a professor of English at Bentley College in Waltham, Massachusetts. Her research and teaching interests include feminist theory and pedagogy, ethics and qualitative research, and women's roles in higher education. Her publications include *Ethical Dilemmas in Feminist Research: The Politics of Location, Interpretation, and Publication; Women Writing the Academy: Audience, Authority, and Transformation;* and several coedited collections: *Ethics and Representation in Qualitative Studies of Literacy,* with Peter Mortensen; *Methods and Methodology in Composition Research,* with Patricia A. Sullivan; and *A Sense of Audience in Written Communication,* with Duane Roen.

Min-Zhan Lu is a professor of English at the University of Wisconsin–Milwaukee. Her teaching and research interests include literary criticism, life writing, and the uses of cultural dissonance in composition. Her essays have appeared in *College Composition and Communication, College English,* the *Journal of Advanced Composition,* the *Journal of Basic Writing,* and elsewhere. Her books include *Shanghai Quartet: The Crossings of Four Women of China* (2001), *Representing the "Other": Basic Writers and the Teaching of Basic Writing* (1999, coauthored with Bruce Horner), and *Comp Tales: An Introduction to College Composition Through Its Stories* (2000, coedited with Richard Haswell).

Harriet Malinowitz is an associate professor of English and founding director of the women's studies program at Long Island University, Brooklyn. She is the author of *Textual Orientations: Lesbian and Gay Students and the Making of Discourse Communities* (1995), as well as articles and reviews in publications including

College English, JAC, PRE/TEXT, Women's Review of Books, Frontiers, NWSA Journal, Feminism and Composition Studies, The New Lesbian Studies, The Terministic Screen, Sissies, and Tomboys, and *The Right to Literacy.*

Susan H. McLeod is a professor of writing and the director of the writing program at the University of California, Santa Barbara. Her publications include *Strengthening Programs for Writing Across the Curriculum; Writing Across the Curriculum: A Guide to Developing Programs;* a multicultural textbook for composition, *Writing about the World; Notes on the Heart: Affective Issues in the Writing Classroom;* and *WAC for the New Millennium: Strategies for Continuing Writing Across the Curriculum Programs,* as well as numerous articles on writing across the curriculum and writing program administration.

Richard E. Miller is the associate director of the writing program and an associate professor of English at Rutgers University. He is the author of *As If Learning Mattered: Reforming Higher Education* (1998), as well as numerous articles in *College English,* including "Faultlines in the Contact Zone" (1994), "The Nervous System" (1996), and "The Arts of Complicity" (1998). He and Kurt Spellmeyer are the coeditors of *The New Humanities Reader* (2002), which seeks to provide the training described in "Teaching after September 11."

Susan Miller is a professor of English and member of the faculty of the University Writing Program at the University of Utah. She teaches writing, cultural studies, and the history and theory of writing. She has recently published articles on composition pedagogy, basic writing instruction, distance curricula in composition; a textbook on writing with computers, written with an undergraduate collaborator *(New Ways of Writing: A Guide to Writing with Computers);* and a study of commonplace books in eighteenth- and nineteenth-century Virginia *(Assuming the Positions).* She is an advisor for the Salt Lake City Community Writing Center and has served as University Public Service Professor. She coordinates the University of Utah's interdisciplinary PhD in rhetoric and composition and an undergraduate cross-curricular minor in literacy studies.

Christine M. Neuwirth is a professor of English and human-computer interaction at Carnegie Mellon University. She has directed Carnegie Mellon's first-year writing course and the masters program in professional writing and has published articles on writing and the pedagogy of writing, primarily with an emphasis on the uses and effects of computer technologies. Her research focuses on computer support for writing and communication, especially computer support for collaborative writing and visualization of electronic mail.

Gary A. Olson, a former writing program administrator at four universities, is the coordinator of the graduate program in rhetoric and composition at the University of South Florida. He is a coauthor, with Joe Moxley, of "Directing Freshman

Composition: The Limits of Authority." His recent books include *Rhetoric and Composition as Intellectual Work* and *Justifying Belief: Stanley Fish and the Work of Rhetoric.*

Mark Reynolds is a longtime faculty member and chair of the humanities division at Jefferson Davis Community College in Brewton, Alabama. He is a past editor of *Teaching English in the Two-Year College.* The author of articles in a number of journals and collections, he is also the editor of *Two-Year College English: Essays for a New Century* (1994). He has served on a number of committees for the National Council of Teachers of English, the Conference on College Composition and Communication, and the Modern Language Association.

Cynthia L. Selfe is a professor of humanities at Michigan Technological University and a coeditor, with Gail E. Hawisher, of *Computers and Composition: An International Journal for Teachers of Writing.* In 1996, she was awarded an EDUCOM Medal for innovative computer use in higher education—the first woman and the first English teacher to receive this award. In 2000, she and long-time collaborator Gail Hawisher were presented with the Outstanding Technology Innovator Award by the Conference on College Composition and Communication Committee on Computers. She has also served as the chair of the CCCC and as chair of the College Section of the National Council of Teachers of English. Her work focuses on the intersection of technology, education, equity, and literacy issues.

Kurt Spellmeyer is the director of the faculty and arts and sciences writing program at Rutgers University in New Brunswick, New Jersey. He is the author of *Common Ground: Dialogue, Understanding, and the Teaching of Writing* and *Arts of Living: Reinventing the Humanities for the Twenty-First Century* (forthcoming). With Richard E. Miller, he coedited *The New Humanities Reader.*

Todd Taylor is an associate professor of English at the University of North Carolina at Chapel Hill, where he has directed the writing-across-the-curriculum program. He edited the *Conference on College Composition and Communication Bibliography: 1984–1999* and was the founding editor of *CCC Online.* His books include *The Columbia Guide to Online Style,* coauthored with Janice Walker; *Literacy Theory in the Age of the Internet,* coedited with Irene Ward; and *Publishing in Rhetoric and Composition,* coedited with Gary Olson.

Edward M. White is an adjunct professor of English at the University of Arizona and a professor emeritus of English at California State University, San Bernardino, where he served long tenures as English department chair and coordinator of the upper-division university writing program. His *Teaching and Assessing Writing* (1985) has been called required reading for the profession; a revised edition in 1994 received the Mina Shaughnessy award from the Modern Language Association "for outstanding research." He is the author of more than seventy articles and book chapters on literature and the teaching of writing and has written, edited, or coedited eleven books, including *Developing Successful College Writing Programs* (1989), *Composition in the Twenty-First Century: Crisis and Change* (1996), *Assessment of Writing* (1996), *Assigning, Responding, Evaluating* (1999), and *Inquiry* (with Lynn Z. Bloom and Shane Borrowman, 2004).

John C. Williams Jr. is the author of *Understanding God's Amazing Grace and the Faith That Receives It.* He is currently employed as a building and grounds Specialist I at Clemson University. He is a devoted husband, father, and man of faith, who listens closely to his God.

Art Young is the Robert S. Campbell Chair and Professor of English at Clemson University. He founded in 1989 and continues to coordinate Clemson's communication-across-the-curriculum program. His most recent and continuing CAC project is "Poetry Across the Curriculum," in which a thousand students and twenty faculty from various disciplines participate. He has coedited five books on writing across the curriculum and was the winner of the Conference on College Composition and Communication's Exemplar Award for 2002.

Index